Praise for *S*

"The richest and most impressiv[e . . . Supre]me Court] since Woodward cowrote [*The Brethren* . . . ab]ute must-read."

[. . . Tim Rut]ow, *Los Angeles Times*

"*Supreme Conflict* gives us a fascinating look at dynamics within the Court, showing how personalities and ideology can affect alliances and debates." —Michiko Kakutani, *The New York Times*

"Ms. Greenburg offers a fresh and detailed account of how the Court works and, relatedly, how presidents decide who gets there. *Supreme Conflict* is by far the most fair-minded portrait of the Supreme Court in a long time, much more rounded and reliable than Bob Woodward's *The Brethren*. . . . [A] tour de force." —*The Wall Street Journal*

"*Supreme Conflict* is a genuinely spectacular feat of reporting . . . a riveting portrayal of why, despite the efforts of both the Reagan and first Bush administrations, the revolution on the Court never quite arrived but remained always just over the hill." —*The New Republic*

"Any book about the court that claims to 'break news,' as Jan Crawford Greenburg's *Supreme Conflict* does, invites comparison [to Bob Woodward and Scott Armstrong's *The Brethren*]. Greenburg's book delivers." —*The Washington Post*

"Jan Crawford Greenburg is one of our finest contemporary students of the Supreme Court. Her important new book provides a rare and incisive look at the personalities and inner workings of today's Court, unveiling in real time the usually-hidden behind-the-scenes mechanics that will influence all of our lives for decades to come."
—Michael Beschloss, author of *The Conquerors*

"Outstanding." —*The National Review*

"Jan Crawford Greenburg draws back the veil on the least public of the three branches of government. Taking us from inside the conference room where the Supreme Court decides its cases, to inside the homes of the high court's newest members as they learned of their selection by the president, *Supreme Conflict* provides riveting reading about an institution that has a profound impact on all of our lives."

—Cokie Roberts, news analyst for ABC and NPR
and author of *Founding Mothers*

"*Supreme Conflict* is filled with details that transform the business of Washington politics into gripping narrative. The book is a must-read for court watchers and political junkies alike."

—*Milwaukee Journal Sentinel*

"Jan Crawford Greenburg raises the curtain on the Supreme Court and shows us things we have never seen before. We get the inside story on how the president's own people sabotaged his effort to put Harriet Miers on the Court. We find out how the relationships the justices forge behind the scenes affect the decisions they hand down and we get new insight into how they reached the decision that led to George W. Bush becoming president in 2000. I can't remember a book where I found out more inside information about anything. This is a masterpiece of reporting that should establish Jan Crawford Greenburg as the preeminent reporter covering the Supreme Court and the law."

—Bob Schieffer, Chief Washington Correspondent, CBS News

"With extraordinary reporting and an irresistible narrative, Ms. Greenburg takes readers beyond locked doors into the private, personal and political dynamics of the Supreme Court. She explains how and why it was what it was and how and why it has now been changed—and in the process, provides surprising and significant new information about its members past and present. Laboring in one of journalism's most difficult gardens—and traditionally one of its least fertile—she has produced a masterful and most important book."

—Jim Wooten, author of *We Are All the Same*

"Jan Crawford Greenburg's eloquent book . . . is the most illuminating account to date of the political and ideological forces that shaped the current Court. Greenburg . . . manages to unlock the door to a famously secret institution. . . . A rich account of the birth of today's conservative Court. Greenburg's window into the genesis of the current Supreme Court, shaped dramatically by the Bush administration, is the sort of rich, balanced account that will add immeasurably to the historical record." —*Pittsburgh Post-Gazette*

"Riveting. *Supreme Conflict* takes you inside one of the most important struggles of our era—the conservative movement's struggle to reshape the Supreme Court. Jan Greenburg writes with a novelist's sense of pace and color, and a journalist's knack of asking the right question. I read *Supreme Conflict* at a single sitting, and learned something new and interesting from almost every page."
—Adrian Wooldridge, coauthor of
The Right Nation: Conservative Power in America

"Jan Crawford Greenburg takes the reader inside not only the Supreme Court but also the Senate and the White House to chronicle the twenty-year battle over the meaning and direction of the Constitution. But this is no twice-told tale: the material is fresh and the rich details will force anyone who has accepted the conventional wisdom about incidents such as Clarence Thomas's first term or the bungled nomination of Harriet Miers to see these and other episodes in a new light. A tour de force!" —Dennis Hutchinson, University of Chicago Law School, editor of *The Supreme Court Review*

PENGUIN BOOKS

SUPREME CONFLICT

Jan Crawford Greenburg is a correspondent for ABC News who covers law and politics for *World News Tonight, Nightline, Good Morning America,* and *This Week with George Stephanopoulos*. She previously served as the Supreme Court analyst for the *NewsHour with Jim Lehrer* on PBS and *Face the Nation* on CBS, and was the chief legal affairs writer for the *Chicago Tribune*. She has covered the Supreme Court for twelve years, and has had extensive interviews with nine of its justices. With high-level sources inside the White House, in the Justice Department, and on Capitol Hill, Greenburg has gained unique access to the leading players in the confirmation battles. She is a graduate of the University of Chicago Law School and has an undergraduate degree from the University of Alabama.

SUPREME
CONFLICT

THE INSIDE STORY OF THE STRUGGLE FOR
CONTROL OF THE UNITED STATES
SUPREME COURT

JAN CRAWFORD GREENBURG

PENGUIN BOOKS

PENGUIN BOOKS

Published by the Penguin Group

Penguin Group (USA) Inc., 375 Hudson Street, New York, New York 10014, U.S.A. •
Penguin Group (Canada), 90 Eglinton Avenue East, Suite 700, Toronto, Ontario, Canada
M4P 2Y3 (a division of Pearson Penguin Canada Inc.) • Penguin Books Ltd, 80 Strand,
London WC2R 0RL, England • Penguin Ireland, 25 St Stephen's Green, Dublin 2, Ireland
(a division of Penguin Books Ltd) • Penguin Group (Australia), 250 Camberwell Road,
Camberwell, Victoria 3124, Australia (a division of Pearson Australia Group Pty Ltd) •
Penguin Books India Pvt Ltd, 11 Community Centre, Panchsheel Park, New Delhi – 110 017,
India • Penguin Group (NZ), 67 Apollo Drive, Rosedale, North Shore 0632, New Zealand
(a division of Pearson New Zealand Ltd) • Penguin Books (South Africa) (Pty) Ltd,
24 Sturdee Avenue, Rosebank, Johannesburg 2196, South Africa

Penguin Books Ltd, Registered Offices:
80 Strand, London WC2R 0RL, England

First published in the United States of America by
The Penguin Press, a member of Penguin Group (USA) Inc. 2007
This edition with a new afterword published in Penguin Books 2008

1 3 5 7 9 10 8 6 4 2

THE LIBRARY OF CONGRESS HAS CATALOGED THE HARDCOVER EDITION AS FOLLOWS:
Greenburg, Jan Crawford.
Supreme conflict : the inside story of the struggle for control of the United States Supreme
Court / Jan Crawford Greenburg.
p. cm.
ISBN 978-1-59420-101-1 (hc.)
ISBN 978-0-14-311304-1 (pbk.)
1. United States. Supreme Court—Officials and employees—Selection and appointment—
History.   2. Judges—Selection and appointment—United States—History.   3. Political
questions and judicial power—United States.   I. Title.
KF8742.G74   2007
347.73'2634—dc22   2006033620

Printed in the United States of America
DESIGNED BY AMANDA DEWEY

To Mom and Dad

CONTENTS

SUPREME
CONFLICT

PROLOGUE

The nine justices emerged from behind the red velvet curtains right on time, as always, at 10 a.m. They are never late or early, no matter how small or big the cases before them. They follow a routine dictated by custom and tradition.

About ten minutes beforehand, the associate justices donned their black robes in a paneled changing room just behind the courtroom and gathered next door in the oak-paneled conference room where they meet to discuss cases. The room is just outside the chief justice's chambers, and as always, he joined them already wearing his robe. Right before the appointed hour, they all shook hands. Then they walked single file behind their chief, in order of seniority, to wait behind those velvet curtains. As the Court's marshal announced "the honorable, the chief justice and the associate justices of the United States of America," an aide swept back the curtains, and the justices stepped into the room.

On this day, June 27, 2005, like all other days on the Court calendar, a hush preceded the marshal's announcement, as if the spectators in the surprisingly intimate marble courtroom suddenly and all at once noticed that it was time. But on this day, the hush seemed more profound, as if the crowd thought it could somehow will the justices into the courtroom a moment or two early. It was a big day, a historic day in the minds of many. All the seats were full, some with top government officials ushered in by Supreme Court police officers, others with people who had camped out overnight in the sticky heat of Washington in late June.

The justices stepped up to their long wooden bench in unison and took their seats in high-backed black leather chairs. The scene was carefully choreographed, but also well practiced. This group had worked together for eleven years. As the justices sat down in their seats, the people in the audience sat up straighter in theirs. Some leaned forward. Everyone, even the justices, looked at the gaunt man in the middle of the bench. It was the last time they expected to see Chief Justice William Rehnquist in that seat, controlling a court he'd led for nineteen years.

Rehnquist was eighty years old, and he was dying of cancer. Many in the courtroom on the last day of the 2004–5 term had come to see him announce the inevitable: He was retiring after thirty-three years on the Supreme Court. The White House had already begun interviewing possible replacements. Journalists had worked up lengthy stories about his legacy, to run when he made his announcement. Former law clerks had considered the remarks they would offer, if asked, about the chief's curious mix of stern leadership and personal warmth. More than one planned to talk about how it was a testament to Rehnquist's willpower and love of the institution that he had managed to finish out the term despite the illness that had weakened him. He was not the kind to leave his ship midcourse; he had steered it home.

None of them truly knew just how sick Rehnquist was. The previous October, doctors had diagnosed him with anaplastic thyroid cancer, the most serious and aggressive form of thyroid cancer. They'd performed a tracheostomy, an operation to make a permanent opening in his throat so he could breathe and eat when the chemotherapy and radiation swelled it shut. Rehnquist did not disclose any details publicly, nor did he make public the grave prognosis his doctors had given him. A younger man, doctors told Rehnquist in the hospital after his diagnosis in October, would have less than a year to live. He'd have perhaps half that.

On that June morning, Rehnquist, who loved to put down a one-dollar bet on almost anything—the amount of snowfall, a football game, a congressional election—had already beaten his odds.

The atmosphere in the courtroom grew tense as the Court turned to the last two cases of the term. Both dealt with whether the Ten Commandments could be displayed on public property. The question had generated enormous controversy across the nation. In Alabama, the state's chief justice had been kicked out of office when he refused to remove a large display from his courthouse. The justices had struggled mightily with these decisions before splitting the difference. They approved a Ten Commandments monument on the grounds of the Texas state capitol in part because it was displayed with dozens of other markers. But they ruled the display unconstitutional in a Kentucky courtroom, where it appeared to take center stage.

Rehnquist announced his opinion in the Texas case, and he struggled to provide even the briefest of summaries. Unable to eat because of his cancer, he'd become thin and stooped, and his skin appeared gray. His trademark booming baritone, which had silenced many a lawyer, sometimes in midsyllable, was gone. His voice now was weak and reedy from the tracheostomy. Rehnquist ticked off the names of the six other justices who'd also written opinions in that Ten Commandments case.

"I didn't know we had that many people on our Court," Rehnquist said slowly, his breathing labored. Then he smiled as he looked to the justices on his left and right, and the courtroom exploded in laughter.

Rehnquist thanked the Court's staff for its work over the term. The audience grew completely still. The other justices peered intently at Rehnquist. This would be the time for the announcement. Rehnquist seemed to pause briefly. Then the marshal banged down the gavel and Rehnquist carefully rose from his seat.

The other justices, looking confused, slowly began to follow. Only O'Connor seemed to have a sense of purpose. She turned and stepped beside her old chief, ready to help him if he needed her arm. Then the old chief shuffled back to his chambers, leaving all of Washington to wonder and wait.

The anticlimax of a non-announcement that morning carried no small amount of apprehension and unease for conservatives and liberals alike. Amid the swirling rumors of retirement and change, conservatives were facing an uncomfortable reality: the Rehnquist Court, with seven justices appointed by Republican presidents, had become a legal and ideological disappointment. Time after time, these justices had refused to sweep aside the landmark liberal rulings of earlier Supreme Courts. In case after case, the justices frustrated conservatives by avoiding clear resolutions of the most controversial issues of constitutional law. Liberals may have seen a Court that put a Republican in the White House, but on the volatile and often emotional issues of abortion, affirmative action, capital punishment, and religion, conservatives were left gasping, often falling just short of their goals. Justices who were advertised and marketed as conservatives turned out to be anything but. Victories at the polls seemed to have no meaning when it came to influencing the direction of the Court.

Despite anticipation of a historic retirement, there was unspoken anxiety on both sides about whether George W. Bush would be able to seize the opportunity for fundamental change. Drama over possible retirements was ratcheted up as conservatives and liberals sensed the moment for changing the Court's direction might again be at hand. Who knew when another such opportunity might come to pass? If Bush had his moment, would he succeed where others—including his own father—had failed?

That morning, change was in the air. But of all the people who had gathered in the courtroom, of all the justices and officials and lawyers and former clerks, only O'Connor and Rehnquist knew how much.

Bush would get his chance.

What would happen next would, after a protracted and sometimes bizarre series of steps and missteps, after strokes of strategic brilliance and acts of folly at the highest levels, produce a profound and lasting alteration to the Supreme Court. The Court that had functioned as a unit for more than a decade, unaltered since the seating of Justice Stephen Breyer in 1994, would be transformed by the departures of these veteran judges, Rehnquist and O'Connor, these old friends from the West. It would be a titanic conflict, one that would turn old allies into enemies, damage reputations, and open bitter wounds, and when the smoke of battle finally lifted, one of the most fateful shifts in the country's judicial landscape in a generation would be a fait accompli, with repercussions as yet unimagined.

1.

DAY'S END

Sandra Day O'Connor was not a woman who sat still. She had grown up under big skies, surrounded by miles of open land, and she liked to get out and see things. In the fall of 2004, she readily agreed to travel to Ottawa with her old friend and colleague Bill Rehnquist to meet with judges on Canada's Supreme Court. Rehnquist invited another justice, Tony Kennedy, and together the group flew there in mid-October.

Rehnquist and his colleagues had just kicked off a new Supreme Court term that had reached a significant milestone. Over its history, the Court has welcomed a new justice on an average of about every two years. Rehnquist's current Court had worked together for a decade, the longest period nine justices had ever served together without a change in membership.

But as Rehnquist, O'Connor, and Kennedy left Washington, change seemed likely. The presidential election was weeks away. George W. Bush was fighting for his political life against a spirited challenge from Massachusetts senator John F. Kerry, with both the president and his challenger pointing to the closely divided Supreme Court to illustrate the campaign's high stakes. With two justices over eighty years of age and two others in their seventies, the next president could get one, two, or even three appointments. It seemed certain in those frantic final stages of the race that the winner of this election would shape the direction of the Court, and with it the country, for decades to come.

On a sunny fall Ottawa day, Rehnquist, O'Connor, and Kennedy spent their time meeting with their Canadian counterparts and touring some of the government buildings, including the Senate and House of Commons. After their official visits, O'Connor wanted to look around the picturesque capital. She was a woman in motion, and she liked to bring people along with her. Every year, O'Connor would take her law clerks on long outings around Washington's landmarks to make sure they didn't miss out, and she encouraged the women to join her aerobics class, which she had started at the Supreme Court just after her confirmation in 1981.

"Let's take a walk," O'Connor suggested to Rehnquist and Kennedy. Kennedy, who joined the Court seven years after O'Connor, was game. But Rehnquist declined. He wasn't feeling well, he said. He had a cold he couldn't shake, some kind of respiratory thing. It had been going on for a while.

Later that day, Kennedy told his wife, Mary, that he thought Rehnquist was unwell. Rehnquist suspected it too. He'd been more tired than usual, and his throat was scratchy. His voice wasn't the same. When he returned home from his Canadian meetings, he went to Bethesda National Naval Medical Center for tests. On Friday, October 22, doctors gave him the news: thyroid cancer, maybe six months.

The next day Rehnquist had surgery to insert a tube in his throat. The Court downplayed the illness, releasing a terse statement the following Monday that Rehnquist had been diagnosed with thyroid cancer and had undergone surgery. Rehnquist, the Court said, expected to be back on the bench the following week.

With barely a week left before the presidential election, the announcement caused surprisingly little stir. Interest groups tried to make the Supreme Court a rallying point with voters. Reporters interviewed doctors who suggested that Rehnquist's days were numbered. But the Court disclosed nothing more, and the story soon died down. By Friday, news that Rehnquist had been released from the hospital barely merited a mention, since the Court continued to insist he was returning to work that Monday.

That claim would prove false. The chief justice's black leather chair, in the center of the Court's bench, would go empty for four months while Rehnquist underwent treatment to reduce the cancerous tumor. He didn't tell the justices about his prognosis, but some of his colleagues assumed he would never again sit beside them in court. Justice John Paul Stevens, the Court's most senior associate justice, took over for Rehnquist in the public sessions and ran the justices' private conferences, where they discuss cases and vote. Stevens even began to relax the terms of the Court's discussions, giving the lawyers and the justices more time to make their points than Rehnquist had allowed.

But Rehnquist, ever the tough old Lutheran, would swear in President Bush during a wintry inauguration ceremony, and he would be back in the courtroom by the end of March. His deep and resonant voice was forever changed, but he allowed no concessions to be made to his weakened condition. He sternly cut off lawyers when their time expired, almost as if he'd opened a trapdoor. He kept a tight rein on the conferences, just as he always had. But he was fading away, his clothes getting looser on his angular frame and his wristwatch dangling near his knuckles when his hands were at his sides.

After Rehnquist had returned to the courthouse and resumed more of his old duties, O'Connor went by her old friend's chamber to talk. Like everyone else, O'Connor thought he would be retiring at the end of the term, and she had reluctantly concluded that she should begin planning her own departure. John, her devoted husband of fifty-two years, was suffering from Alzheimer's disease, and he was becoming increasingly frail. She wouldn't be able to stay on the Court indefinitely, she confided to Rehnquist. "I might have to do this," O'Connor said.

But Rehnquist surprised O'Connor. Despite his obviously weakening condition, he hadn't looked that far ahead into his own future. "We don't need two vacancies," he said. "But let's just wait. Let's talk later."

O'Connor and Rehnquist had been friends for more than fifty years, since their days together at Stanford Law School. They'd come from very different places—he was the A student from Wisconsin who'd been an army weatherman; she was the Arizona cowgirl who roped and rode horses with the boys. But Rehnquist had a quick wit, and O'Connor loved a good joke, so the two socialized often. Since Stanford didn't have on-campus housing for women graduate students, O'Connor and other women students lived in a co-op apartment. Rehnquist and his friends would visit and help with dinner. Afterward, the group would play charades, a game Bill Rehnquist would enjoy his entire life, especially with his law clerks.

After law school, Rehnquist clerked on the Supreme Court, and he received lucrative job offers from private law firms. O'Connor, also a star student at Stanford University and its law school, didn't enjoy similar treatment. She had completed her schooling in six years instead of seven, having spent her fourth year as an undergraduate earning credit in the law school, and she had earned top grades. But she had just one law firm interview, and the partner asked her how well she could type.

"Well, medium," O'Connor told him. "I can get by, but it's not great."

The partner told her, "If you can demonstrate that you can type well enough, I might be able to get you a job in this firm as a legal secretary. But, Ms. Day, we have never hired a woman as a lawyer here, and I don't see the time when we will."

O'Connor declined the typing test and, contrary to popular legend, didn't even get an offer for the secretarial job. Knowing where to wage her battles, she turned her sights to the district attorney in San Mateo

Valley and eventually persuaded him to hire her as a lawyer, after she wrote him a long letter and told him she could set up a desk in his secretary's office.

That December, on her family's cattle ranch in Arizona, she married the charming John O'Connor, whom she'd met on the *Stanford Law Review*. She became the sole breadwinner while her husband finished law school. When the O'Connors moved to Phoenix several years later, she still couldn't find work at a law firm, so she became heavily involved in volunteer work while she reared three sons, and then hung out her own shingle. She and John also developed a close group of friends, including Rehnquist and his wife, Nan, who also had settled in Phoenix. The families played bridge together, picnicked in the desert, enjoyed frequent dinners, and even participated in play readings.

About the time the Rehnquists were moving to Washington in the late 1960s, after Bill Rehnquist took a high-ranking Justice Department job in the new administration of Richard Nixon, O'Connor made the transition from committed Republican Party supporter to political candidate. In time she would become majority leader of the state senate—the first woman to serve in such a position in American history.

When President Nixon nominated Rehnquist to the Supreme Court in 1971, O'Connor was as surprised as everyone else. She'd written Nixon just three weeks earlier and urged him to put a woman on the Court. But O'Connor quickly turned all her efforts to supporting her close friend, lobbying Arizona leaders and writing letters in support. In a speech on the floor of the state senate, she joked that her only regret was that the president's choice "doesn't wear a skirt." But he was "one of the most brilliant legal minds in the country," she said, and she predicted that he might someday become chief justice. After Rehnquist's confirmation, O'Connor and her husband flew to Washington for his swearing-in ceremony. It was O'Connor's first time in the Supreme Court.[1]

Rehnquist had been on the Court nine years when newly elected

President Ronald Reagan got his first Supreme Court nomination. Reagan had said during his 1980 campaign that he wanted to nominate a woman to the Court, and his attorney general contacted Sandra Day O'Connor, then a midlevel state court judge.

"It had nothing to do with me," O'Connor said. "He was hoping to get votes from women, I assume, and rightly so." Attorney General William French Smith had kept a little piece of paper underneath the phone on his desk with names of possible nominees on it. Whenever he heard of a prospect, he'd jot down the name, and O'Connor's made it onto his handwritten list. She isn't sure how. Maybe through Chief Justice Warren Burger, whom she'd come to know through a presidential commission they'd served on together? Or through her old law school classmate Rehnquist? "Probably because there were not that many women judges, much less many Republican women judges," O'Connor said. "Face it. Where are you going to find them?"

Shortly after Potter Stewart told the White House he would be stepping down, Smith called O'Connor at home. She was in bed, recovering from a hysterectomy. "Could you come back to Washington to talk about a vacancy?" Smith asked. He did not say for the Supreme Court, but O'Connor knew what he meant.

"Well, I've just had surgery," she told Smith. "I'll have to check with the doctor. If he says okay, then yes."

O'Connor's doctor gave her permission to go, but only if she promised not to lift anything, not even a handbag. She flew out by herself several days later to begin a barrage of interviews with lawyers and staff in a hotel several blocks from the White House, so no one would see her. Smith told her that night that she would be meeting with Reagan in the White House the next day.

"Well, how do I get there?" she asked. Smith said he'd have his secretary pick her up where it was convenient. Before her surgery, O'Connor had planned to be in Washington for meetings with a medical advisory group. Since she was in town, she figured she might as well attend the meetings. The next morning, she left one of the group's sessions and stood outside a People's drugstore on Dupont Circle, where she waited for her ride to meet the president.

She talked with Reagan for forty minutes, with his top advisers sitting in the background. At first they discussed cattle and ranching and general things, like how much they enjoyed riding a good horse. Reagan then asked a few questions about law, though nothing of major substance. Do you understand the role of a legislator, Reagan asked, and the role of a judge? The question is a classic for conservatives, who think liberal judges act too much like politicians and decide issues that don't belong in court. It was a question O'Connor felt she was well qualified to answer. "I understood that about as well as anybody could," O'Connor said, "having been both." O'Connor remembers thinking that the conversation seemed fun for Reagan, and she enjoyed it herself.

When the interview ended, she went to the airport to catch her flight back to Arizona. "And I breathed a big sigh of relief. I thought, 'Wasn't that interesting, to meet all those people in the Oval Office?' " O'Connor said. She also felt sure she wouldn't get the job, especially with a friend from Arizona who also had gone to Stanford Law School already on the Court. "I was thinking it was so unlikely. I just thought it was not remotely likely. It was my husband who said, 'Of course they'll ask you. Don't be ridiculous.' "

A week later, Reagan reached her in her chambers in Phoenix. "I'd like to announce your nomination tomorrow, Sandra," Reagan said. O'Connor had gone from a young woman out of law school who couldn't get a job because of her sex to a judge who was going to be a Supreme Court justice because of it. "My heart sank," she said.

"It was such a massive undertaking, and I wasn't a bit sure my background and experience would enable me to do the job well enough to say yes," O'Connor explained. "You don't want to do a lousy job. I'd never worked at the Court. I wasn't a law clerk there. I didn't know it. I didn't have a practice that took me to the Supreme Court." O'Connor and her husband, John, were happy in Arizona. "To uproot ourselves and move to Washington, D.C., for me to start this massive new undertaking was a daunting prospect, and not one that filled my heart with joy," O'Connor recalled.

O'Connor was a little shaky when she hung up with the president. She immediately called her husband at his office. He was not ambivalent. "You have to do this," he told his wife. He had great faith and trust, and he told her she couldn't say no, despite her instincts. "You'll do fine."

So the O'Connors went to Washington. The pressure was overwhelming at times. As a midlevel state court judge, O'Connor was not particularly well versed in some of the constitutional concepts senators wanted to talk about. Administration lawyers gave her binder after binder, filled with notes and cases and talking points. She met with senators during the day, studied the binders at night, and practiced with lawyers the next morning. Then she started again. She lost so much weight that her clothes became loose on her already thin frame.

After Reagan nominated her, O'Connor called on Rehnquist, as well as then–chief justice Burger, whom she'd come to know through judicial conferences, to ask what she might expect during the Senate confirmation process. O'Connor had been so involved in helping Rehnquist with his own battle a decade earlier that she never thought twice about calling him now that she was in the same position. But neither Rehnquist nor Burger felt comfortable, as sitting justices, talking with her while her nomination was pending. "The sense then, and I think today, was if you're nominated, you stay away," O'Connor said.

But unlike the more controversial Rehnquist—who was hit with charges that he had opposed the landmark *Brown v. Board of Education*—O'Connor did not need her friend's input. Despite grumbling from conservative senators worried about her views on abortion, O'Connor was confirmed unanimously.

Rehnquist was more conservative than O'Connor from the beginning, but his attitudes toward the Court and the law were similar to her own. A new day brought a new case. No grudges, just move on.

O'Connor always admired that about Rehnquist, and after Reagan appointed him chief justice in 1986, her appreciation for him only grew. Rehnquist ran the Court with great efficiency.

The new chief justice was a master of the short statement at the Court, and he demanded brevity from fellow justices in their conferences. Rehnquist made it known that he expected less talk than his predecessor Burger had allowed. He found endless debate unproductive, and he believed the justices could best exchange legal reasoning and ideas in written memos and drafts. Whenever Rehnquist thought a justice went on too long in conference, he would simply cut him off. "It will come out in the writing," he'd say.

"Bill Rehnquist was concerned about efficiency. He didn't want to waste time. You could raise your hand, but it was not encouraged," O'Connor said of the conferences. "I thought Rehnquist's push for efficiency was a pretty good thing—to get on with the task and get the work done."

O'Connor voted often with Rehnquist in her early years, when he was the Court's most conservative member. Later, as chief justice, Rehnquist moderated his position on some issues, and O'Connor did as well. But as O'Connor entered her second decade on the Court, she began being pulled further left. Her voting patterns looked almost the same, but they didn't tell the full story. Increasingly, she was holding the conservatives back, staying on their side, but refusing to embrace sweeping rulings. By the early 1990s, Rehnquist found himself losing her vote on many of the era's major cases, as O'Connor became more liberal.[2] Unlike Burger, who would invite O'Connor to tea when he wanted her vote, Rehnquist kept his distance.

As chief justice, Rehnquist rarely pushed the independent O'Connor, even when she sided with liberals on social issues. Despite their long friendship—and the number of times he needed a fifth vote—it was a rare instance when Rehnquist picked up the phone to press his views. Conservative critics of Rehnquist grumbled that he wasn't putting his all into the job. He could have been more effective in managing O'Connor, they complained, instead of just standing by while his friend abandoned them on the cases they cared about the most.

It wasn't Rehnquist's style to lobby. Once, in Clarence Thomas's first year on the Court, the new justice was struggling with a case over the plight of thousands of Haitians who'd fled their war-torn country on boats for the United States. The George H. W. Bush administration ordered the coast guard to intercept them and return them directly to Haiti. Lawyers asked the justices to step in and stop the coast guard. Thomas was anguished. He sympathized with the Haitians. He called Rehnquist for advice, and the chief referred Thomas to a favorite poem by Arthur Hugh Clough. "Say not the struggle naught availeth," the poem begins, urging fortitude in the face of battle. It then ends on a hopeful note: "Westward look, the land is bright."

Thomas made a copy of the poem and slid it under the glass top of his desk, where he's kept it. He joined seven other justices and declined to intervene in the plight of the Haitian boat people. "I am deeply concerned about these allegations" of mistreatment in Haiti, Thomas wrote in a separate opinion explaining why the Court would not step in. "However, this matter must be addressed by the political branches, for our role is limited to questions of law."[3]

When Rehnquist did press, he could be effective. He cared deeply about states' rights, and beginning in 1995 he'd convinced other justices to join him in scaling back Congress's power. The Court generally was divided on those cases 5–4, and O'Connor, the former state legislator, was a solid ally. But five years later Rehnquist worried he would lose her vote in a critically important states' rights case that challenged the federal Violence Against Women Act.[4] The law allowed women to sue in federal court if they were physically assaulted because of their gender. Opponents said those lawsuits belonged in state court.

Rehnquist worried that O'Connor was wavering, and he felt compelled to approach her. Although O'Connor typically sided with him on states' rights issues, she also strongly supported women's rights. The case forced her to choose sides between two of her causes, and supporters of the law urged O'Connor to take theirs. But Rehnquist was the more effective lobbyist. O'Connor called him in his chambers late one afternoon to tell him she would be casting her vote with the chief. He hung up the phone with satisfaction. "Well, we got it," he said.

But even in those states' rights cases when O'Connor remained with her chief, the other justices seemed to be pulling back. Ten years after Rehnquist first tried to lead a "federalism revolution," the justices held up a stop sign and said that Congress could trump the states on law-enforcement issues. The Court ruled that the federal government had broad powers to prohibit the use of marijuana for medical purposes, even if the states wanted to allow it.[5] Antonin Scalia and Anthony Kennedy joined the Court's four liberals in supporting federal power in the case.

That case, decided at the end of the 2004 term, effectively ended Rehnquist's efforts to rein in Congress. Dying of cancer, he was in no condition to fire off one last rhetorical volley for states' rights. O'Connor and Thomas wrote the dissents instead.

The decision also seemed to signal the end of the Rehnquist Court. With the chief's expected retirement, George W. Bush would finally get the chance to put his stamp on the Court. But Bush wouldn't immediately change its direction. He would be replacing a conservative with another conservative, albeit a leader of his choosing.

That year had been difficult for the Court. Rehnquist, so stern in private settings, was a well-liked leader, and the justices had developed a warm and easy rapport over the years, even though they grappled with the most divisive issues of the time. Liberal justice Ruth Bader Ginsburg affectionately called Rehnquist "my chief," and as he deteriorated before their eyes, they suffered along with him.

His illness was ever present. Even in the private conferences, Rehnquist's breathing was strained, and he frequently had to clear his tracheotomy tube. Some of the justices felt constrained from strongly disagreeing over the cases during those conferences. And the other justices ended up writing more opinions.

O'Connor had several important ones. Although she sided with the liberals to order the Ten Commandments removed from a county courthouse,[6] she wrote a blistering dissent in a landmark dispute over property rights.[7] The liberal justices, joined once again by Justice Anthony Kennedy, had allowed a Connecticut town to force residents from their homes so they could sell the land to developers and collect more property taxes.

O'Connor said the decision meant "nothing is to prevent the state from replacing any Motel 6 with a Ritz-Carlton, any home with a shopping mall, or any farm with a factory." Her opinion may have been in the minority on the Court, but public outcry against the decision was immediate. Legislatures began passing laws to block the dire scenario O'Connor predicted.

The trials of the 2004 term behind her, O'Connor seemed to be looking ahead to another year on the Court. She had hired her law clerks for the next term, and had scheduled her public speeches so they didn't conflict with the days the Court was in session.

With the end of June approaching, O'Connor went back to talk to Rehnquist. He'd been coming to court every day, but she, like the other justices, still believed the chief would be retiring soon. She'd begun to think she would spend one more year on the Court before retiring herself. Rehnquist had been emphatic in their earlier discussion: The Court didn't need two retirements at the same time. Her guess was that he would announce his retirement, allowing her to stay one more year.

She guessed wrong.

"I want to stay another year," Rehnquist told O'Connor.

Years earlier, Rehnquist had vowed not to linger at the Court, that no man was bigger than the institution he served. Now, facing death, Rehnquist wasn't ready to leave a job that defined his life. "Say not the struggle naught availeth," went the words of his favorite poem. "Westward look, the land is bright."

Rehnquist was not ready to give up. But he then delivered a message she had heard before, this time with a stunning implication: "And I don't think we need two vacancies."

O'Connor, the trailblazing jurist who was arguably the most powerful woman in America, was caught off guard. Rehnquist's implication was clear: She must retire now or be prepared to serve two more years. Her opinions had determined the direction of the Court, reshaped American culture, and preserved the constitutional right to an abortion. But now Rehnquist, ravaged by cancer and desperately ill, was unilaterally deciding both of their fates. He would stay, and she should either step down now or be prepared to serve longer than she wanted.

The seventy-five-year-old O'Connor had been willing to remain another year, but because of her husband's illness, that would be it. Since the day he'd met Sandra Day, John O'Connor III had spent his life providing unconditional love and support. Unlike his wife, he never doubted that O'Connor would get the nomination after she met with President Reagan. And he never doubted that she could handle the job, even in those early days when, as a new justice, she couldn't sleep and lost weight from the pressure of being the first female on the highest court. O'Connor had no idea, absolutely none, how she would hold up in the face of historic pressures. She soon received the answer: her husband.

Sandra O'Connor had always imagined that she and John would retire to Arizona, where they'd kept a home the entire time they'd lived in Washington. They'd spend more time with their grandchildren, on the golf course, and traveling around the world. But now it was clear that wouldn't happen. The face of retirement had changed. John was battling Alzheimer's, the same debilitating disease that crippled and killed the president who had nominated O'Connor as an associate justice two decades earlier. It was her turn to support her husband, before the disease stole him from her for good.

She hadn't thought she'd be retiring at the end of the term, but it soon started to sink in. "Well, okay," O'Connor said, deferring to her old friend and chief. "I'll retire then."

With that exchange, the fading Rehnquist delivered to conservatives the vote they had craved for more than a decade. Now George W. Bush and his Republican Congress could begin the realignment of the Supreme Court. Bush would not be replacing a conservative with a conservative. He would replace the justice who often dictated the direction of the Court.

After twenty-four years on the Court, O'Connor had become the justice to watch. Rehnquist may have occupied the center seat on the bench, but O'Connor was the justice in the middle. With the Court divided 4–4 on critical issues, her vote often determined the outcome of important cases. Lawyers crafted their arguments to appeal especially to her, knowing that as O'Connor went, so went the Court. So broad was her power that journalists and law professors stopped talking about the "Rehnquist Court." It was instead, they said, the "O'Connor Court." Her vote had preserved the constitutional right to an abortion[8] and the use of affirmative action in college admissions.[9] Her vote had helped keep religion out of the public square.[10]

When O'Connor took her seat in the courtroom that last Monday in June, she knew that William Rehnquist was staying put. She had reconciled the events of the past month and, as she looked out on the packed courtroom, understood that this day would likely be her last on the bench. She may have been ambivalent about the timing, but "you make the decision, and you live with it," she explained in an interview. She had already thought about what she would say in her letter to President Bush. "I wanted to convey one simple thing: that I'd decided to retire and that I respected the Court," O'Connor said.

But O'Connor also understood the power of her vote, and she anticipated the battle that would ensue over her successor. She planned to tell Bush that she would remain on the bench until the Senate confirmed her replacement. She wasn't willing to risk leaving the Court short one member. She didn't want the Court deadlocked. "I did that deliberately," O'Connor said. "I had no intention of leaving the Court in a mess. I chose those words deliberately."

Two days after the justices exited the courtroom, leaving Washington speculating over when Rehnquist would quit, O'Connor called the Court's marshal, Pamela Talkin, into her office. O'Connor had specific instructions. She had a letter for President Bush. Talkin should keep it in the Court's safe until Friday, then deliver it to the White House.

Some of the justices have speculated privately that O'Connor waited until Friday to announce her retirement in order to give Rehnquist a chance to retire first. But they are mistaken. O'Connor and her husband, John, were leaving town that day, and she wanted to be on her way before the news reporters descended. She had seen the crush of cameras outside Rehnquist's home, camped out for a photograph on the day of his expected retirement announcement. She was determined to avoid that public spectacle.

Talkin, who is the first woman to oversee the Court's operations and security as marshal, called White House Counsel Harriet Miers at the White House the next day. Miers, Bush's longtime adviser from Texas who'd come to Washington in 2001 to work in his administration, had become counsel only months before. But she knew the kind of justice Bush wanted to appoint, and she'd been involved in the discussions over possible replacements for Rehnquist. The conversation didn't take long. "I need to deliver something, a letter, from a justice," Talkin told Miers.

It was a call Miers had expected. All week the White House had waited for Rehnquist to make his announcement, and it had already lined up a handful of contenders for Bush to interview to replace him. But the White House had begun to doubt Rehnquist would leave.

Talkin, on O'Connor's instructions, didn't tell Miers who had written the letter. She agreed to hand-deliver the letter to Miers in the White House the next morning at 10:30.

When Miers hung up the phone, she quickly notified Bush and Vice

President Dick Cheney, who were having lunch, and then told her deputy, William Kelley. Only a few months into the White House job, Kelley had deep Supreme Court experience, having argued before the Court as a lawyer in the Bush and Clinton administrations and having served as a law clerk to Burger and Scalia before that.

Most of the work was done. Top White House officials, including Cheney, had been interviewing possible nominees to replace Rehnquist for the past two months, and they had winnowed down the list to a handful. Kelley had played a critical role in analyzing prospective nominees and their opinions and writings, to advise Bush on whether they'd remain solidly conservative once on the Court.

Talkin and officials in the court's public information office arrived early the next day, as did Miers and her team in the White House. Miers called Talkin again to ask if she could bring the letter fifteen minutes earlier than scheduled. Talkin agreed, and then she delivered the stunning news. "The letter," she told Miers, "is from Justice O'Connor."

The revelation came as a jolt, but it would be a mistake to say that Miers was shocked. With no news from Rehnquist, some—notably the *Weekly Standard*'s Bill Kristol—had already speculated that it would be O'Connor who would step down. Seasoned Court watchers didn't believe it, nor did O'Connor's friends. But Miers saw it as her job to anticipate every possible contingency, and O'Connor's retirement—though unlikely—was one she'd considered.

O'Connor had told only a handful of people about her plans. Not even her three boys knew. She'd written them letters several days before and timed them to arrive at their homes Friday, when everyone else heard the news. As Talkin was breaking the news to Miers, O'Connor's farewell letters were hitting the other justices' desks.

O'Connor's secretary called Ginsburg's chambers. "You're going to get a letter from Justice O'Connor," she said. "You should open it right away."

Ginsburg was stunned. Kennedy, upon getting the letter, walked down the hall and gave O'Connor a hug. Clarence Thomas quickly called his wife, Ginni, who worked at the conservative Heritage Foundation, with the news. Minutes later, Thomas called back and asked his wife to urge her Heritage colleagues—frustrated by years of O'Connor opinions—not to say a negative word about her in the press.

Thomas, like the other justices, had grown fond of O'Connor. Depending on the age of the justice, the pioneering O'Connor was invariably described as a mother hen or a sister, the one who organized their lunches and kept things moving along. Even as the Court took up contentious issues that divided the justices as they divided the nation, the justices remained collegial. They credited O'Connor for much of that. They would miss her.

An hour later, one of the Court's Cadillac sedans whisked Talkin down Pennsylvania Avenue and into the White House, where she handed Miers the letter of resignation.

Before Talkin made it back to her office, Bush called the Court to speak with O'Connor and thank her for her service. The two spoke briefly. Bush invited her to the White House, but she declined. She had a plane to catch.

"For an old ranching girl, you turned out pretty good," Bush told O'Connor. "You're one of the great Americans."

O'Connor found herself overcome with emotion, and her voice began to break.

"I wish I was there to hug you," Bush said.

Minutes later, O'Connor walked out of the courthouse with John at her side and headed to Ronald Reagan Washington National Airport. The era of the so-called O'Connor Court was over.

Bush now had his chance. The battle would be epic. A new justice could provide the deciding vote on cases involving abortion, affirmative action, and religion. But the stakes, if anything, were even higher. O'Connor's retirement could change not only the Court's direction, but its very role in American life. For the past fifty years, beginning under the leadership of Earl Warren, the Court had confronted America's most pressing social controversies. The Court showed little hesitation in interjecting itself into those disputes and attempting to solve the nation's most vexing problems from the bench, even if that meant wresting them away from the state legislatures and the Congress.

In the 1950s, civil rights groups increasingly turned to the courts because elected officials did little or nothing to stop pervasive and virulent discrimination against African Americans. The Supreme Court responded with *Brown v. Board of Education* in 1954, which dismantled "separate but equal" facilities for blacks and whites throughout America. Segregation was outlawed by *Brown,* and only because the Warren Court ignored critics and intervened.

But the Court did not stop there. It began to see itself as a vital protector of rights and liberties, including those not specifically addressed in the Constitution. It recognized greater rights for criminal defendants. It imposed limits on religious expression. It identified new constitutional rights to privacy. Its role in American society grew. It became a moral compass.

Liberals believed that was an entirely proper role for the Court, especially since the other branches of government had failed so miserably in the area of civil rights. The Court was supposed to protect the rights of the minority against the will of the majority. If judges would not, they said, perhaps no one would. That approach encouraged the justices to identify new constitutional rights, especially in situations the document's framers could never have imagined two hundred years earlier. As society changed, the understanding of the Constitution should change with it, liberals believed, and the justices should help foster the progression.

Conservatives saw a Supreme Court that had arrogantly grabbed power for itself. By deciding those issues and creating new constitutional rights, conservatives believed, the justices usurped the role of elected officials, who were closer to the people and more accountable for their decisions at the ballot box. That struck at the heart of democratic participation, they believed. After all, voters aggrieved by their elected officials could campaign for change. But if the Court's unelected judges made all the decisions, the electorate had no leverage and little incentive to get involved in the debates.

As it happened, many politicians came to welcome the Court's intervention in contentious issues. It often saved them from making the tough calls. A politician could vote for extremely strict regulations on abortion, for example, knowing a court would step in and reverse them. His vote would have no practical impact, other than as a campaign slogan. A Maryland state senator candidly summed up that sentiment during a 2006 debate in his state legislature over whether to allow gay marriage, an issue that had bitterly divided his constituents. "I'm just hoping and praying the courts will step in," he said.[11]

For four decades, Republican presidential candidates had campaigned on constraining the Supreme Court's role in American life. But once elected, they'd had little success in doing so. The Warren Court soared so high and fast that it created a draft that swept the next Court, led by conservative Chief Justice Burger, right up with it. When Rehnquist took over in 1986, conservatives assumed his Court would pull back. Instead, it merely slowed down the constitutional crank, without turning it back the other way.

Sandra Day O'Connor's retirement offered a long-awaited opportunity to finally change the Court's direction—but only if conservatives didn't blunder through the process as they had in the past.

Justices—especially presumed conservative ones—have sometimes surprised the presidents who appointed them. Theodore Roosevelt said he could "carve out of a banana a Judge with more backbone" than Oliver Wendell Holmes. Harry Truman suffered a stinging setback when two of his four appointees voted to strike down his claims of presidential power to seize the nation's steel mills in 1952, and he called Justice Tom Clark "my biggest mistake." Dwight Eisenhower reportedly said his two worst mistakes as president both sat on the Supreme Court: William Brennan and Earl Warren, who became the ideological leaders of the most left-wing court in history. "Packing the Supreme Court simply can't be done," Truman said. "I've tried it, and it won't work."

Ronald Reagan made four appointments to the Supreme Court, but he failed to reverse the legacy of the liberal Warren Court. Nor did Richard Nixon, who also nominated four justices, including Rehnquist. Nixon, like Reagan, deliberately made his nominations to reverse the Court's direction. But Nixon ended up with yet another liberal court— and he appointed a justice, Harry Blackmun, who would write *Roe v. Wade,* a decision that would outrage conservatives for decades to come and change forever the tenor of confirmation hearings.

Change does not come easily in an institution that, once set on its course, moves with all the speed and agility of an oil tanker.

Rehnquist himself tried to explain in speeches in the mid-1980s why presidents so often fail to transform the Supreme Court. Beyond legal principles that can constrain justices from readily overturning previous decisions, Rehnquist speculated that new issues come before the Court that the justices—and the appointing president—simply never considered. Then there is public opinion. The justices work in an insulated atmosphere in the courthouse, but they go home and read the papers and talk about current events. Just as one planet can affect the orbit of another, public opinion "will likely have an effect upon the decision of some of the cases decided within the courthouse," Rehnquist said in a 1986 speech.

But conservative leaders, long focused on turning those tides of public opinion in their direction, have always grumbled that its influence always pulls justices one way: toward liberal elites in the media, especially the editorial pages of the *New York Times,* and at law schools, where most prominent academics see the Warren Court as the standard-bearer.

The Rehnquist Court had proven deeply disappointing to the Right. Justices billed as conservative proved not to be; justices who were solidly conservative shifted the court in unexpected ways. In both its reasoning and results, the Court failed to live up to conservative expectations and at times acted directly contrary to them. With seven Republican-appointed justices, the Rehnquist Court had refused to overturn *Roe v. Wade,* which guaranteed a woman's right to an abortion. It reaffirmed *Miranda v. Arizona,* a 5–4 Warren Court decision that required police to give warnings against self-incrimination to criminal suspects in custody.[12] It would not bring down the curtain on affirmative action.[13] It put greater restrictions on the death penalty[14] and created new rights for gays and lesbians,[15] expressly overturning earlier decisions in the process. It imposed sharper limits on presidential power than ever before.[16]

By the end of Rehnquist's tenure as chief justice, his court was decidedly not conservative. With O'Connor and Kennedy at its center, the Court was willing to identify new rights in the Constitution and take on all those nettlesome social issues that conservatives thought should be decided by legislatures. The Rehnquist Court didn't hesitate to take on the most hotly debated public issues of the time—abortion, gay rights, affirmative action, the death penalty, presidential power, the separation of church and state. Sometimes the decisions were narrow. Sometimes the justices split the difference between two strongly argued extremes.[17] But more often than not, on the most volatile issues, the Court did not take the conservative path.

Like the Republicans in the political branches, who have flouted ethics laws, increased the size of government, and shown no discipline in cutting runaway spending, the Supreme Court under Rehnquist went astray from conservative legal principles. Over the years, the O'Connor Court became increasingly willing to inject the Court—and the Constitution—into explosive public disputes. The justices came to believe that judicial wisdom could help decide the right policy. Their opinions didn't have the aggressively progressive tone of the Warren Court's decisions, which profoundly reshaped constitutional rights and protections in criminal law, civil rights, race relations, free-speech rights, and religion, but they produced significant liberal victories.

That's not to suggest that the Court was liberal. If anything, it was jurisprudentially unmoored. During Rehnquist's reign, the justices were in a constant struggle over which of their competing legal theories was most relevant. They had their own philosophies about the law, so the Court could legitimately be characterized as liberal one day and conservative the next. They tended to think of themselves as individual justices first, and less like a court of nine working to find consensus in the law. The Court was ideologically adrift, and its course usually depended on which way O'Connor—and to some extent, Kennedy—chose to go.

More often than not, on the big cases involving contentious social issues, O'Connor or Kennedy—or both of them together—would join the four liberals to rule against conservative positions. Only two of the justices who took the liberal path were Democratic nominees. The other four were appointed by Republicans. President Ford appointed John Paul Stevens, a maverick whose vote became solidly liberal after his first decade on the Court. Reagan tapped swing justices O'Connor and Kennedy. George H. W. Bush selected David Souter, one of the Court's most predictably liberal members.

As chief justice, Rehnquist was unable to build consensus and forge coalitions on key cases, even with his old friend O'Connor. At times, the once-fiery dissenter seemed to care more about a case's outcome than about the principled legal reasoning it took to get there, disappointing conservatives like Scalia, who would bluntly note the inconsistencies. In a 1998 case, Scalia accused the Court, with Rehnquist in the majority, of taking an approach it had specifically rejected only the year before. "The changes are attributable to nothing but the passage of time (not much time, at that), plus application of the ancient maxim "That was then, this is now,' " Scalia wrote in a dissent joined by Thomas.[18]

Unmoored as the Rehnquist Court appeared to be, however, few would argue that it was more expansive in granting rights than the Burger and Warren Courts would have been—with the possible exception, ironically, of *Bush v. Gore,* which ruled that the Florida recount in the disputed 2000 presidential election violated equal protection. During Rehnquist's remarkable thirty-three-year judicial career, he eventually molded other justices to his strong law enforcement views. His Court imposed limits on affirmative action and narrowed the use of redistricting designed to increase minority representation. It allowed more religious expression, including school vouchers for parochial schools. He also led a Court that was more assertive about its own authority, and more willing than any other Court in modern times to invalidate federal legislation that infringed on the states' concerns.

But the Rehnquist Court didn't dig up the foundation cemented by more left-leaning Courts and justices. Some of Rehnquist's victories, especially in scaling back congressional power over the states, had little practical impact. The way conservatives saw it, his Court did little to impede the liberal agenda, and in many cases actively furthered it. On one key social issue after another, the Rehnquist Court seemed bent on frustrating those who had long dreamed of restoring the Court to what they saw as its proper place in the system of government.

Perhaps that is why most liberal criticism of the Supreme Court focused more on fears about where the Court was headed than where it actually stood toward the end of Rehnquist's tenure.

Academics have written about the Rehnquist Court's surprising liberal legacy. Some have attributed its shift left to the Court's ruling in *Bush v. Gore,* which ended the bitterly contested 2000 presidential election and handed the presidency to George W. Bush.[19] That decision opened the Court to withering criticism for deciding the case on politics, not law. Those denunciations may have made the Court's centrists even more wary of being cast as predictable conservatives, a concern that would push the Court even further left in the remaining years of Rehnquist's tenure. But the suggestion that O'Connor and Kennedy voted with the Court's liberals only in the years after *Bush v. Gore,* in order to counter allegations by the media and law professors that they had been driven by rank partisanship, ignores a decade of their earlier rulings on social issues.

Still, the 2000 election was without question a watershed event for the Court. The outcome of the race came down to fewer than a thousand votes in Florida. Al Gore initially conceded defeat on election night when it appeared that Bush had carried the state and won the presidency, but the balloting was so close, the stakes so high, that Gore withdrew his concession and decided to challenge the results and ask for a partial recount.

The legal battle captivated the nation, as television networks aired endless images of election officials hand-counting the ballots, often holding them up to the light and squinting quizzically to discern the vote. Bush opposed the recount, arguing that it was illegal under state law and the federal Constitution. His partisans also made much of the fact that Gore and his lawyers had asked that a recount be conducted not in the entire state, but only in a few heavily Democratic Florida counties where they suspected those squinting at hanging chads might "find" enough additional votes to hand the election to Gore. Lower courts agreed with Bush, but the Florida Supreme Court ordered the recounts to continue.

Entire books have been written on the Supreme Court's decision in *Bush v. Gore,* but the outcome is not that complicated. The five most conservative justices joined together to block the recount of votes in Florida, essentially calling the election for George W. Bush. The conservatives believed that the Florida Supreme Court had brazenly thumbed its nose at an earlier unanimous U.S. Supreme Court decision by ordering the recounts to continue without any standards for conducting them. The conservatives said the process was so arbitrary that it violated basic concepts of equal protection, a secondary argument Bush's legal team had made. This was a startling decision from justices who had spent their careers resisting such broad constitutional claims.

The Court's four most liberal justices sided with Gore, refusing to join a more narrow opinion by Rehnquist that upbraided the Florida Supreme Court for ignoring their directives. The liberals said the justices should stay out of the process and emphasized states' rights—that the Florida courts and the Florida officials should handle a recount which would determine the presidential contest. It was a stunning claim coming from the four, who had vehemently opposed previous Supreme Court decisions giving states greater powers.

The decision produced deep divisions in the Court and outraged liberals, law professors, and editorial writers, all of whom accused the conservative justices (though not their liberal counterparts) of deciding the case based on their political views. Although every justice had taken a position at odds with his or her stance in the past, the blow to conservatives was particularly severe. The decision also seemed to represent the kind of result-driven outcome the conservative legal movement had long opposed.

The conservative legal movement prided itself on strictly following its methods of interpreting the Constitution, even when it produced results conservatives didn't like. But the unsigned opinion in *Bush v. Gore* seemed to many like a result-oriented approach, good for one day, and one case, only.

The Court's liberal justices still believe *Bush v. Gore* was a political decision, and they privately question whether the outcome would have been the same if it had been *Gore v. Bush,* with the Republican candidate calling for a recount. They contend that the Court would never have reviewed the case in the first place if the parties had been reversed.

But the conservative justices say politics didn't drive them. Kennedy says he took a long walk around the hallways of the Supreme Court and imagined how he would have seen the case if the parties had been reversed. He concluded that he would have decided it the same way. The conservative justices believe that the country was in crisis, and they insist that they had a duty to step in and make the hard decisions. The Florida Supreme Court was a rogue state court "off on a trip of its own," as O'Connor puts it, ordering up recounts but without clear and uniform standards for doing it. The justices, she argues, had no choice but to step in.

"A no-brainer! A state court deciding a federal constitutional issue about the presidential election?" Kennedy exclaimed, in an interview nearly six years later. "Of course you take the case."

The Supreme Court didn't ask to get involved, defenders like Kennedy and O'Connor say. It was Al Gore who started the recount battle. "It would be odd if the people that brought the litigation would later say the courts shouldn't intervene," Kennedy says today. "We didn't say the case should go to the court. Those were the other parties that made that decision for us. And for us to say, 'Oh, we're not going to get involved because we're too important,' well, you know, that's wrong."

O'Connor is less forceful in her analysis. She ruefully notes that subsequent media recounts of the disputed ballots indicated Bush would have won Florida.[20] The outcome would have been the same, she says, even without the Supreme Court's involvement. "It's not correct to say the Court determined the result. The voters determined the result, and it never changed," O'Connor says today. "Could we have done a better job? Probably. But it wouldn't have changed the result."

Whether the decision elected a president or not—and media recounts of ballots in the contested counties support O'Connor's contention—this was a Court that possessed a sweeping sense of its role in refereeing disputes of enormous national importance. A judicial approach that had infuriated and motivated conservatives for decades was entirely pleasing to them as *Bush v. Gore* unfolded. And if the conservative justices were driven by a political or ideological motive to rule in a way that guaranteed Bush's election, their decision paid multiple dividends. It gave the new president a chance to appoint two or three justices who would hold a much more restrictive view of their roles on the bench.

The Court stayed together for five years after *Bush v. Gore*, denying George W. Bush a nomination in his first term. In that time, the Court's moderates embraced sweeping liberal rulings on key social issues, further disappointing conservatives. With Sandra Day O'Connor's retirement, Bush would now have the chance to succeed where his father and so many other Republican presidents had failed. If he got it right, he could make history. The burden of reshaping the Supreme Court would be placed on Bush's administration and his GOP majority in the Senate. The battle for the Supreme Court's future was about to begin.

2.

SETTLING FOR TONY

The courtroom crackled with tension on the final day of the Court's 2003 session on the last Thursday in June. Lawyers and gay-rights activists had arrived early to get a prime seat, nervously whispering as they waited for the justices to emerge from behind the velvet curtains. There were few smiles, and there was little small talk. Veteran lawyers who had devoted their entire careers to fighting for the constitutional rights of gays and lesbians looked grim. They had gathered to hear a case that many in the courtroom believed to be a referendum on their way of life: whether states could prosecute gays and lesbians for having consensual sex.

Several of the lawyers felt almost ill from anxiety, their hearts pounding and stomachs churning, when the Court's marshal struck the gavel and said, "the honorable, the Chief Justice and the Associate Justices," as the nine entered the chamber. The attorneys had been waiting on the decision for weeks, and although the Court refuses to tell the public which cases it will be deciding on a given day, everyone knew this was the day the gay-rights case would be decided. It was, after all, the close of the Court's session, the Court's final chance to hand down a decision before the justices took their summer break.

As the justices plowed through the far less significant cases announced that morning, anxiety built to almost unbearable levels. Justice Breyer finally finished delivering a lengthy lesson in a criminal case, and Chief Justice Rehnquist's voice boomed through the courtroom. Justice Kennedy, he said, would announce the opinion in No. 02-102, *Lawrence v. Texas.*

Anthony Kennedy leaned forward in his chair and began summarizing the issues in the case. It came about after Houston police officers, responding to what later was proven to be a false report that a man was "going crazy" with a gun, entered the apartment of fifty-five-year-old John Lawrence, a medical technologist. When they found Lawrence having sex with his partner in the bedroom, police arrested both men and took them to jail.

Kennedy's voice was strong and forceful, with an almost indignant edge, and the breadth of his opinion quickly became clear. In 1986, the Court had upheld a similar Georgia law that made sodomy a crime. That case, *Bowers v. Hardwick,* was "not correct when it was decided, and it is not correct today," Kennedy said.

The gay-rights lawyers and leaders in the courtroom could scarcely contain their elation: History was being made, and they were on the winning side. Kennedy continued.

"This case does involve two adults who, with full and mutual consent from each other, engaged in sexual practices common to the homosexual lifestyle," he said. "The state cannot demean their existence or control their destiny by making their private homosexual conduct a crime."

Kennedy was offering an apology. As he expressed regret for the previous decision that had denied gay men and women the right to make intimate and personal choices, several of the lawyers in the front rows of the courtroom began weeping openly. Kennedy's opinion, which the Court's four liberals joined, would help gays to attack all forms of discrimination, including laws that banned same-sex marriage.

Rehnquist, Scalia, and Thomas endorsed a harsh dissent that accused Kennedy of signing on to the "so-called homosexual agenda" and taking sides in the "culture war." Thomas, in a separate dissent of his own, called the law "uncommonly silly" and said he would repeal it if he were a state legislator, but that it wasn't unconstitutional. Even O'Connor, the Court's other moderate, thought Kennedy had gone too far. She agreed with the result, but refused to sign on to his sweeping opinion overturning *Bowers.*

Once again Anthony Kennedy had crossed the ideological line, disappointing the conservatives who had supported him. And he didn't hesitate this time. Kennedy acknowledges that he agonizes over his opinions, but he didn't on that one. The right result was so obvious, he later told Thurgood Marshall's wife, that he wrote the decision over the course of one weekend. Remarkably, a man once perceived as a staunchly conservative justice, appointed by Ronald Reagan to return the Court to a more limited role in society, had no reservations about drafting the most sweeping opinion in support of gay rights in U.S. history. By offering constitutional protection to gays, Kennedy opened the courthouse door for countless legal battles in the coming decades.

Kennedy had come a long way from his earliest days on the Supreme Court, when the *New York Times* called him a "predictable conservative"[1] and the *Washington Post* said he was "as conservative as any justice nominated by President Ronald Reagan."[2] Those early returns had raised conservatives' hopes. But the lawyers who'd studied his record before Reagan nominated him knew all too well the kind of justice he would likely become.

Kennedy's confirmation in 1988 came only after a spectacular combination of strategic blunders and humiliating revelations that led a White House in the final months of Ronald Reagan's presidency to grab desperately on to the last confirmable man standing. Adamantly opposed by high-ranking officials in the Justice Department, Kennedy had stood by quietly as other prospects were destroyed or self-destructed. His president, wounded and weakened, had little choice but to send him out to the battlefield next, even while the carnage was still being carried away. Kennedy is living proof that despite a president's efforts to change the direction of the Court, politics—both in the White House making the nomination and in the Senate voting on confirmation—sometimes force a different path.

In the days after Lewis Powell announced his retirement back in June 1987, no conservative dreamed that the best Reagan could do to replace him would be a moderate California federal judge named Anthony Kennedy. The administration was determined to change the direction of the Court, and Powell's retirement had given conservatives a momentous opportunity. His replacement would provide their fifth vote to begin reversing all those liberal decisions Reagan had campaigned against, from bans on school prayer to a constitutional right to abortion. The administration lawyers were fully on board with Reagan's promises to change the direction of the Supreme Court. They had been keeping lists of nominees for several years, after instituting a rigorous system for judicial selection. Kenneth Starr had overseen the effort in the early years, with a team of lawyers that included a young John Roberts. Starr's group aggressively pursued judicial candidates who shared the administration's conservative judicial philosophy, and carefully screened candidates by asking detailed hypothetical questions. The process had proven ruthlessly efficient in the lower federal courts, where scores of young nominees would soon become conservative icons.

The efforts intensified once Ed Meese became Reagan's attorney general in 1985. Reagan's longtime friend wasted no time in making the issue his own, writing and speaking extensively about the kind of judges the White House should nominate. Meese trumpeted "originalism," a way of interpreting the Constitution that limits a judge's focus to the document's exact words and the original understanding of its meaning. The only rights an originalist judge will typically recognize are those specifically mentioned in the Constitution's text. Under this restrictive approach, cultural and social issues would be decided not in courts but in legislatures, which conservatives say are better suited to implement the people's will. That's the kind of justice Ronald Reagan wanted to nominate, and both his legal and political teams appreciated the significance of their decisions.

"The stakes here are immense—whether or not this President can leave behind a Supreme Court that will carry forward the ideas of the Reagan Revolution into the 21st century," Patrick Buchanan, the White House communications director, wrote in a 1985 memo to Donald Regan, Reagan's chief of staff. Political advisers like Buchanan also knew that a successful Supreme Court nomination would bring other rewards, including a chance to score political points with the conservative groups that turn out to vote on election day.

"Given the cruciality of the Supreme Court to the Right-to-Life Movement, to the School Prayer Movement, to the anti-pornography people, etc.—all of whom provide the Republicans with the decisive Presidential margins—the significance of this first nominee is not easy to exaggerate," Buchanan wrote in another memo, midway through Reagan's second term.

When Chief Justice Warren Burger retired in 1986, the year before Powell, Reagan not only had a chance to tap a solid conservative who would lead the Court into the next century, but also could reward political backers and solidify their support. Burger's retirement could not have come at a better time for the White House. Reagan was at the height of his popularity, with near-record-setting approval ratings, when advisers began searching for a replacement. In a Gallup poll at the time, 68 percent of Americans approved of Reagan's job performance—making him more popular than any other president midway through his second term since Franklin Roosevelt. Journalists began filling column inches speculating whether Congress would respond to the president's popularity by voting to repeal the Twenty-second Amendment, which limits presidents to two terms in office.

But Warren Burger's retirement set in motion a chain of events that would ultimately thwart Reagan's goal of remaking the Court. Decisions made that year would sow the seeds for Kennedy's nomination a year later. Burger had told Reagan in a private meeting about a month before the end of the Court's session that he would be stepping down. He'd offered up six names as possible replacements, including Justices William Rehnquist and Byron White, as well as Judges Robert Bork and Antonin Scalia, both of whom were serving on the same D.C.-based federal appeals court.

Bork had been on the shortest of short lists for at least a decade, back to 1975, when Gerald Ford instead nominated Chicagoan John Paul Stevens at the urging of his attorney general, Edward Levi. Others in the Justice Department had wanted Bork then, but Levi, the former dean of the University of Chicago Law School, insisted that Stevens was the better choice. Bork was too controversial in those years immediately after Watergate because as solicitor general he'd carried out President Nixon's orders to fire special prosecutor Archibald Cox. Stevens, a Chicago-based federal appeals court judge, was above reproach; he had even been counsel to a special commission that investigated ethics complaints against members of the Illinois Supreme Court. Scalia had emerged only more recently as a contender, having joined the appeals court in 1982 after working in the Ford Justice Department, where he held Rehnquist's old job, and teaching law at the University of Chicago.

A couple days after Burger spoke to Reagan, Meese met with Reagan's White House counsel, Peter Wallison, to discuss the contenders. Historically, presidents had sought nominees who shared their ideological goals, but they didn't go to great lengths to analyze how an appointee would rule as a justice. That changed as the Supreme Court became more involved in social issues. Presidents began seeking nominees they thought would reflect their own positions. In the Reagan White House the goals were clear: They sought candidates who would be certain followers of Reagan's philosophy of judicial restraint. Meese urged Wallison to talk to William Bradford Reynolds, the controversial head of the department's civil rights division, about his work in researching prospective nominees. They agreed to have a short list of candidates ready for the president when they met with him ten days later.

Reynolds had taken over Starr's role in leading the group that screened prospective judicial nominees after Starr had become a judge on the D.C.-based federal appeals court. At Meese's direction, the group thoroughly examined more than a dozen Supreme Court prospects. It focused on sitting federal judges who'd run the gauntlet of the Judiciary Committee and the full Senate and had proven conservative credentials.

But by the week's end, Rehnquist, Bork, and Scalia had emerged as the obvious front-runners. The other nominees weren't seriously discussed, although two conservative Justice Department lawyers, Richard Willard and Carolyn Kuhl, pushed for Kennedy. Both had clerked for Kennedy on the California-based federal appeals court and believed his integrity and experience as a judge would make him a good justice. But Willard did not oversell Kennedy, emphasizing to his colleagues only that Kennedy would be a "good administrator" and would "get along with others on the court."

The Justice Department also averted a bid by Senator Orrin Hatch, who'd made it known to the White House that he was interested in the nomination for chief justice. Lawyers knew they needed a reason for rejecting the conservative Utah Republican, so Justice Department lawyer Michael Carvin came up with one. He wrote a memorandum for the file, taking the position that any senator who had voted for a judicial pay raise, as Hatch had, was disqualified from getting the office.

Wallison and Reynolds spent two hours in early June talking at the Justice Department about the leading candidates. Rehnquist was considered the "paradigmatic example" of a judicial conservative during his fourteen years on the Court and was the top choice for chief, according to a memo summarizing the events, but Reynolds worried that he was "tired and probably would not want the added administrative burdens of the chief justice position."

Scalia and Bork were neck and neck to take Rehnquist's seat as associate justice. "Both," as one administration lawyer put it, "were perfect." Both were leading conservative intellectuals with well-developed views on the law and how to interpret the Constitution. Both believed courts should have a limited role in American life and step into disputes only when the elected representatives—whether in Congress or in the state legislatures—infringed on freedoms that were expressly written in the Constitution. Under that approach, both would denounce judges who created any "right" not specifically found in the Constitution, such as the right of privacy to have an abortion or the right to engage in homosexual conduct. Both, the administration believed, would readily vote to overturn Supreme Court decisions they thought were clearly inaccurate or unprincipled. That meant both would overturn *Roe v. Wade.* Indeed, Justice Department lawyers were so confident of Bork's views on the subject that they wrote in one internal memo, "he would not hesitate to overturn constitutional aberrations such as *Roe v. Wade.*"

"Bork possesses monumental intellectual and scholarly credentials and has personally reexamined many of the broad, fundamental legal and jurisprudential issues of our time," the lawyers wrote in a background memo about the potential nominee. He also was "extremely eloquent and persuasive, both in print and in person," a "talent that will serve him well in building a consensus supporting conservative principles on the court."

Scalia, too, was "extremely personable . . . articulate and persuasive," the lawyers wrote in a separate memo, although, as an appeals court judge he was "potentially prone to an occasional outburst of temper," making it "conceivable he might rub one of his colleagues the wrong way."

But on substance, the two were almost identical. Although Scalia had not "focused on the 'big picture' jurisprudential questions to quite the same extent as Bork," his writings reflected "a fundamental, well-developed theory of jurisprudence," the lawyers wrote in a separate memo outlining his views. "Scalia's judicial philosophy," the lawyers wrote, "almost precisely mirrors that of Bork." If they differed at all, Scalia was slightly more conservative, they concluded.

For Reagan's advisers, the politics of the nomination turned on age and compatibility. Scalia edged out Bork on both. "It came down to the ten years," one top official later explained. Scalia was almost a decade younger than Bork, and even though he smoked and drank, he also exercised regularly. Reynolds and his team concluded that Scalia was likely to be on the Court longer than Bork because he was in better health—an important consideration if Scalia was to be Reagan's last nomination.

They also thought Scalia was a better nominee to stand alongside Rehnquist. Advisers had some concern that Rehnquist, the Court's most ardent conservative, would be controversial. As the first Italian American nominated to the Court, Scalia could be an easier sell than Bork, and he would give Reagan a political boost.

"While Bork is an ex-Marine and a brilliant judge, I would lean to Scalia for the first seat," Buchanan wrote to Don Regan. "He is an Italian-American, a Roman Catholic, who would be the first Italian ever nominated—a tremendous achievement for what is America's largest ethnic minority, not yet fully assimilated into the melting pot— a minority which provides the GOP its crucial margins of victory in New Jersey, Connecticut and New York."

With advisers narrowing the focus—and all leaning toward Scalia to take Rehnquist's job as associate justice—Reagan met with his top advisers in early June. A key concern, according to a written summary of the meeting, was the "problem of finding candidates who were likely to adhere to the President's philosophy of judicial restraint after they had been appointed to the Supreme Court." O'Connor, for example, had said the right words during her interview and Senate hearing. But having been a midtier state court judge, she hadn't grappled with the big federal constitutional questions or written about theories of constitutional interpretation. Her opinions were already proving disappointing to conservatives.

By that point, O'Connor had been on the Court five years. She'd been a consistent conservative vote at first, but she had begun to move away from the values of the conservative president who nominated her. Administration lawyers were starting to have "serious concerns about the depth and consistency of her commitment to principles of judicial restraint and fundamental constitutional values," as they put it in one memo. "Her most glaring weakness has been in the religion cases," the lawyers said in one memo, because she "has consistently taken the indefensible position that legitimate efforts to accommodate religion" violate the Constitution. O'Connor had voted to strike down educational programs benefiting religious schools, laws that required a moment of silence in public schools, and laws that required employers to excuse employees from working on their Sabbath.[3]

The administration lawyers were also worried about affirmative action. O'Connor, they wrote, had a "troublesome propensity to file concurring opinions seeking to dilute the force of opinions condemning" racial quotas. An especially disquieting case involved a group of white teachers from Michigan who had challenged their school district's employment policy as unconstitutional race discrimination.[4] Under the policy, minority teachers could keep their jobs over more senior white teachers if it was necessary to maintain the school's racial balance. The Court struck down that race-based plan by a 5–4 vote, with O'Connor joining the conservatives. But O'Connor's separate opinion in that case alarmed the administration lawyers. O'Connor not only refused to go along with the moderate Powell's blistering condemnation of racial quotas, but even sought common ground with the liberal dissenters. O'Connor believed the justices weren't as divided on the issue of affirmative action as it seemed and concluded that the Court "is at least in accord" in believing affirmative action programs by public employers are constitutional.

O'Connor's separate opinion infuriated Meese's Justice Department, which believed it had "undercut" the conservative cause and weakened the ruling's forcefulness. "This concurrence demonstrates an error in strategic judgment as well, because it attempts to create a 'consensus' among various justices where there clearly was not one," Justice Department lawyers wrote after the O'Connor opinion in 1986. "Such 'diplomatic' efforts are inevitably doomed to failure and simply provide the dissenters with further ammunition in future cases."

Importantly for future Court nominees, O'Connor's moderate shift served as a warning to administration lawyers: There were real risks in selecting an unknown, undefined nominee, especially with so much on the line. Political considerations must line up with the legal ones.

Reagan said he wanted to talk to Rehnquist to gauge his interest, but choosing between Bork and Scalia wasn't so simple. Reagan initially wanted Bork. He'd long assumed that Bork, the nation's leading conservative jurist, would be his next nominee as an associate justice. But when his advisers sketched out the politics, Reagan found Scalia intriguing. He liked that Scalia was young enough to serve on the court for a long time, and would be the first Italian American appointee.

Reagan met with Rehnquist three days later. Burger's plans still weren't public, but Rehnquist did not seem surprised when Reagan told him the news.

"You're the unanimous choice of all of us," Reagan continued. He asked Rehnquist to think about taking the job. But Rehnquist did not need to weigh his options; he accepted the nomination on the spot. "I'd be honored," he told Reagan.

Reagan moved to the next issue. He'd obviously need to appoint a new associate to take Rehnquist's place. What about Scalia or Bork? Reagan asked.

Rehnquist declined to take a side. He told the president he had "high regard" for both men.

Reagan turned to his advisers after Rehnquist left the Oval Office. He wanted to meet with Scalia. Don Regan called Scalia and set up a meeting with Reagan for June 16, four days away.

In their meeting at the White House, Reagan got right to the point. He described the circumstances of Burger's resignation and his plans to nominate Rehnquist to take his place. "You're the choice of all of us," he told Scalia, just as he'd told Rehnquist four days earlier.

Scalia said he would be honored to accept, and Reagan concluded that he'd introduce his new nominees to the nation the next day.

Even though neither nomination would affect the balance of the Court—Rehnquist replaced the conservative Burger, and Scalia the even more conservative Rehnquist—the process quickly became contentious. But instead of focusing on the new nominee and his views, the liberal groups focused their attention on Rehnquist, attacking his Supreme Court opinions on race, privacy, federal power, and criminal law. They also accused Rehnquist of intimidating and harassing minority voters when he worked as a poll watcher in Arizona in the 1960s. Those charges came on the heels of allegations that Rehnquist was insensitive to civil rights, based largely on a memo he'd written in 1952 as a law clerk to Justice Robert Jackson. In the memo, Rehnquist wrote that he believed *Plessy v. Ferguson,* the infamous 1896 case that preserved "separate but equal" accommodations for blacks and whites, was "right and should be reaffirmed." Rehnquist said the memo was written to reflect Jackson's views, not his own. But liberal critics—and Jackson's secretary—flatly rejected that explanation.

Rehnquist's nomination attracted the strongest recorded opposition in the history of the Senate for a chief justice; thirty-three senators ultimately voted against him. But Scalia, the new nominee, slid unnoticed under the radar. Despite his strong views, he was confirmed unanimously.

But time would soon prove that Reagan and his troops had made an egregious error. The former baseball announcer had selected the wrong leadoff man. In hindsight, his choice of Scalia over Bork was a strategic blunder that would thwart Reagan's efforts to remake the Supreme Court. By nominating Scalia first, alongside the controversial Rehnquist, the White House used up all of its political advantages. With Reagan at the height of his popularity and Republicans controlling the Senate, Bork would have been confirmed alongside Rehnquist—

leaving the more loquacious and charming Scalia to emerge for the next nomination, all but daring senators to reject the court's first Italian American nominee.

Instead, Bork's chance came a year later, when Powell concluded he would retire after almost sixteen years on the Court. Nominated by President Nixon, Powell had become a key "swing" vote who sometimes sided with liberals, sometimes with conservatives. Unlike replacing Burger, following Powell with a solid conservative would change the direction of the Court—and the nation.

Now Reagan was by no means assured the easy confirmation he'd enjoyed with Scalia the year before. The political tables had turned upside down. Democrats had pulled off the impossible in the November elections, taking over eight seats in the Senate for a commanding 55–45 vote margin. Republican senator Strom Thurmond had relinquished control of the Judiciary Committee to Delaware senator Joe Biden, whose new title as chairman gave him the ideal platform to drum up liberal support for a presidential bid. Liberal interest groups promised all-out war over judicial nominees. "It will stop them dead in their tracks in reorganizing the judiciary," vowed the influential Nan Aron, of the liberal Alliance for Justice, the week after the election.[5]

Reagan, too, was weakened from the year before. The Iran-Contra scandal had become public in November, and his approval ratings had tumbled. By June, when Powell retired, the number of people saying Reagan hadn't told the truth about Iranian arms sales reached 69 percent, and Reagan's approval ratings fell nearly 20 points. Americans had also shifted blame to Reagan for budget deficits and said Democrats could better solve the problem.

Struggling to emerge from scandal and regain his footing, Reagan replaced his top advisers in the White House with outsiders. Howard Baker, the former Tennessee senator, took over for Regan as chief of staff, and A. B. Culvahouse, Baker's law firm colleague, came in as White House counsel.

Powell's retirement was not entirely a surprise. He'd suffered from health problems, and journalists had long speculated that the Virginian would step down. But Powell's timing was hardly ideal. For an inexperienced and embattled Reagan White House, it would be a kind of perfect storm, one of the biggest Supreme Court battles in history.

The moment Powell's resignation letter reached the White House, Justice Department lawyer Carvin, a New Yorker whose quick wit and colorful stories took the edge off his blunt style, rushed in to give the news to Chuck Cooper, the head of the Office of Legal Counsel. Cooper, who'd clerked for Rehnquist, was an Alabama native with a genteel southern accent and crisply starched shirts. Though differing in styles, the two were united in their belief that only conservative judges practicing judicial restraint should be nominated by Ronald Reagan. They quickly called Reynolds, who had just lost a bruising Senate confirmation bid to be the third-highest official at Justice after senators had accused him of seeking to roll back civil rights. Cooper and Carvin had one word for Reynolds when he answered the phone. "Bork," they said in unison.

Reynolds's response was swift: "Done."

Unlike in the George W. Bush administration, the Justice Department wielded great influence over judicial nominations. Ed Meese had assembled a group of lawyers—Reynolds, Cooper, Carvin, Doug Kmiec, and Sam Alito—who shared his views about judicial restraint and the role of the federal system and the Supreme Court's limited role within it.

No judge was a stronger proponent of that approach than Robert Bork. Meese did not have to sell Reagan on his nomination when Powell stepped down. In the West Wing later that afternoon, Culvahouse summoned his top lawyers and asked for an updated list of possible candidates. He told them to focus on "minorities, women, Democrats, and senators" and think through "confirmability issues." Robert Bork's name "should be on the list," Culvahouse said. He didn't need to add that the D.C. judge should be at the top.

After sifting through potential nominees, the group gathered early Saturday morning for assignments, and each lawyer was asked to focus on a specific nominee. Again Bork was at the top of the list. The group immediately focused on his role in the "Saturday Night Massacre," when Bork followed President Nixon's orders to fire special Watergate prosecutor Archibald Cox. Nixon was forced to turn to his solicitor general after his attorney general and deputy attorney general, Elliot Richardson and William Ruckelshaus, had refused. Now, thirteen years later, Culvahouse would have to assign a Reagan White House lawyer to investigate the matter.

In addition to Bork, Senator Hatch was again on the list, as was Senator Howell Heflin, an Alabama Democrat, although they were added largely for the benefit of the senators themselves and not because they were ever viewed as serious contenders. A couple of women judges were added to the mix, along with five men, including, again, Anthony Kennedy.

Much of the work involved updating research that had been put together for Reagan the year before, when they'd gone through the process and selected Rehnquist and Scalia. At every turn, Bork was the obvious next choice.

In a memo outlining Bork's views, the White House lawyers described him as the bright light of judicial conservatism, a leading thinker with impeccable logic and a powerful writing style. Bork also happened to be "a tremendously warm human being and very witty," the lawyers wrote, as well as "responsive, evenhanded and respectful" of all the lawyers who appeared in his courtroom. "Even liberals respect Bork's intellectual force," the lawyers wrote in a memo to Reagan.

He had few negatives, or so they believed. His only "disturbing opinion" in the eyes of the Justice Department was a case involving a libel lawsuit against columnists Rowland Evans and Robert Novak.[6] Bork had sided with the columnists and urged the court, as the lawyers put it, to "expand the already extraordinary protection afforded the media" in libel suits. That case had him parting ways with the more conservative Scalia, who accused Bork of "sociological jurisprudence" in siding with the press in the libel case.

But the White House treated that as positive. "The media will also be kind to Bork because of his strong support for the First Amendment in a recent libel decision," the White House lawyers said.

Years later, the administration memos appear breathtakingly naïve. Confident in Bork's impeccable academic qualifications, the administration utterly failed to anticipate the controversy his nomination would create and thus had no strategy to defend Reagan's favorite pick. Rather than sailing onto the Court, as anticipated, Bork met overwhelming resistance and was incapable of winning over his many critics. Although his defeat came at the hands of a Democrat-controlled Senate, six Republicans also voted against him. The 58–42 Senate vote against Bork was the largest margin of defeat ever for a Supreme Court nominee.

The nomination was an abject failure at every level. The White House, with Baker and Culvahouse both new to their jobs, never developed a strategy to sell Robert Bork to the senators and the American people. As a result, Democrats were able to define the nominee as a Stone Age extremist who would turn the clock back on civil rights for women and minorities. Though shrill attacks against nominees are often exaggerated by the Left and Right, Bork's critics recognized what Reagan did. Robert Bork was in the intellectual vanguard of judicial restraint. His constitutional method was at the very center of the conservative movement. He had provided the underpinnings for Meese's entire approach for reshaping the judiciary away from what conservatives saw as the gross excesses of the Warren Court. He would change the direction of the Supreme Court.

Unprepared for the conflict and facing an unanticipated firestorm of criticism, the White House inexplicably chose not to defend Bork's constitutional approach to the law. It was a debate many conservatives wanted to have. They felt judicial activism had placed too much power in the hands of unelected judges and deprived the people, through their elected representatives, of making the decisions at the center of democracy. But rather than launch that ideological battle, White House officials desperately tried to paint Bork as a Lewis Powell "moderate," which he decidedly was not. That ridiculous strategy only played into the hands of Democrats by making Bork's conservative legal philosophy appear radically removed from the mainstream.

Overconfident of Bork's intellectual superiority and his ability to handle the Senate hearings, administration officials yielded to their nominee's demands when it came time to prepare for the hearings. Unlike the grueling, days-long "murder board" sessions of today, when nominees are confronted with the most provocative questions law professors and White House lawyers can formulate, Bork's preparation largely consisted of a few sessions in his living room with Reynolds and Ray Randolph, another Justice Department lawyer. If either made suggestions on how to respond to senators more diplomatically, Bork would just smile. He saw no reason to pull punches. "I'll say it the way I'm going to say it," he'd respond. That overconfidence would wreck Robert Bork's lifelong dream of sitting on the Supreme Court.

When confronted with the real questioners at the televised Judiciary Committee hearings, Bork did himself no favors. He came across as arrogant and dismissive, playing into the hands of his opponents, who effectively portrayed him as cold, uncaring, and unsympathetic to the problems of ordinary Americans. He got no respect from liberals and no strong support from the media, and his answers to the senators' questions made him seem anything but warm, witty, and responsive.

A White House postmortem was harshly critical of Bork's performance, all but screaming frustration at his failure to better explain his views on the law. Instead of stressing the democratic aspects of his jurisprudence—and driving a wedge between northern liberals and southern Democrats—Bork had "responded to politically charged innuendo with legal esoterica."

"The nominee should take his case directly to the American people. Bork totally missed this opportunity," policy analyst Dinesh D'Souza wrote. "When senators asked him whether he felt crime was a blight on this country, instead of giving examples of serial murderers set free on technicalities, Bork said that criminal law was not his specialty." In the memo, D'Souza imagined the debate he and other conservatives thought they would have. "When senators harangued Bork about state laws requiring forced sterilization and other such atrocities, Bork should have replied, 'Senator Kennedy, your question presumes a profound lack of faith in the American people. Do you imagine that the American people lack the good sense to pass laws under which they can live? In which state do you expect forced sterilization laws to pass?' "

But that argument was never offered, that debate never engaged.

The battle over Robert Bork redefined and reshaped the Senate confirmation process and influenced the decisions of future presidents and the preparation of future nominees. It galvanized the public interest groups, which have since turned judicial battles into key fund-raising opportunities. But in the days following the historic Senate vote, none of this was clear. What was clear instead was that the White House was not ready to concede defeat—or to back away from a fight. "My next nominee for the court will share Judge Bork's belief in judicial restraint—that a judge is bound by the Constitution to interpret laws, not make them," Reagan said after the Senate vote.

Administration officials had known for weeks that Bork was doomed, and they'd begun thinking through the next step and pulling out the notebooks that contained the files on other possible contenders. Baker was saying the Bork fight illustrated that only a bland, indistinct candidate was confirmable, but lawyers in the Justice Department and in some quarters of the White House insisted that Reagan should nominate another strong conservative. Baker, the former senator used to cutting deals and compromising, may have wanted an acceptable moderate, but to the legal team, Supreme Court nominations weren't about political compromise.

For a time, the political advisers also saw another upside in a hard-line conservative. "We have to remember that bland homogeneity is precisely what the political left wants. They would much rather have milquetoast than conservatism of any stripe," D'Souza wrote his boss, Domestic Policy Adviser Gary Bauer, in another memo nine days before the Bork vote. "For the president to appoint a moderate would be to reward the kind of lynch mob that has strangled the Bork nomination. Even worse, it would be a powerful and haunting statement of acknowledgment that the President's agenda is no longer salable to the American people."

In the press and in the White House, Anthony Kennedy was emerging as a leading contender. Willard and Kuhl were persistently making the case for him, as was new federal judge Alex Kozinski, a strong conservative and, like Willard and Kuhl, a former law clerk. And there were Kennedy's connections to Reagan from his days in Sacramento as governor. Baker and Culvahouse thought he was the best alternative.

But Kennedy had fierce opposition in the Justice Department and in some quarters of the White House, especially among those who believed strongly in Scalia and Bork and shared their views that courts should have a limited role in American life. Tony Kennedy was no Scalia, they believed, and he was no Bork. Based on his appeals court decisions, they quickly concluded that he would be more like O'Connor—willing to inject courts into disputes they thought better left to legislatures and too eager to identify "rights" not expressly written in the Constitution. "There was no verve, no broader perspective," said one high-ranking Justice Department lawyer. "He was getting B reviews."

The confidential memos lawyers prepared on Kennedy at the time presented what they called "serious" and "disturbing" questions about his views on the Constitution. These memos, especially those written by Justice Department lawyers, are in marked contrast to the glowing written reviews Bork and Scalia received. They make clear that many in the administration knew precisely the kind of justice Anthony Kennedy would be—one who turned out to be a tremendous disappointment to conservatives.

In vetting prospective nominees, lawyers in the Justice Department and White House reviewed all the candidates' written court decisions and articles, as well as speeches and other public statements. They then wrote up lengthy reports on the finalists and placed them in three-ring binders for high-level advisers to digest. The research on Kennedy turned up several opinions they found unsettling.

One case centered on naval regulations prohibiting homosexual conduct.[7] The navy's policy was blunt: "Members involved in homosexuality are military liabilities who cannot be tolerated in a military organization. . . . Their prompt separation is essential." That meant mandatory discharge for any known gay person in the navy. Several people who'd been discharged filed a lawsuit, arguing the policy was unconstitutional.

Kennedy wrote the opinion for the appeals court panel, and he "somewhat grudgingly" upheld the regulations banning gays and lesbians, as one Justice Department lawyer explained in an early memo. More troubling, Kennedy also "spoke very favorably of privacy rights," the lawyer said, in what would prove to be a telling observation. By contrast, Bork had firmly upheld the navy's regulations when he confronted the issue in a different case before his D.C.-based federal appeals court.[8]

"Judge Kennedy . . . cited *Roe v. Wade* and other 'privacy right' cases very favorably and indicated fairly strongly that he would not uphold the validity of laws prohibiting homosexual conduct outside of the context of the military," Justice Department lawyer Steve Matthews wrote in a memo to the judicial selection group. "This easy acceptance of privacy rights as something guaranteed by the Constitution is really very distressing."

Another case involved a Seattle mother, Clara Penn, who was arrested and charged with distributing heroin from her home.[9] Police searched Penn's home after an informant said she was distributing drugs and using her children to help deliver them. They had no luck at first—until an officer offered her five-year-old son five dollars if he would show them where his mother kept the drugs. The boy led police to a glass jar full of heroin buried under some soft sod in the family's backyard.

The trial judge threw out the evidence, but the federal appeals court reversed his decision and sided with the officers. Kennedy thought the police practice was "pernicious in itself and dangerous in precedent." He wrote what he called an "emphatic" dissent, chastising police for the "severe intrusion upon the relation between a mother and a child" and warning that "indifference to personal liberty is but the precursor of the state's hostility to it."

The California judge's sweeping language disturbed Reagan's lawyers. But they were even more concerned that he chose to cite a report from Amnesty International to bolster his views. Conservatives generally believe that such citations should have no place in judicial opinions. Judges should look to the Constitution and the words of the state or federal laws at issue, they believe, and not to foreign laws or obviously partisan outside sources. But Kennedy had referred to the Amnesty International report as authority for his argument that "the assault on the parent and child bond is relentless and deliberate in many countries of the world." It did not help that the liberal advocacy group had made Ronald Reagan's support for the Nicaraguan Contras one of their top causes while Kennedy was under consideration.

The Justice Department also took issue with Kennedy's record on separation-of-powers cases, suggesting he saw the courts as having too expansive a role. "Generally, he seems to favor the judiciary in any contest between the judiciary and another branch," Matthews wrote, pointing to three of Kennedy's opinions that had "one or more substantial weaknesses."

But the set of cases presenting "some of the most disturbing aspects of Judge Kennedy's jurisprudence," Justice Department lawyers wrote, involved claims of new constitutional rights. Those cases suggested Kennedy would be too willing to accept novel claims of constitutional protection, beyond what the Constitution specifically provided.

Yet, even with the Justice Department's deep reservations, Kennedy was gaining momentum in the White House, where Baker and Culvahouse were advising against another fight. At Justice, lawyers began searching frantically for "someone who can trump Kennedy," as one put it. But none of the other nominees whose resumes were in the notebooks seemed much better. Federal appeals court judge Patrick Higginbotham, for example, had already been endorsed by Democratic Texas senator Lloyd Bensten, and the last thing they wanted to do was reward Democrats who had defeated Bork. Laurence Silberman, a highly regarded federal appeals court judge, was too boldly conservative, as was Judge Ralph Winter—a "mini Bork," as one lawyer put it. The others were either too old or not predictably conservative.

Outsiders, too, began pushing their favorites. Senator Warren Rudman, the New Hampshire Republican, called White House officials and made the case for state court judge David Souter. Carvin wrote a short memo against Souter, arguing that he was unknown and had not done anything sufficiently impressive as a state official or state court judge to merit even brief consideration. No one in the administration gave Souter a second thought.

Douglas Ginsburg was a different kind of stealth nominee. From his days heading up the Justice Department's antitrust division, Ginsburg was well known to administration officials and those on Capitol Hill. But his legal views were not. He hadn't done the kind of writing or public speaking that had gotten Bork into so much trouble. When Cooper and Carvin tossed out his name as a possibility, it was like a light turning on in a darkened room.

Ginsburg was conservative and confirmable, the "almost perfect" choice, as they put it in one memo. At forty-one, he would be one of the youngest justices in history. He was Jewish, which could moderate liberal opposition. He had a distinguished academic record as a law clerk to Justice Thurgood Marshall and a professor at Harvard Law School. He'd been confirmed twice by the Senate within the past two years, and the members and staffers on the Judiciary Committee liked him. He had solid political skills and got along with even the most ardent Democratic congressmen when he was in the administration. He was moderate in style and epitomized judicial temperament in ways that Bork did not.

Politically, other advisers felt strongly that Reagan could not be seen as accommodating the forces that had defeated the Bork nomination. Ginsburg, a new judge on the same D.C.-based appeals court as Scalia and Bork, was a clearly confirmable candidate who would leave the Bork opponents as ultimate losers in the fight. His nomination would help send the message that, as one adviser put it in a memo to the White House, "there is no profit in taking on a wily and still-powerful president."

As the Bork nomination was falling apart, Carvin asked Justice Department lawyer James Swanson, who'd recently clerked for Ginsburg on the appeals court, to write a memo analyzing Ginsburg's legal views and judicial decisions. Kennedy's name had appeared on short lists dating back to the O'Connor nomination, but Ginsburg had never been mentioned as a possible nominee—not once. His name did not appear in any of the Supreme Court files, even on the longer lists of names lawyers had compiled over the years. The White House had briefly vetted him when Reagan nominated him to the D.C.-based federal appeals court, but he had not taken the next step up the ladder to prospective Supreme Court nominee.

The lawyers in the Justice Department had to convince Meese, who also knew Kennedy from Sacramento and liked him. Meese summoned his legal team to his office after the Judiciary Committee's vote on Bork. It was clear that Bork would not get through the Senate, and they wanted to be ready to move quickly. Willard argued for Kennedy; Reynolds, for Ginsburg. After Willard made his case, Reynolds asked how he thought Kennedy would stack up with the Court's other justices.

"He should be as good as O'Connor," Willard said, "but not as conservative as Rehnquist." In 1987, O'Connor was still seen by many outside Meese's Justice Department as a solid conservative. Especially notable was her position on abortion. O'Connor had refused to join the Court's more liberal justices in 1983, when they struck down an Ohio abortion law that required minors to get parental consent, imposed twenty-four-hour waiting periods, and required doctors to perform second-trimester abortions in the hospital. Rehnquist and White joined her dissent.[10]

Willard hadn't grasped the growing dissatisfaction among administration lawyers who cared less about the abortion issue than about the overall role of the Supreme Court in American life. They had real concerns that O'Connor was not going to be the kind of conservative they'd hoped.

Willard's comparison of Kennedy to O'Connor energized Meese to support Ginsburg, although he had been leaning that way from the beginning. Meese had seen Ginsburg laboring in the vineyard as an assistant attorney general in the antitrust division, getting to the office at 7 a.m. and doing a masterful job articulating Reagan's positions on competition. His academic credentials were impressive. And he was young and likable: Bob Bork without the negatives.

Carvin and Cooper also started pushing senators to turn the tide against Kennedy. They called Dennis Shedd, Strom Thurmond's staffer, and told him Reagan was deciding between Kennedy and Thurmond's longtime favorite, South Carolina federal judge William Wilkins. "Kennedy's taking the lead," they told Shedd. Thurmond immediately got on the phone with the White House. "Anybody," he said in his slow southern accent, "but Anthony Kennedy."

They made a similar call to Randy Rader, a lawyer on Orrin Hatch's staff, saying Kennedy had the edge over Hatch's preferred nominee, Texas federal appeals court judge Edith Jones. Hatch then placed a similar call to the White House. He didn't want Anthony Kennedy.

Meese and Reynolds also reached out to Reagan's trusted adviser William French Smith, who had been attorney general and was back in California. Smith agreed to call Reagan. Reynolds asked Carvin to write Smith's talking points for the call.

"Mr. President, I've known you a long time. This is your legacy. I know Anthony Kennedy, and he won't be there in the trenches," Smith told Reagan during the phone call. "When we're sitting on the beach twenty years from now, I want to be able to look you in the eye and say we put in place the people you wanted on the Supreme Court."

In the White House, Chief of Staff Baker was still resisting the hard-core conservatives, including federal judges like Silberman. Kennedy appealed to Baker as an easy confirmation. But Baker, who'd been chief of staff for only six months, did not have Reagan's ear. Meese did, and he went to the Oval Office and put all his cards on the table. "I've known Tony since Sacramento," he told Reagan. "I can't look you in the eye and say he's the kind of justice you want on the Supreme Court."

"That's funny," Reagan responded with a twinkle. "William French Smith called an hour ago and said the same thing."

After talking to Smith, Reagan had all but decided to nominate Ginsburg. But Baker valiantly made his best case for Kennedy. He would be easier to confirm. He was engaging and personable—he even dressed up in Federalist garb when he taught *Marbury v. Madison* to his law students at the University of the Pacific in California. Politicians from the state Democratic Party had offered their support.

But Reagan decided to follow the advice of his most trusted advisers. Kennedy, who had come in for an interview with Reagan, flew back to Sacramento knowing he would not get the job.

Ginsburg's age was considered the only possible stumbling block. Anticipating the criticism, advisers wrote talking points about other youthful justices, including liberal giant William O. Douglas, who was forty when nominated in 1939. They also considered planning an event to be called "Young Leaders in American History," so Reagan could comment on the "youthfulness of the founding fathers." "He would make the point that if age were the test we would still be a British colony without our Constitution, and that Ginsburg's age should be a positive, not a negative factor," Reagan's domestic affairs team advised in a memo.

But instead of making his age a positive attribute, Ronald Reagan found himself having to explain away how Ginsburg had "erred in his youth." The "youth culture" of the 1960s and 1970s caught up with

Ginsburg and sent his prospective nomination crashing on the rocks. Six days after his nomination, when Ginsburg started making the rounds with senators, National Public Radio's Nina Totenberg reported that Ginsburg had smoked marijuana while he was a professor at Harvard in the mid- to late 1970s. Although he'd been through several FBI background checks—and had just been through the confirmation process for the federal appeals court—Ginsburg hadn't thought to disclose his marijuana usage. The FBI didn't ask potential nominees whether they'd "used" drugs, as agents do today. Instead, the question was "Have you ever abused alcohol or drugs?" Ginsburg truthfully answered no.

Ginsburg's nomination quickly spun out of control, and he told Reagan on November 7 that he would withdraw. He was never formally nominated to the Supreme Court.

Ed Meese was devastated. Under his leadership, a dope-smoking controversy had followed the failure of the Bork nomination. He had embarrassed the president, and he felt personally responsible. He knew the White House couldn't run the risk of another withering defeat, because, with the next presidential election now less than a year away, time pressures were enormous. If the hearings encroached too closely on the elections, Senate Democrats could simply refuse to confirm anyone. The conservatives in the Justice Department stood down. The Bork-Ginsburg fiasco was complete. Meese gave in to Baker.

Now the fact that everything about Kennedy was milquetoast suddenly seemed like the greatest of virtues in this battered White House. Kennedy lived with his wife, Mary, and their three children in the same Sacramento house he grew up in. He had dutifully assumed his father's law practice in 1963, when his father died suddenly. He was the picture of moderation. Even his physical appearance—medium brown hair and eyes, nondescript glasses—was bland.

Reagan and his advisers knew that Kennedy would get the nod even before he boarded his plane for a flight back to Washington. White House staffers had already written three different newspaper opinion pieces heralding his nomination. They were just waiting for the official announcement before they contacted potential supporters who would sign their names to the pieces.

But the White House first had to make sure the straight-arrow Kennedy—whose more colorful father had once offered to pay him a hundred dollars if he ever had to pick his son up at the police station—was the man he seemed to be. For days, White House staffers had been compiling questions to unearth any potentially embarrassing information. They came up with hundreds of them, focused largely on sex, drugs, and money. The questions were astonishingly personal and intrusive. Did you have sex in junior high? High school? College? If so, how many different women? Where? Did you use contraception? Were there pregnancies? Any abortions? Did you contract venereal disease? Did you engage in homosexual activity? Aberrational sexual activity? Has your wife ever had an abortion? Have the two of you engaged in "kinky" sex?

They tried to think of everything that possibly could become an issue during the confirmation. Did you ever use alcohol or drugs? Sniff glue? Attend parties where drugs were used? Have herpes? Did you ever have any traffic tickets? Drink and drive? Use guns? Have fistfights? Engage in cruelty to animals?

And after all the detailed questions, there were the big catch-alls. They asked Tony Kennedy to reveal the most unpleasant or embarrassing thing that happened to him while in high school. In college. In law school. As an adult. Then they turned to his family—his parents, children, siblings—and asked him similar questions about them.

The interview, on Sunday, November 8, took three hours. Culvahouse asked most of the questions, but Baker, Meese, Reynolds, and Ken Duberstein, the deputy chief of staff, also were there. By the end of it, they were certain Kennedy had nothing in his closet.

Kennedy met Reagan late Monday afternoon in the residence of the White House, after spending most of the day with FBI agents poring over his background. Reagan knew Kennedy from their days in

California—as governor, he'd even asked Kennedy to draft a proposed tax-cut initiative. Reagan had also recommended Kennedy to Gerald Ford, who put him on the San Francisco–based federal appeals court in 1975, when he was thirty-nine years old. Although Ford was the president who first put him on the federal bench, Kennedy always gave Reagan credit for his career as a judge. Culvahouse had provided a list of questions, but Reagan had crossed one off: He didn't care what Kennedy thought were "the political issues that you think the Supreme Court will face over the next five to ten years." His questions were purely personal.

Reagan and Kennedy sat together. Reagan's top advisers—most of the men who'd grilled Kennedy the day before—sat off to the side of the room. Reagan looked closely at Kennedy, and he paused, as if to stress the importance of the question he was about to ask. "Is there anything in your background," Reagan asked, "that might create problems for you if you were nominated to the Supreme Court?"

"No, sir," Kennedy said, with emphasis.

Reagan announced Kennedy's nomination in a news conference at the White House two days later, after the FBI had finished its work. "The experience of the last several months," Reagan said, "has made all of us a bit wiser."

Reporters asked a beaming Kennedy, with his wife and three children standing nearby, what he thought of the two failed nominations.

"I'm delighted by this nomination," Kennedy said. Over the next two decades, many of the same liberal groups and editorial pages that had been skeptical of his nomination would instead find themselves sharing that sentiment.

With the defeat of Robert Bork and Douglas Ginsburg, Reagan's chance to redirect the Court had passed. But conservatives brought their disappointment upon themselves. The decision to nominate the more politically salable Scalia before Bork was a critical misstep. The White House compounded the problem the next year when it failed to anticipate the opposition from well-organized interest groups and adequately prepare Bork for the onslaught he would face. When Bork went down, the White House again blundered in sending up a new and untested candidate in Ginsburg, instead of going back to prospective nominees on the original short list like the solidly conservative Laurence Silberman, whose previous legal work would have yielded some support from liberals and organized labor. As a result, by the end of the second failed attempt to replace Lewis Powell, Reagan was left with little choice but to turn to a man even his own advisers doubted would be the kind of justice the president had vowed to nominate. Those doubts soon would be realized.

3.

FALSE HOPES

Joining the Supreme Court is an extraordinary intellectual challenge for anyone, even an experienced federal appellate judge like Anthony Kennedy. Like Dorothy, a new justice isn't in Kansas—or a lower federal or state court—anymore.

The work is overwhelming at first. Since the Court typically gets involved only in issues that divide the judges in the different lower courts, it makes sense that cases reaching the Supreme Court would pose tough questions. The pressure on the justices to write legally precise opinions is much greater than in the lower courts. The rights of millions can rest on a word or phrase.

And then there's the public attention. Nominees to the Supreme Court usually work in obscurity in the lower courts, and they're completely unprepared for the harsh glare of the spotlight. To be thrown into the public arena, constantly attacked by editorial writers, protesters of all stripes, and posturing politicians, is a monumental adjustment. Journalists and academics scrutinize and analyze every move.

When Sandra Day O'Connor joined the Court in 1981, seven years before Kennedy, the spotlight was particularly bright. Washington and the world wanted a closer look at the Court's first woman justice, and invitations to luncheons and dinners and meetings arrived by the barrelful. Her two secretaries couldn't keep up with the mail. O'Connor's work as a state court judge hadn't prepared her for that. Her staff members, also new to the Court, didn't know their way around well enough to guide her. She'd taken all three of the incoming law clerks Potter Stewart had hired before he retired, and she brought with her a young female lawyer from her husband's Arizona firm. With no experience between them, it was inevitable that mistakes would be made. They were.

After she was sworn in, O'Connor's first order of business was poring over thousands of appeals that had accumulated over the summer, when the Court was on its three-month break. At the Supreme Court, those appeals are called petitions for certiorari, and they're filed as lengthy, detailed legal briefs in which a party that lost in a lower federal court or in a state court explains why the Supreme Court should step in and hear the case. These so-called cert petitions provide the last chance for the losing litigant. If the Supreme Court denies cert, the result below stands. The opposing lawyer also files a brief, urging the Court not to hear the case. Both sides explain the issues and the lower court decision, and then they set out their respective legal arguments on why they should prevail. If four justices agree, the Court will hear the case. But getting those four votes is almost impossible: The Court receives more than nine thousand cert petitions a year, and it agrees to get involved in fewer than one hundred cases.

Just after O'Connor moved into her new chambers, Court employees delivered copies of thousands of cert petitions. O'Connor and her clerks stacked the briefs in sequential order, by their case numbers, all over the floor of her chambers. But the justices don't always discuss the cases in numerical order, as O'Connor would find out. Her troops had spent days organizing a system that proved worthless. Throughout her first term there would be other missteps, some greater than misdirecting staff in a filing system. "There's no how-to-do-it manual for a

Supreme Court justice," O'Connor said. "I had no concept about a lot of it, and a lack of understanding about the other."

The other justices had introduced themselves and volunteered their help whenever needed. But O'Connor didn't even know what to ask for. The justices operate independently, almost as if they were each running their own law firms, with their own clerks and staff and law books. O'Connor, so accustomed to building consensus and bringing people together back in Arizona, felt isolated from her colleagues and the outside world. "It's a totally academic commitment," O'Connor said. "When you enter the Court, you are entering a world of serious judicial and academic endeavors. You're closing the door to a lot of other things."

O'Connor spent an inordinate amount of time in the first couple of years reviewing the law clerks' memos about the cert petitions, struggling with whether the justices should step into a case or whether the lower court decision should stand. O'Connor had never worked in a federal court, so she was unsure what cases were right for the Supreme Court's review.

Mere disagreement with a lower court decision wasn't always enough. The justices also looked to see whether the issue had split the various lower courts that had considered it. And just because the justices refused to hear a case didn't mean they agreed with the lower court's decision. Sometimes they wanted to wait and see how other lower courts would handle the same issue. After reviewing the cert petitions for a few years, a justice can get a good sense of what cases deserve review, but not, as O'Connor learned, at the beginning.

After hearing arguments her first week, O'Connor joined the eight other justices in the conference room outside Chief Justice Warren Burger's chambers to discuss the cases and cast their votes. No one else is permitted in the room during those conferences, so the justices can speak freely and in complete confidence. O'Connor vividly remembers how she felt, taking her seat at that conference table with the other justices. In one of those first cases, the justices divided 4–4. She had to cast the deciding vote. "Now that's the moment of truth—not all the rest of the stuff. It's being at that conference table to talk about how we're going to resolve the case that's been argued that week," she recalled. "That's the time when all this comes home to roost. Now, you're deciding."

Writing those early opinions can be like walking a minefield. If the reasoning and the writing weren't hard enough, a new justice can unknowingly offend a colleague simply by referring to a case he has long opposed. Or she can use language that just rubs him the wrong way. In one of O'Connor's early cases, Harry Blackmun sent her a written memo asking her to eliminate a word in one of her criminal-law decisions:

"You should be warned . . . that I wage a campaign, thus far successful, against the use of the word 'parameter.' (I will not join an opinion in which that word appears.)," Blackmun wrote in early 1982. "I am also waging a campaign, thus far totally unsuccessful, against the current popular misuse of the word 'viable.' My decade with the medical profession makes me sensitive to this."

O'Connor made her way through. She was a reliable conservative at first. She was strongly law-and-order, and she voted most often with Rehnquist, then the Court's most conservative member. Rehnquist moderated his views somewhat when he became chief, but in 1981 he was championing the conservative cause while standing alone in the field. So often did he end up writing a solo dissent that his law clerks had given him a small Lone Ranger doll.

O'Connor found herself seeing things his way more than she agreed with any other justice. In her first term she voted with him 82 percent of the time—more often than she agreed with Lewis Powell, considered a centrist, or Burger, a solid conservative. Her second term, she was even more solidly with Rehnquist—86 percent of the time. The third term, she voted with her friend 92 percent of the time. The two Stanford graduates agreed on cases about as often as did William Brennan and Thurgood Marshall, liberal icons whose votes were considered indistinguishable. But over the years, that would change.

Kennedy, too, voted like a reliable conservative when he first joined the Court, siding with Rehnquist and Scalia more than with anyone else. Like O'Connor, he was in the spotlight. But Kennedy watchers were not merely the curious. He was under the glare of critics. Kennedy's first few months on the Court were unusually challenging. The lingering effects of the brutal Bork hearings continued to polarize America's view of the Court. Kennedy sounded like a moderate during his Senate hearings, but no one knew for sure. After all, he'd been nominated by Ronald Reagan and was a Californian whose outlook was presumably well known to the president's men, like Ed Meese.

The stakes were high. If Kennedy was a reliable conservative, Chief Justice Rehnquist would presumably have his fifth vote. With Byron White, O'Connor, and Scalia already on his side, Rehnquist could revisit those issues he'd addressed in his dissents, starting with *Roe v. Wade.*

Since the Senate didn't confirm Kennedy until early February 1988, a mountainous backlog of work awaited him after he was sworn in. In those years, the Court would hear about 150 cases each term, twice the number it hears today. When Kennedy came on board, half of those cases had not been argued. Powell had retired at the end of the prior term, so only eight justices had participated in the other half. In four of those cases, the Court had divided 4–4. The justices would hear them again, and the newest justice would cast the deciding vote on all four.

And then there were the reams of cert petitions that awaited Kennedy's review. The Court had put aside all the petitions that had gotten three votes from other justices. A fourth vote by Kennedy meant the case would go on the Court's docket. A vote against meant the lower court decision would stand. By definition, these were the closest cases for deciding whether to grant cert—and there were four hundred of them. Rehnquist, in perfect earnestness, asked his new colleague to finish them up by the next week.

With the crushing workload, Kennedy had no time to get acquainted with his new colleagues. Blackmun extended a welcome. Showing all of his avuncular charm and only a trace of his touchiness, Blackmun sent Kennedy a friendly note welcoming him to the "good old #3 Club." He and Kennedy were the club's only members, since each was his president's third choice for the seat.

Although Kennedy may have felt overwhelmed by the work of a justice, he certainly looked the part of one. More than Reagan's first two choices for the seat, Kennedy resembled the man he had replaced. Like Powell, he was tall and patrician, with the lawyerly appearance and perfect manners one would expect from a traditional Republican Supreme Court justice. Like Powell, Kennedy began his career in private practice and had spent most of his life in a single, provincial state capital (Powell in Richmond, Kennedy in Sacramento). Like Powell, Kennedy would be committed to the court's customs and traditions of collegiality. Neither man was a career academic or theoretician like Antonin Scalia or Robert Bork. Neither had worked in the Justice Department, as Rehnquist and Scalia had done. And both men, perhaps because of their backgrounds, would find themselves moving away from the ideological edges of the Court and toward its center as their careers progressed.

The new Court of nine justices began hearing oral arguments only four days after Kennedy took his oath of office. The second week Kennedy was on the bench, the justices took up a race-discrimination case that would be one of the most controversial of the term. Kennedy would learn quickly that a single vote could trigger a political hurricane, one whose fury would be directed straight at the justice casting the decisive vote.[1] Kennedy would be the target of vicious criticism by special-interest groups and by some of America's most powerful editorial pages. Some went so far as to invoke the specter of segregation and accuse the earnest, mild-mannered Kennedy of betraying the promise of racial equality. The allegations shocked the new justice as unfair and unwarranted, far removed from the judge he had been, and provided a powerful early lesson for a brand new justice sensitive to criticism.

The case involved a lawsuit by Brenda Patterson, a former file clerk in a North Carolina credit union who claimed the company's president had discriminated against her. After being the target of racial insults, Patterson was laid off. Her lawyers sued the company under one section of a nineteenth-century law that Congress had passed to protect newly freed slaves' right to enter contracts and buy and own property. In the early twentieth century, federal courts allowed blacks to use the laws to challenge government discrimination, such as statutes that prohibited them from buying property in white-owned neighborhoods. Later, courts began interpreting the laws to invalidate plainly discriminatory terms in private contracts, such as restrictive covenants in real-estate deeds.

In 1968, the heyday of the Warren Court's boldly progressive rulings on civil rights, the justices dramatically expanded the century-old law to cover purely private forms of discrimination that didn't involve government action.[2] The timing was peculiar, since Congress had just created new remedies for addressing racial discrimination by passing the Civil Rights Act of 1968. Having taken the lead in breaking down segregation in *Brown v. Board of Education* and other landmark cases, the justices on the Warren Court had become accustomed to acting as an agent of change in the area of civil rights, even after the Congress and the president began passing laws outlawing discrimination. Despite the new laws, the Court remained an active player in the civil rights debate, just as it had when Congress and the White House refused to protect minority rights.

In the coming years, the federal courts continued to expand the reach of the nineteenth-century law. The Supreme Court, then led by Chief Justice Warren Burger, extended it even further in 1976 to require that private schools admit black students.[3] The law soon became the preferred method for employment discrimination claims as well. Some justices were concerned that there seemed to be no logical stopping point for lawsuits, and they began debating internally in the 1980s whether the 1976 case had grown beyond any reasonable bounds and should be overruled. Powell, who had brokered a compromise on affirmative action and was in the majority in the 1976 case, had even written a memo suggesting that it might be time to reexamine the issue.

Two days after the Court heard Brenda Patterson's claim, the justices gathered in their conference room to discuss it. Rehnquist, who started the discussion, said he didn't see how Patterson's lawsuit was appropriate under the law, which was limited to making and enforcing contracts. Perhaps, he said, it was time to rein in the old law and overrule those earlier cases. Following Rehnquist's lead, the justices quickly moved from talking about Patterson's racial-harassment claim to a sweeping discussion of whether they should hear the case again. None of the parties had asked them to reconsider the old cases, but they thought the time had come. White, Scalia, and O'Connor voted with Rehnquist in favor of hearing the case again. The Court's four most liberal justices—Brennan, Marshall, Blackmun, and Stevens—were against it.

That left the tie-breaking vote to the junior justice, who by Court tradition is always the last to speak. Kennedy cast his deciding vote with the conservatives. To Kennedy, revisiting the 1976 case seemed reasonable, since the law providing protection to the plaintiffs was now stretched beyond recognition. Besides, the nineteenth-century law was supplanting modern civil rights laws aimed at correcting the same problems.

But Kennedy's newfound critics didn't see it that way. When the justices announced they were rehearing the case to consider scaling back the old law, liberal justices came out blazing, suggesting the new conservative majority was motivated by politics. "I can find no justification for the bare majority's apparent eagerness to consider rewriting well-established law," wrote Blackmun. John Paul Stevens predicted dire consequences, writing that the decision to rehear the case would have a "detrimental and enduring impact on the public's perception of the court as an impartial adjudicator of cases" and that the harm "may never be completely undone."

Civil rights groups were stunned. No one had asked the Court to rethink these established cases, and few had been particularly critical of them in Congress or in law journals. The outrage came swiftly. The Court's announcement was taken as a sign that the new right-wing majority was getting ready to embark on a campaign to dismantle years of progressive rulings. "Casting a Shadow over Civil Rights," blared a *New York Times* headline. In an editorial, the newspaper wrote, "To reach out to unsettle settled law—to declare that a promise redeemed a century late may yet be broken—is ominous, no matter what the court ultimately rules."[4]

For those who had worked so hard to derail Robert Bork's nomination, the Court's decision to review a line of decades-old cases was a staggering disappointment. Kennedy now appeared to be Robert Bork without the beard. If civil rights were on the table, so, too must be abortion. "Bork was beaten because he posed a threat to reopen precedents," William Robinson of the Lawyers' Committee for Civil Rights Under Law told *U.S. News & World Report.* "Now, Kennedy has voted to do that in his very first civil-rights case. It's very disheartening."[5]

Kate Michelman of the National Abortion Rights Action League told the magazine the case was an "ominous sign" and gave antiabortion groups hope that "the Court might reconsider a subject that isn't so secure as civil rights."[6]

As a newcomer to the Court, Kennedy was taken aback by the fury. The new justice had not expected that a single vote to reconsider an obscure civil rights law could cause such an uproar. The debate over the arcane law had seemed straightforward in the Court's conference room. Since modern state and federal civil rights laws were now on the books and were specifically designed to redress employment discrimination, why was he now enemy number one to America's left wing?

In just a few months on the Court, Kennedy emerged as one of the most conservative of the justices. He sided with Scalia and Rehnquist more than with any other justice. At term's end, editorial writers and liberal special-interest groups were predicting he would ban abortion, eviscerate the rights of minorities, and set the Court—and the country—back fifty years. The press had decided that the new justice would be, in the words of *U.S. News & World Report,* "the moving force behind the shift [to the right]—if it comes."[7] Dean Geoffrey Stone of the University of Chicago Law School remarked: "Those five votes have the power to overrule an awful lot of law."[8] Blackmun summed up his opinion of his new colleague in his private conference notes for a death penalty case in April. When Kennedy sided once again with Rehnquist, Blackmun wrote, "Here we go," as if to suggest that Kennedy was already becoming a tiresomely predictable right-wing vote.

It seemed the Rehnquist Revolution had begun.

That fall the Court opened its 1988 term with a docket crammed with cases that could launch a judicial counterrevolution. It appeared that the most progressive of the Warren Court rulings were endangered. With Kennedy as the fifth vote, conservatives believed the Court was finally poised to shift right. The Court would be hearing major cases on affirmative action, capital punishment, free speech, and civil rights. It would also confront the most divisive issue in America: abortion.

For Democratic operatives who had been seeking to capitalize on the new Court's controversial decisions, the outlook became even grimmer with the collapse of Michael Dukakis's 1988 presidential campaign. Four more years of Republican nominees would surely place the Court in conservative hands for a generation.

But by the end of the term, Kennedy's first full session, the Court would produce a series of decisions that yielded conservative results but little in the way of enduring methodology. There would be nothing conservative to match such liberal landmarks as *Roe v. Wade.* At most, Kennedy's first full term on the court would be a harbinger of a more conservative future. But it ultimately would fail to provide even that.

In mid-October, however, the justices' concerns were more immediate. They heard the *Patterson* reargument in a circuslike atmosphere, as the same groups that had killed Bork's nomination a year earlier flooded the justices with friend-of-the-court briefs. One of those briefs was filed on behalf of sixty-six members of the Senate—including not only the majority and minority leaders, but also seven members of the Senate Judiciary Committee who had so recently praised Kennedy for his moderate view of the law.

The conference after the rehearing took on a tone much different from the one held the spring before, when Kennedy had first joined the Court. This time, Rehnquist was more circumspect. He told his colleagues that although the 1976 case was wrongly decided, the Court must weigh the importance of stare decisis, a legal principle that limits the Court from readily overturning past decisions. As the justices went around the table expressing their views, it became clear that even those who had voted to rehear the case had lost enthusiasm for taking the remarkable step of overturning an established line of civil rights cases.

The most emotional remarks came from Thurgood Marshall, who had argued scores of landmark civil rights cases during his remarkable career as the preeminent civil rights attorney of his time. Marshall rarely gave his opinions at conference, but on that day, he spoke in highly personal terms. He went through the bitter history of segregation, and reminded his brethren that the Supreme Court had had to end racial separation because Congress would not. Marshall told of how the infamous *Plessy v. Ferguson* decision, which had permitted the division of blacks and whites in public facilities so long as they were "separate but equal," had "destroyed all progress" and "left negroes to the tender mercies of the South." "You do not know what we have been through," Marshall said. Under the existing laws, he continued, blacks "couldn't fly a kite." Presidents and Congress had done nothing through the years; only the federal courts had. "And you want to reverse this?" Marshall asked incredulously.

By the time it was Kennedy's turn to speak, the Court was prepared to unanimously reaffirm the 1976 case. But it was divided 4–4 on the original question in Patterson's case: whether to extend the law further and permit her claim for racial harassment. Kennedy began by saying that reviewing the old cases had helped him think through the issues. He now found that rather than wanting to overrule the 1976 case, he agreed with it and thought he "could have been with the majority" in the original case. Blackmun was so startled that he wrote two exclamation points beside his notes on Kennedy's position. Kennedy was ready to reverse the lower courts and allow Brenda Patterson to proceed with her racial-harassment claim, extending the old law once again. With Kennedy's support, the liberals had a majority of one.

Or so they thought.

As the senior justice in the majority, Brennan was in charge of assigning the opinion, and he assigned it to himself. Rehnquist asked Justice White to prepare a dissent.

But Kennedy began to waver almost immediately. He rejected the hard-line conservative position, but was equally uncomfortable with Brennan's sweeping approach. When Brennan circulated his draft opinion, three justices quickly joined it. Kennedy did not.

Months passed without word from Kennedy. Blackmun viewed the silence as an ominous sign and asked a law clerk to snoop around about the reasons for the delay. The clerk reported back that one of Kennedy's clerks had "boasted" that he'd persuaded Kennedy to change his mind by telling him "Justice Brennan has been 'sticking it to him' all year long, and that Justice Kennedy would be wise to return the favor." The clerk later told Blackmun about rumors of negotiations among O'Connor, Kennedy, and Scalia.

In his personal journal, Blackmun complained on April 21 about "games being played" in the *Patterson* case. The next day, his journal entry stated somewhat cryptically, "The Reagan crowd cabal re: Patterson—SOC—AS—AMK." Five days later, Justice Kennedy circulated an opinion of his own. He was rejecting Brenda Patterson's racial-harassment claim and siding with the conservatives.

When the dust finally settled, White withdrew his dissent, and Kennedy's opinion became the majority decision. Rehnquist, White,

O'Connor, and Scalia joined him, reaffirming the 1976 case, but excluding racial-harassment claims like Patterson's.[9]

It left the Court's liberals disappointed and angry at Kennedy.

If the clerk's rumor memos sound a little like a strangely formalized version of the notes passed around during high school study hall, it should be kept in mind that the clerks weren't very far from high school themselves. The most conventional path for a Supreme Court clerk is to earn spectacular grades at a good college and a very good law school and then clerk on a federal appellate court for one year. Most clerks are thus still in their mid-twenties, and clerking on the Court is one of their first professional experiences in the law.

Kennedy blames some of the clerks, though not his own, for much of the rancor in the contentious 1988 term. The clerks that year had a difficult time distinguishing a personal from a professional disagreement and were "hostile and fractious," Kennedy says. They understood the law, he says, but not the traditions of the Court.

Another reason for the tension on the Court that year may have been that the Court's two remaining liberal standard-bearers, Brennan and Marshall, were in a state of physical and mental decline. To the consternation of the other justices, Brennan would bring with him to conference a written speech about each case to read aloud. Marshall spoke little, and what he said was not always relevant. The weakened condition of Brennan and Marshall meant that their clerks weren't as well supervised as in previous years.

It also meant that Stevens and Blackmun were left by themselves to ward off what they saw as the coming conservative revolution. But Stevens was an iconoclast, and Blackmun could be a difficult colleague. Neither man possessed the charm and charisma of Brennan and Marshall in their prime.

Kennedy's retreat back to the conservatives in Brenda Patterson's case occurred the day after the Court heard oral arguments in a landmark abortion case that conservatives hoped would mean the end of

Roe v. Wade. If the new justice thought his motives had come under attack in the civil rights case, he had no idea what bitterness a major abortion hearing could generate. The case, called *Webster v. Reproductive Health Services,*[10] undoubtedly contributed to the sharp dissents coming from the Blackmun chambers that year. It was a frontal assault on the constitutional right to an abortion.

For better or worse, Harry Blackmun will be forever remembered as the justice who wrote *Roe v. Wade.*[11] Even liberal scholars have said his opinion in *Roe* rested upon questionable constitutional foundations. It was also idiosyncratic—it might be the only Supreme Court decision in history to consider the views of "the Ephesian, Soranos, often described as the greatest of the ancient gynecologists"—but it got seven votes in 1973. Only Byron White and Rehnquist, in his second year on the Court, dissented. But even Rehnquist's dissent was respectful toward his new colleague, praising the opinion for bringing "to the decision of this troubling question both extensive historical fact and a wealth of legal scholarship."

The *Roe* decision, which determines elections, triggers marches, inspires bombings, and is alternately described as the greatest advancement for women's rights in our time or the *Dred Scott* of the twentieth century, did not produce a particularly fierce debate on the Court when it was first decided. Although it was controversial from the start, opposition to *Roe* built throughout the 1970s. It wasn't until the 1980 presidential election that *Roe* practically hijacked the entire American political system.

To determine when restrictions on abortion were constitutional, Blackmun first divided pregnancy into trimesters. States could not interfere with a woman's decision to abort in the first trimester, Blackmun wrote, but they could do more to intervene as the pregnancy progressed. In the second trimester, states could impose regulations to promote safety, such as requiring doctors to perform abortions in hospitals. By the third trimester, when the fetus can live outside the womb, states could prohibit abortions entirely, except when necessary to protect the mother's health or save her life.

Blackmun knew his opinion in *Roe* would be controversial, but he did not remotely anticipate how the ruling would define him as a public figure. The mail to Blackmun's chambers contained stunning quantities of personal missives on the subject of abortion. Some were threatening enough that Blackmun eventually acquired a security detail. Blackmun didn't toss the letters in the trash: He kept and cataloged them. He even replied to some. He soon began asking prospective law clerks the same question during his interviews: "How would you feel about clerking for the author of *Roe v. Wade*?" As *Roe* came to define him as a jurist, he became increasingly sensitive to criticism of it. Each time it faced the chopping block, he adopted a posture as the Court's stalwart defender of women's reproductive rights and the sanctity of precedent.

Shortly after the Court agreed to hear the *Webster* case, the new George H. W. Bush administration had quickly stepped in and urged the Court to overturn *Roe*. It was an invitation many thought the Court would accept. Rehnquist, White, and Scalia had already made clear that they opposed *Roe*. O'Connor had sidestepped the issue, though she had made statements deeply critical of *Roe* and had proposed an alternate standard. Kennedy was widely expected to vote with the conservatives. Even those conservative lawyers who had recommended against his nomination thought he was solidly opposed to *Roe*. Though they hadn't asked, Kennedy had implied as much in his meetings with Justice Department lawyers. What's more, the Court had signaled that it was willing to aggressively rethink old cases, as Brenda Patterson's case made clear.

Antiabortion forces were cautiously optimistic. They believed they had five votes.

The case drew press and publicity to the Court in a way that few other cases ever had, and set a record for the largest number of friend-of-the-court briefs ever filed in a single case. There were seventy-eight of them. Hundreds of thousands marched on the Mall in Washington in support of *Roe*, setting a record at that time for an abortion rally. The Court was flooded with mail urging the justices to take one position or the other, as well as coat hangers to symbolize the dangers of illegal abortion and enlarged photographs of aborted fetuses. NBC even aired a docudrama, *Roe v. Wade*, starring Holly Hunter as Norma McCorvey (aka Jane Roe) and Amy Madigan as her attorney, Sarah Weddington.

The *Webster* case challenged the constitutionality of a Missouri abortion law that began by asserting that human life "begins at conception." The law imposed a number of restrictions on abortion, including prohibiting people who worked in public medical facilities from performing or recommending abortion unless it was necessary to save a woman's life. The law also required doctors to run tests to determine whether the fetus could survive outside the womb before they performed an abortion after the twentieth week of pregnancy.

The justices were unsettled in their conference in late April when they discussed the case and how to handle it. The provision that most sharply divided them was the requirement that doctors test a fetus's viability. The Court's four supporters of *Roe*—Brennan, Marshall, Blackmun, and Stevens—were adamant that it was unconstitutional. The remaining five justices all thought the provision should be allowed, but they couldn't agree on why or how.

White and Scalia indicated they were prepared to overrule *Roe*, but they didn't think it was necessary to decide the case, and neither did Rehnquist. O'Connor implied that she wouldn't go that far, saying she wanted to "adhere to what I have written" in the past on abortion. Then it was Kennedy's turn.

The fetal-testing requirement is "probably invalid under *Roe*," Kennedy said. He'd taught *Roe* for fifteen years, he said, and "on pure stare decisis, I would leave it alone." It was a clear win for Blackmun's *Roe*.

On the other hand, Kennedy said, *Roe* continued to "do damage to the Court and judicial review and the conception of a judge's proper position and role." The abortion debate really should return "to the democratic process." Now Kennedy was sounding more like Scalia.

But it was important to protect the rights of young women, Kennedy continued. Was that a point for *Roe*? Perhaps, Kennedy concluded, the Court should just change *Roe*'s standard—"its method and structure"—for evaluating when an abortion law is unconstitutional.

The Court would soon find the opinions in *Webster* to be as jumbled as Kennedy's in conference. Rehnquist wrote an opinion that allowed the testing and threw out Blackmun's three-trimester framework. But he didn't explicitly say he was overruling *Roe*. Kennedy joined that opinion, as did White and Scalia. O'Connor refused to go along, and tried her hand at a separate opinion. In the end, the Court's fragile conservative majority could never find common ground to do the very thing their appointing presidents had wanted. To the surprise of conservatives and liberals, *Roe* would survive its first major challenge with a new Court.

But perhaps the result in *Webster* wasn't so shocking after all. The Court responded as it often does when the justices sense a particular issue is drawing them too far into the political arena and beyond their comfort zone: It had reached a result, but with only a confusing, unpersuasive, and nonprecedential opinion to justify it. In that, it resembled the Court's later work in *Bush v. Gore*. But unlike the unsigned opinion in *Bush v. Gore*, the four-justice *Webster* opinion hadn't provided a decisive answer to the jurisprudential question confronting the Court. It had only staved off the debate for a subsequent confrontation and, quite possibly, for a new justice.

Because Kennedy had voted with the three conservatives, it was widely assumed that he would, when the time came, join Rehnquist, White, and Scalia in voting to overrule *Roe*. But Kennedy's comments in the justices' private conference were revealing: Even then, he appeared to be articulating two irreconcilable positions. At the time, the weirdness of the four-justice *Webster* opinion, which didn't overturn *Roe* but proposed a different way of analyzing abortion cases, was widely seen as a failed effort to hold on to O'Connor's vote. But its restraint may also have helped the Court maintain Kennedy's support.

In her separate opinion, O'Connor argued that *Webster* did not require the Court to confront *Roe*. Rehnquist's opinion, she said, violated the general principle that the Court should avoid deciding constitutional questions whenever possible. That drew a memorably ferocious reply from Scalia. He flatly asserted that her argument for why the Court should avoid confronting *Roe* "cannot be taken seriously," since she had done the very thing she was admonishing against in earlier cases.

It was a stinging rebuke. Like Kennedy, O'Connor was sensitive to harsh criticism aired for public consumption. She thought it was unnecessary, and she bristled when she found herself on the receiving end of what she saw as a personal attack. It also made her wary. Scalia wasn't the first on the Court to push Sandra Day O'Connor away by offending her.

In O'Connor's first term on the Court, William Brennan excoriated the newest justice for one of her early opinions. He flatly accused her of misapplying a case on prisoners' rights, called *Rose v. Lundy,* that she'd written only a month before.[12] O'Connor was offended by the attack because she didn't believe she had misapplied the case. She thought Brennan had been trying to manipulate her.

"Sic transit Gloria Lundy!" Brennan wrote in the second case, picking up the Latin phrase *sic transit gloria mundi,* which means "thus passes the glory of the world." "In scarcely a month, the bloom is off the Rose."[13]

Brennan's law clerks had inserted the language in his dissent, and Brennan didn't remove it. He later said it was an oversight. Regardless, O'Connor never forgot it—or his accusation. Brennan, legendary for his powers of persuasion, never made headway with O'Connor from then on. He also helped keep the Court's first female justice in the conservative camp longer than she might have been otherwise. That would become clear in the years to come, after Brennan retired from the Court.

O'Connor soon would find herself offended by Scalia's brusque language. Rehnquist was concerned that his younger conservative champion was starting to push her away just as Brennan had done a few years before—but now in the other direction. After Bork was defeated, Rehnquist had worried that the administration would nominate another forceful personality to take his place. Rehnquist was relieved to see the calm-tempered Kennedy come on board instead.

Years later, after she retired from the Court, O'Connor refused to specifically address Scalia's pointed criticism. Instead, she spoke "generally." "I do not like having strong, almost abusive language used in appellate decision making. I think it does not help the collegial process," O'Connor said in an interview. "I understand the writer wants to write in a way that will capture the minds and hearts of readers to his or her point of view. That's why it's done, I suppose. But I am not in favor of using language that engenders long-term divisions."

The *Webster* abortion case was announced on the last day of the term. In the final weeks, the Court had released a number of other controversial 5–4 decisions, with Kennedy solidly behind conservatives on almost every explosive issue that year. The term before, twelve cases had split the Court 5–4. In the 1988 term, thirty-three cases divided the Court 5–4. In nineteen of those, the new conservative majority of Rehnquist, White, O'Connor, Scalia, and Kennedy carried the day.

In one civil rights case, for example, the five-justice Rehnquist bloc made it harder for employees to sue under federal law if they believed a neutral company policy unfairly affected them because of their race. In dissent, a flame-throwing Blackmun questioned whether the majority "still believes that race discrimination—or, more accurately, race discrimination against nonwhites—is a problem in our society, or even remembers that it ever was."[14] In two separate capital cases, the Court

refused to block the execution of killers who were mentally retarded or
were as young as sixteen when they committed their crimes.[15] Those ex-
ecutions, the Court said, didn't violate the Eighth Amendment's pro-
hibition on cruel and unusual punishment.

Kennedy's first full term on the Court was sometimes regarded as
the year that a new conservative majority on the Court began to leave
its mark on the law. "The Year the Court Turned to the Right," said the
New York Times, pronouncing it a "watershed" in modern Court history. "Rarely has a single Supreme Court term had such an unsettling
effect on the political landscape," the *Times* wrote in a front-page news
story. "For the first time in a generation, a conservative majority was
in a position to control the outcome on the most important issues,"
the story said. "On all these issues, it was the vote of Anthony M.
Kennedy . . . that made the difference."[16]

But for all the shrill speeches and jarring headlines about Kennedy's
contributions to the new conservative majority, the Court did little that
would cheer the Republican base for long. Some decisions were outright
liberal victories, such as *Texas v. Johnson,*[17] which struck down flag-
burning statutes in forty-eight states on First Amendment grounds,
and *Allegheny County v. Greater Pittsburgh ACLU,*[18] which created new
limitations on the public display of religious symbols. In *Allegheny
County,* a fractured and somewhat long-winded Court held 5–4 that the
Constitution's establishment clause did not allow a crèche in a place of
prominence in a local courthouse, but that it did permit a menorah, a
Christmas tree, and a sign saluting liberty together just outside a government office building. Kennedy wrote a powerful dissent, accusing
the Court of adopting a new test that was intuitively ridiculous—"a jurisprudence of minutiae" that would require the Court to decide future
cases "using little more than intuition and a tape measure."

Ambiguous decisions like *Webster* weren't particularly great tri-
umphs for the Right, either. The case applied minimal limits to *Roe,* but
it ultimately upheld the landmark decision. In terms of expectations,

liberal special-interest groups were privately pleased that they had survived a term when the Court reviewed so many explosive cases.

Even in cases where the conservatives prevailed, the victories turned out to be largely pyrrhic. The civil rights cases that had so bitterly divided the Court would eventually be the target of new legislation by Congress. Two years later, it would pass the Civil Rights Restoration Act of 1991 to reverse the consequences of several of the Court's decisions. The justices themselves have since overturned both death penalty cases decided in the 1988 term, ruling that the states and federal government can't execute juveniles or the mentally retarded.[19]

Like the Rehnquist Court itself, the ideological impressions left by Anthony Kennedy would evolve through the years. After his first fourteen months on the Court, the *Washington Post* said, Kennedy was "at least as conservative" as Robert Bork and had "moved the court's center much farther to the right than anyone had expected."[20] The man who appointed him, Ronald Reagan, had to be pleased. In his first full term, Kennedy voted with Rehnquist 92 percent of the time, more than any other justice. As the *Boston Globe* reported, "If the Supreme Court has embarked this year on a historic rightward shift, as most agree it has, much of the credit or blame goes to the newest justice, Anthony M. Kennedy."[21]

Expectations from conservatives were high; perhaps the defeat of Robert Bork had made no difference. They were wrong. Unknown to outsiders, Kennedy had spent his first term trying to straddle the divide between the Court's two blocs—especially on the divisive abortion and civil rights cases. His middle-of-the-road, split-the-difference approach to deciding cases was consistent with his record as an appeals court judge, as his opponents in the Justice Department were all too aware when he was nominated.

That fall, with George H. W. Bush beginning his first year in the White House, conservatives were confident. Reagan, they believed, had remade the Court. Bush would give them insurance runs, since he had promised to continue Reagan's efforts to reshape the Supreme Court. Bush would get two chances to add to the five votes the conservatives now counted as their majority. They didn't know that Kennedy, the staunch conservative who provided Rehnquist with his fifth vote to lead a revolution, would eventually rethink his positions on abortion, religion, and the death penalty. That reality—bitter to conservatives— would become evident soon enough.

4.

THE DEVIL YOU DON'T

White House counsel C. Boyden Gray had just walked into his Georgetown home and was changing into tennis clothes when his phone rang. It was John Sununu, President Bush's chief of staff. He spoke quickly. The Supreme Court's liberal stalwart, William Brennan, had just sent a letter to the president announcing his retirement. Bush was on Air Force One, traveling back to the White House from a West Coast trip, and he wanted to meet for breakfast the next morning to talk about possible nominees. He planned to settle on one within forty-eight hours.

The unexpected news giving Bush his first nomination made conservatives euphoric. The charming Brennan, nominated by Republican president Eisenhower, had long anchored the Court's liberal bloc. His persuasive personality and clever writing style made him one of the most influential justices in the twentieth century. At eighty-four, he had no plans to retire. But he'd suffered a slight stroke after a fall, and he'd reluctantly concluded he would step down after thirty-three years as a justice.

For conservatives, Brennan's retirement gave George H. W. Bush the chance of a lifetime. Brennan's retirement wasn't like replacing one conservative with another, as Reagan had done with Scalia. It was not even like replacing the moderate Lewis Powell, as Reagan had done with Kennedy. It was that rare moment when a conservative president was positioned to replace a liberal giant.

Moreover, Brennan's departure, conservatives believed, would leave the Court's three other liberals—Marshall, Blackmun, and Stevens—without their leader, making it almost impossible for them to peel off a justice from the majority. It would give conservatives a dramatic opportunity to cement their majority and firmly take ideological control of the Court—a takeover they thought they could secure when the ailing Marshall followed Brennan into retirement.

But for Bush, the timing presented significant challenges. He was negotiating a tax increase that had infuriated his conservative base and was particularly painful in light of his campaign rhetoric: "Read my lips: No new taxes." At the same time, he was considering vetoing the civil rights bill that had overturned the Court's controversial decisions from the year before—an action that would inflame liberals against him. Confronted with opposition from both ends of the political spectrum, the president did not want the kind of bruising fight over the Supreme Court that Reagan was willing to endure.

Bush also wanted to move quickly to avoid the mistakes made by Reagan three years earlier when he nominated conservative firebrand Robert Bork to the Court. Bush thought Reagan had moved too slowly in announcing Bork as the nominee, giving Democrats like Massachusetts senator Ted Kennedy ample time to prepare an onslaught of speeches and prepared statements attacking the nominee from the moment he was announced. Kennedy had rushed to the Senate floor within an hour of Bork's nomination, ominously envisioning, in his now famous "Robert Bork's America" speech, a land where "women would be forced into back-alley abortions, blacks would sit at segregated lunch counters, rogue police could break down citizens' doors in midnight

THE DEVIL YOU DON'T

raids, schoolchildren could not be taught about evolution, writers and artists could be censored at the whim of government." Kennedy's depiction of the newly nominated jurist, considered one of the harshest personal attacks ever on a Supreme Court nominee, came to define Bork more than any of the White House's talking points.

Bush would not make that mistake. He wanted an announcement by Monday.

"Who do you like?" Sununu asked Gray.

"I like Starr," said Gray. "He's the best person. And he's confirmable."

Kenneth Starr was Bush's solicitor general and ran an office of lawyers who represented the administration's position before the Supreme Court. Starr had been in the job less than a year, after Attorney General Dick Thornburgh persuaded the federal judge to leave his life-tenured post on the prestigious D.C.-based federal appeals court. He'd explained the move to quizzical associates as simply honoring the wishes of the president. "You can't turn down a request by the president," he'd said.

Although Starr would later become known for his controversial pursuit of President Clinton as independent counsel, he was widely viewed at the time in Washington simply as a first-rate intellectual who valued hard work and collegiality. Affable and diligent, he enjoyed the intellectual rigor of the appeals court. But administration officials told him he would be on the shortest of short lists for the Supreme Court and lured him over. Though nothing was promised, the implication was clear in the White House: Starr was the front runner. Gray, the patrician Bush adviser whose family had made its fortune in tobacco and banking in North Carolina, assumed others saw Starr the same way.

After hanging up with Sununu, Gray rushed back to the White House and assembled his legal team in his office in the West Wing. The year before, he'd instructed his staff lawyers to compile biographies on a dozen nominees, but few other than Starr warranted serious consideration. Gray spent that night reviewing background materials to get ready for the next morning's meeting with Bush, Sununu, and Thornburgh.

Down Pennsylvania Avenue, in the Department of Justice, Thornburgh was conferencing with his closest advisers, including Deputy Attorney General Bill Barr and J. Michael Luttig, who was head of the Office of Legal Counsel. The president had wanted to meet immediately, Thornburgh told his advisers, but had agreed to give them the night to winnow down a list. "I want a notebook I can take to the president at 7:30 in the morning," Thornburgh said.

Thornburgh was the former two-term governor of Pennsylvania, a seasoned politician who was seen as a possible presidential candidate himself. He'd become attorney general in the waning days of the Reagan administration, after Meese left under an ethics cloud, and Bush had kept him on. Thornburgh relied heavily on Barr and Luttig to broker the relationship with the White House, and the men had developed close relationships with a number of high-level officials. Gray liked them both and respected their judgment.

On paper, Barr and Luttig were quite different, but in person they made a formidable pair. Senior Justice Department officials referred to them as "the Bulldogs." Barr was an Ivy League–educated native New Yorker who once reportedly punched a high school classmate in the face for making an offensive comment about the pope. He'd worked at the Central Intelligence Agency and was a domestic policy adviser in the Reagan administration. Luttig was pure Texas. He grew up in Tyler, the son of an engineer, and still carried his sharp twang after years on the East Coast. He would later become a prominent federal appellate judge and himself a prospective nominee, but he was prone to rivalry, and his elbows were as sharp as his intellect.

Both men were forceful and quick, and neither had much patience at the Justice Department for people who lacked focus or street smarts. They saw the law the same way, and they quickly came to share the same negative opinion of Starr, whose conservative worldview was often cloaked by his moderate temperament. He was soft and bookish in appearance; his values had been shaped in rural Texas, where he grew up the son of a Church of Christ minister. Administration officials, especially Barr and Luttig, believed him to be a decent man, but one who could be maddeningly squishy and unfocused. Those traits could be disastrous in a would-be conservative Supreme Court justice, making him more susceptible to drift to the left after the first criticism from liberals in the media and in academia.

After the meeting with Thornburgh, Luttig quickly called his deputies together for an all-night session. They set up long tables in his office and pulled out all the materials they'd gathered on prospective nominees. His team, working with lawyers in Gray's office the year before, had written twenty- to thirty-page memos on each, summarizing their backgrounds and legal views. But they hadn't summarized or synthesized them. Luttig spent that night writing two-page executive summaries to go in front of the memos, and he put the documents in a large notebook for Thornburgh to take to Bush on Saturday.

At the White House the next morning, the president's most powerful legal advisers gathered for breakfast with Bush in the private residence. He was eager to discuss the prospective nominees, who'd been narrowed down to a manageable half dozen and represented a diverse array of backgrounds and experiences. But even before the coffee was poured, Thornburgh made his views known. "Starr is unacceptable," Thornburgh said flatly.

The declaration jolted the breakfast session.

Thornburgh had been troubled by Starr's disputes with his closest advisers, Barr and Luttig, who were adamant in their opposition. Barr and Luttig thought Starr was too malleable, and they clashed with him in style and substance. "Ken is Ken," they'd say, with some irritation, after Starr would deliver verbose and meandering briefings on cases or legal issues.

But there were also sharp substantive divisions. Thornburgh's deputies had sparred bitterly with Starr the previous summer over issues involving presidential power, and both men had come to believe he wasn't reliably conservative enough for a lifetime appointment on the Supreme Court. At the time, Barr headed up the Office of Legal

Counsel, having beaten Luttig out for the job when Bush first took office. Barr had asked Luttig to leave his law firm to become his deputy, and the two became close friends.

The issue dividing the three was a federal law that permitted private citizens to sue for fraud against the federal government. It authorized private people to act as bounty hunters of sorts, tracking down defense contractors and others who might have defrauded the United States government and then suing them on its behalf for damages. If the individual won the lawsuit, he would get to keep up to 30 percent of the penalty, with the rest going into the U.S. Treasury. Laws with similar provisions had existed since the Constitution itself was written. The particular law in question had first been signed by President Lincoln, and a bill to strengthen its private-lawsuit provision in 1986 overwhelmingly passed Congress and was signed by President Reagan.

Nonetheless, Barr and Luttig thought the law infringed on presidential authority, the final straw in a series of court decisions and other laws eroding executive authority. Congress, they contended, had illegally encroached on executive power to prosecute wrongdoers. But new solicitor general Starr concluded that any challenge to the law would be quixotic at best. Barr and Luttig were furious that Starr wouldn't take their side. They came to think he rejected their position in part to avoid antagonizing Senator Charles Grassley, a populist Republican from Iowa who had sponsored the 1986 amendments to the law and who served on the Senate Judiciary Committee. Consciously or not, Starr, they thought, had put his own interests above the president's, possibly because he was envisioning appearing before that very committee as a Supreme Court nominee.

The showdown over presidential power set a pattern which continued after Barr became deputy attorney general the next year and Luttig moved into Barr's old job. From that point forward, Starr was the odd man out.

Thornburgh slammed the door shut that Saturday morning, insisting to Bush and to other advisers that Starr was unsuitable for the

Supreme Court. He suggested he felt so strongly about it that he was willing to resign.

His forceful stand against the odds-on favorite floored Gray, who'd walked into the residence assuming the meeting would be brisk and cordial and end with Starr's being tapped as Bush's first Supreme Court nominee. But Thornburgh's uncompromising position doomed Starr's chances. A president could—and years later, when Bush's son occupied the White House, would—make a nomination over his own attorney general's opposition. But Gray knew at that moment that Starr could not survive with such open and broad-based opposition in the Justice Department.

That ended the discussion—and the Supreme Court prospects—of Kenneth Starr.

The men moved on to the next nominee: federal appeals court judge Laurence Silberman, who had been considered by Reagan for the Lewis Powell seat. Bush had his own concerns about Silberman. Part of it was timing: Silberman had been part of a three-judge panel that the day before had sided with Lieutenant Colonel Oliver North in throwing out his criminal convictions arising from the Iran-Contra affair. Bush knew that Silberman would be too controversial. But Bush also had qualms about Silberman's prickly, in-your-face style. Once, while serving as ambassador to Yugoslavia in the mid-1970s, Silberman received a threatening letter from a Canadian supporter of Yugoslav president Tito, and he fired off a blunt response on his official letterhead: "I have received your letter of Aug. 4," Silberman wrote. "Kiss my ass. Sincerely."

Bush, ever the former diplomat, took offense. He personally vetoed Silberman, leaving him to make his mark on the U.S. Court of Appeals for the D.C. Circuit, where he would welcome newly appointed Judge Clarence Thomas before his ascension to the Supreme Court—and start a running feud with a young Judge Mike Luttig. The grudge match between Silberman and Luttig, which stemmed from their efforts to hire the same law clerks, would help doom Luttig's chances to reach the high court in 2005.

"What about Clarence Thomas?" Bush asked the group. Thomas had just joined Silberman on the D.C.-based federal appeals court, and Bush liked him. Bush also liked the idea of nominating an African American for Brennan's seat, because it would be seen as a pick based on merit, not as a quota pick based on the race or gender of the justice he replaced.

But Gray and Thornburgh swiftly intervened. "It's too soon for Clarence," Gray argued, agreeing with Thornburgh that Thomas needed more judicial experience. He could wait, because he was young enough to be on the short list for years to come.

The list dwindled rapidly, and the conversation turned to Sununu's favorite. In his home state of New Hampshire, David Souter was widely seen as the resident legal genius, a former Rhodes Scholar and Harvard Law School graduate who had all the eccentric qualities that come with unconventional brilliance. Sununu had put Souter on the state supreme court, largely as a favor to Senator Warren Rudman, an old friend. Rudman had been honorary chairman of Sununu's campaign for governor, and Sununu believed his support had helped him win the race.

On election night in 1982, a grateful Sununu embraced Rudman and made a vow. "Warren," he said, "anything you want in this state, you got."[1] Rudman had a ready response: Nominate David Souter to the New Hampshire Supreme Court. Rudman, who had been the state's attorney general, had made Souter his deputy in 1971. Working closely together—sometimes talking ten to fifteen times a day—the two came to share a deep affection.[2] Rudman thought of Souter as "a very special younger brother" with a fierce intellect.[3]

"Warren, it's done," said Sununu, even though he didn't know Souter.[4] When a vacancy opened up the next year, Sununu tapped Souter, as he'd promised.

Souter's nomination to the Boston-based federal appeals court in 1990 also stemmed from political payback. New Hampshire voters had resurrected Vice President Bush's presidential candidacy after he'd taken a beating in the Iowa caucuses in 1988, finishing an embarrassing third behind Senator Bob Dole and television evangelist Pat Robertson. Barbara and George Bush flew to New Hampshire after the stinging defeat, and Governor Sununu greeted them with assurances that Bush would win in his state. Sununu helped craft a strategy that put Bush on the offensive, attacking his challengers and emphasizing his pledge of no new taxes. The voters responded just as Sununu had predicted.

Once in the White House, Bush showed his thanks by making Sununu his powerful chief of staff. Sununu then turned his sights on the obscure Souter. "I want David Suter for this job—soon," Sununu wrote, with a glaring misspelling, to Deputy Chief of Staff Andy Card in November 1989, as the White House was looking for nominees to the Boston-based federal appeals court. Card wrote "for action" at the top, and he forwarded the note to Gray. The next month, Souter came to Washington for an interview at the Justice Department and the White House. Bush nominated him to the federal bench in early 1990.

Rudman, too, was pushing Souter for Brennan's spot. When he heard that Brennan had retired, he immediately called Sununu. It was, Rudman told Sununu, "a chance to do something important for America."[5] But Rudman was a moderate Republican who strongly supported abortion rights. Some of Bush's top advisers didn't trust him. They knew he supported Souter, but they didn't know about his back-door conversations with Sununu and, later, with Bush. That information would have made them more suspicious of Souter and much less willing to get behind him as the nominee.

Bush flipped in his notebook to the thirty-page memo on Souter. The memo, written by deputies in Luttig's office, raised no red flags about the reclusive judge. He was so new to the federal bench that he'd barely heard a full day of arguments as a federal appeals court judge. Summarizing Souter's New Hampshire Supreme Court opinions, the Justice Department attorneys concluded that he acted like a judicial conservative, using a "text-based, original-intent approach" to interpret the state constitution. Those opinions revealed a "jurisprudence grounded in judicial restraint," the lawyers said approvingly. That approach reflected Souter's "strong pro–law enforcement philosophy" and a "measured approach to the recognition of new procedural rights." Souter's method also produced a "pro-business philosophy," apparent in his cases involving employment rights and corporate liability, the lawyers said.

Luttig's two-page summary was more cautious. The first case he mentioned, a decision that homosexuals had a constitutional right to operate day-care centers, was the one that had disqualified Souter three years earlier in the eyes of the Reagan Justice Department. Souter had joined a majority that said the state couldn't pass a law excluding gays and lesbians from operating those facilities.[6] "Because of his brief tenure on the federal bench, there is no real basis on which to evaluate his views on many of the key issues that would come before him on the Supreme Court," Luttig wrote in his summary. It was a point that Luttig made repeatedly about Souter.

Other than the one involving day care, the lawyers found no troubling cases to suggest that Souter would drift to the left once he got on the Court—unlike Anthony Kennedy's review two years earlier, when Justice Department lawyers unearthed what they saw as obvious warning signs. But they did caution Bush that little was known about Souter's views and that he had "not had occasion to set forth any generalized views upon the principles that should govern interpretation of the federal Constitution."

Sununu didn't show his hand in that breakfast meeting, though he noted that Souter's scant record would avert the kind of battle waged over Bork just three years before. Sununu strongly supported Souter, but he saw the other advisers ably narrowing Bush's focus. He decided to wait and make his pitch when Bush was down to a couple of prospects.

At the end of the breakfast, Bush didn't formally announce that he'd settled on his finalists, but the list clearly was focused on two: Souter and Edith Jones, a judge on the New Orleans–based federal appeals court whose solid conservative record made her the favorite of Barr and Luttig.

Gray rushed back to his office, where his staff was waiting to begin more intensive preparation. "Starr's out," Gray told his stunned staff. "Look at the rest of the list."

As the White House lawyers were combing through the files of Souter and Jones, Rudman reached Bush. "You've just appointed this man to the First Circuit Court of Appeals, and he can easily be confirmed for the Supreme Court," Rudman told him. "I can guarantee that he has no skeletons in his closet, and he's one of the most extraordinary human beings I've ever known." [7]

Bush didn't say so, but Rudman's words pushed just the right buttons. Souter was clean and confirmable—two critical factors for a nomination so close on the heels of the controversial Bork and the disgraced Ginsburg. With Democrats controlling the Senate by a comfortable 55–45, Bush did not want controversy.

Hours later, Bush asked to see Souter and Jones. Gray tracked them down—Souter in Manchester, New Hampshire, and Jones in her hometown of Houston—and asked them to fly to Washington the next day.

Rudman, worried Souter would miss his flight, drove him to the Manchester airport Sunday morning. As Souter, carrying his battered suitcase, got out of the car, he turned back to Rudman with a pained look on his face. He opened up his wallet and showed Rudman that he had only three dollars, so Rudman gave him a hundred dollars and joked that he "ought to pin a tag on you . . . that says, 'Please take this boy off the plane in Washington.' " [8]

Luttig picked Souter up at Dulles International Airport, outside Washington. The White House was so worried about leaks that Luttig was told not to go inside the terminal to meet him. Instead, he pulled to the curb and waited for Souter to come outside. Luttig did not even identify Souter to his wife, Elizabeth, until the two were inside his home, where Souter was to spend the night.

At dinner that night, Luttig found Souter gracious and confident, though a bit socially awkward and incapable of reading his southern hosts. Elizabeth offered Souter a glass of wine, even though the Luttigs don't drink.

"That would be nice," he said, and Elizabeth went off looking for a bottle.

She returned with a Cabernet Sauvignon bearing a fancy label. "The only bottle we have is the one Chief Justice Burger gave Mike to have on a special occasion," she said with a rueful smile, waiting for Souter to politely decline, as would be expected of a man raised with southern traditions. Warren Burger was Luttig's mentor and saw him as almost a son. He'd given Luttig his first real job out of college, as his assistant, and later encouraged him to go to law school. Luttig had been saving that bottle.

New Englander Souter missed the cue. "Oh, well, that would be nice," he said.

Elizabeth opened the wine, and the three spent the dinner talking about New Hampshire.

The next morning, Souter met with Gray and Thornburgh, and he made a strong impression on both men. Gray and one of his top assistants, Lee Liberman, had interviewed Souter over lunch in the White House in December, shortly before his nomination to the U.S. Court of Appeals for the First Circuit. Liberman had realized Souter would be a potential short lister because of his relationship with Sununu, so she had been eager to meet him. She cared deeply about the courts and took seriously her job of vetting nominees. As a University of Chicago Law School graduate who'd clerked for Scalia and was a founding member of the Federalist Society, the conservative legal group, Liberman had sterling academic and conservative credentials. Gray considered her brilliant, and trusted her views.

Liberman was fairly impressed with Souter. He came across as a judge who took a formalistic view of the law, not the liberal approach that the Constitution is a "living" document that evolves with society.

She also was predisposed to favor Souter, since she believed he had been considered by the Reagan administration for the seat eventually taken by Kennedy. In her office files, she'd kept a copy of a *New York Times* article that proclaimed Souter "now near the top of the list" of possible Supreme Court nominees in the wake of the failed Bork nomination. "A New Contender Is Seen for Court," the headline revealed. "Souter, on Top Bench in New Hampshire, Is Said to Be High on Reagan's List."[9] The entire article, written the day before Reagan nominated Kennedy, focused on Souter, calling him an "appealing choice" who was "said to be something of a protégé" of Rudman's. It was based entirely on an unnamed "Senate source."[10]

But the story was erroneous. The Reagan White House never considered Souter a serious contender, despite what Rudman and others may have thought. The *Times* story also listed William Wilkins as a possible nominee, but the White House had included him only as a nod to Strom Thurmond, who had long pushed for his nomination.

Even with that apparent endorsement, Liberman wasn't overly enthusiastic at first. Souter's record was sparse, and he lacked the academic sparkle of her mentors, Scalia and federal appeals court judge Frank Easterbrook, a University of Chicago Law School professor who Liberman had hoped would be the nominee. Souter also said some conflicting things. In an interview with a Massachusetts legal publication after he became a federal appeals court judge, Souter said he did, in fact, view the Constitution as a living document. The article said Souter veered away from using conservative terms like "strict constructionist" to characterize his thinking. "On constitutional matters, I am of the interpretivist school," Souter told the *Massachusetts Lawyers Weekly*. "We're not looking for the original application, we're looking for meaning here. That's a very different thing."[11]

But Souter said a very different thing in 1986, when he was a justice on the New Hampshire Supreme Court and wrote a dissent that sounded like one of Scalia's. The language of the Constitution should be understood "in the sense in which it was used at the time of its adop-

tion," Souter said, in a case involving the New Hampshire Constitution.[12] "The court's interpretive task is therefore to determine the meaning of the . . . language as it was understood when the framers proposed
it and the people ratified it as part of the original text."

In their session Monday morning, Gray and Thornburgh found
Souter extraordinarily congenial, although they did worry that he had
no life-defining cases, when he'd taken an unpopular stand and weath-
ered the storm. Luttig was especially troubled and took the strongest
stand against Souter of anyone in the administration. Souter simply did
not have a sufficient record for the nomination. "I cannot tell you who
he will be as a Supreme Court justice," Luttig told Thornburgh and
Gray. "On federal law, there's nothing. We're drawing the most specific
inferences based on the most pedestrian state cases possible."

But in the White House, Sununu was ready to make his case with
Bush. When he nominated Souter to the state supreme court, he was
looking for "someone who would be a strict constructionist, consistent
with basic conservative attitudes," Sununu told Bush. "I'm sure he
would do the same thing when he encountered federal questions."
"What he says and does is what he is. No pretense, no surprises."[13]

Sununu's characterization of Souter more accurately described
Jones, a favorite of conservatives. She had been general counsel of the
Texas Republican Party before becoming a judge, and she had a well-
established track record after only five years as a federal judge. But she
didn't have a forceful advocate to match Sununu.

After their meetings in the Justice Department, Souter and Jones
went to the White House. Souter met with Bush in the residence early
that afternoon for about forty-five minutes, talking about his judicial
approach and general view of the court system.

Bush had talked earlier in the day to Jones about many of the same
things, and he found himself liking her better than Souter. He could understand her views on the law. Where Souter was obtuse and indirect,
Jones had been more straightforward and easier to understand. But
Jones was young and almost brittle in appearance. She was just forty-

one, and her slight frame made her appear even more youthful. And as a University of Texas Law School graduate, she lacked the Ivy League credentials—Harvard and Harvard Law—that lawyers in the White House counsel's office instinctively valued. Souter, the product of elite northeastern private schools, was seen as more scholarly. "Brilliant," the advisers all pronounced.

As Sununu was pushing for Souter, Gray and Thornburgh were worrying about Jones and how she'd handle the intense pressure of a Judiciary Committee hearing. Her conservative credentials would also mean more of a fight, and Bush didn't want that—even though he could have won it: Jones's nomination would have put southern Democrats in the impossible position of voting against a bright law-and-order woman judge at a time when the Supreme Court did not have one justice from the South.

For an hour, Bush sat alone with a yellow legal pad, making a list of pros and cons. The reclusive New Hampshire judge, cast as the more scholarly of the two, seemed more suited to have the title of justice. He was the kind of man who would devote his life to the Supreme Court.

At 4:15 p.m., Bush asked Souter into his private office, just next to the Oval Office, and formally offered him the job. Less than an hour later, Bush stood at the lectern in the White House briefing room and introduced the obscure judge to the Washington press corps. Souter stood quietly at his side with his arms crossed. He looked slightly stunned as reporters fired questions at Bush about abortion and whether *Roe v. Wade* was history.

Bush was pleased that reporters were surprised by how quickly he made the nomination. Advisers immediately characterized it as the mark of a forceful leader. Vice President Dan Quayle, who earlier in the day had argued that Jones was a better choice, told the College Republican National Committee later in the week that the nomination "is just the latest example of [Bush's] decisive executive style."

But the description of Souter as a brilliant legal scholar and deserving replacement for his friend Bill Brennan was too much for Thurgood

Marshall. Three days later, Justice Marshall derisively told Sam Donaldson of ABC News that neither he nor Brennan had ever heard of
Souter—even though Brennan was responsible for overseeing matters
on Souter's court, the U.S. Court of Appeals for the First Circuit. He said
he "didn't have the slightest idea" why Bush had nominated him. "I just
don't understand what he is doing," Marshall groused of Bush. "I don't
understand it."

Donaldson emphasized that Souter might replace Brennan, the
Court's revered liberal icon.

"I still never heard of him. When his name came down, I listened
on television. And the first thing, I called my wife. 'Have I ever heard
of this man?' She said, 'No, I haven't either.' So I promptly called Brennan, because it's his Circuit. And his wife answered the phone, and I told
her. She said, 'He's never heard of him, either.' "[14]

Those words stung Souter. He deeply admired both Brennan and
Marshall, and had told friends he considered Marshall "one of the giants of the century."[15]

The conservative and liberal groups that had mobilized over the
Bork nomination didn't know what to make of Souter either. Conservatives were skittish. Sununu, Bush's envoy to the Right, assured them
in private meetings that the obscure judge with the monastic lifestyle
was a "home run." The White House communications office was crank-
ing out editorials that portrayed Souter as a tough law-and-order judge
who believed judges had a limited role in society.

As Sununu was seeking to firm up support, the moderate, prochoice
Rudman was reaching out to neutralize the opposition. Rudman believed Souter would not overturn *Roe v. Wade,* and he spoke privately
with Ralph Neas, who, as executive director of the Leadership Conference on Civil Rights, had mobilized the opposition to Bork. Souter,
Rudman assured Neas, "will be fine" on privacy and civil rights issues.
Neas and others who had worked against Bork were also hearing from
their contacts in New Hampshire that Rudman was right. Souter, they
were coming to believe, would be fine.

It fell to the abortion-rights groups to come out against Souter. They assumed that any nominee the prolife John Sununu supported was certain to overturn *Roe v. Wade,* and they promptly opposed him. STOP SOUTER OR WOMEN WILL DIE, one flyer screamed. "We find him a devastating threat," said Eleanor Smeal, president of the Fund for the Feminist Majority.

Advisers in the White House and Justice Department were beginning to have their own doubts. Having learned from the Bork debacle, they subjected the new nominee to mock questioning to simulate what he would face in the Judiciary Committee. In these preparation sessions with administration lawyers, Souter did poorly. At times, he leaned back in his chair and mumbled incoherent answers. White House lawyers felt a sense of panic. "My God, did we ever pick the wrong person," Gray said after one session.

At the same time, reporters began unearthing personal details about Souter. His eccentric qualities started to seem outright bizarre. He was so frugal that he'd let his aging farmhouse, with its sagging porch and peeling paint, almost fall apart. He drove a worn-out Volkswagen for so long that his former colleagues on the New Hampshire Supreme Court believed "he would die in that car." He once got so upset about an increase in his electric bill that he indignantly brought it to court to show the other justices. The bill had just topped thirty dollars. The other justices were paying well over two hundred dollars a month for electricity, and some were surprised Souter even received a bill. "They figured he was still out there reading by the wood stove," one of his colleagues said.[16]

Luttig and the lawyers on his staff, after hearing yet another story that detailed his solitary style, looked at each other with alarm.

It wasn't until the hearings that different concerns began to emerge. Souter wowed Senate Democrats with a performance so flawless that, years later, a Democratic administration would ask its own Supreme Court nominee to watch a videotape of it as an example of "what to do."

But it wasn't Souter's presentation that alarmed conservatives this time. It was his thinking about the law. Listening to Souter testify, Liberman had a sharply sinking feeling as she heard him heap fawning praise on Brennan, defend the rulings of the liberal Warren Court, and reject the conservative legal theories of Scalia. Even Ruth Bader Ginsburg, years later when she was preparing for her own confirmation hearings, was struck by Souter's responses—and how far he was from the "strict constructionist" Bush portrayed him to be.

David Souter instead sounded much like the man he was to replace. When Democratic senator Herb Kohl of Wisconsin asked Souter how he would remember Brennan, Souter could have politely expressed admiration for Brennan's legal skills and his prominent role in the development of American law. Instead, he gushed: "Justice Brennan is going to be remembered as one of the most fearlessly principled guardians of the American Constitution that it has ever had and ever will have," Souter said. "No one following Justice Brennan, absolutely no one, could possibly say a word to put himself in the league with Brennan. All you can do is to say what perhaps once Justice Brennan said, 'I will do the best I can.'"

Charles Grassley, a strongly antiabortion lawmaker, found himself growing increasingly irritated. He'd raised concerns early on about whether Souter was conservative enough for the lifetime appointment to the Supreme Court, and he was determined to make Souter explain himself. He had asked Souter a series of easy, leading questions about how conservatives view the proper role of the courts, an outlook that rejects the idea that "the courts, rather than the elected branches, should take the lead in creating a more just society."

But Souter declined to walk the conservative line. "Courts must accept their own responsibility for making a just society," he said, sounding much like the man he was replacing. "The courts are going to be forced to take on problems which, sometimes, in the first instance, might better be addressed by the political branches of government." If the other branches refuse to address a "profound social problem" that raises a constitutional issue, Souter said, then "ultimately it does and must land before the bench of the judiciary."

"The law of nature and political responsibility, constitutional responsibility, abhor a vacuum," Souter told Grassley.

Pennsylvania senator Arlen Specter, a moderate Republican, was openly amused at the exchange. He described Souter's remarks to reporters during a break: "I don't think you'll find a more liberal statement anywhere. It was out of Brennan's left pocket."[17]

But Grassley and other conservatives were now downright uneasy. Souter was sitting there, talking about how courts have to fill vacuums when the legislature fails to act. Grassley went back and questioned Souter again when the hearing resumed Monday morning. "As it hit me on Friday, [your testimony] seems to me more the terminology likely to come from a judicial activist," Grassley told Souter. "If we are going to have a Supreme Court that thinks it can fill vacuums every time there is a perceived problem, then . . . you are going to be a very busy person because democratic self-government does not always move with the speed or the consensus or the wisdom of philosopher kings who might best fill those vacuums." If that's your approach as a Supreme Court justice, Grassley continued, "then you are coming dangerously close to acting like a politician. Would you please clarify the use of the term vacuum, or, even better, rephrase it in favor of something different?" Grassley pleaded, as he and the senators on the committee laughed.

Souter smiled. "I think you're giving me a hint, Senator."

But Souter then proceeded to defend the Supreme Court's power to identify new unwritten rights that aren't specifically mentioned in the Constitution. He referred to *Brown v. Board of Education,* the landmark 1954 ruling that outlawed "separate but equal" racially segregated schools. Thurgood Marshall had argued the case before the Court. "If you simply read the text of the Constitution and somebody said, 'Where does it refer to school desegregation?'—of course you would not have found anything," Souter said. "But I think that clearly implicit in the text of the Constitution itself was the proper basis for the court's exercise of its jurisdiction."

Grassley, growing impatient, pressed Souter to name any case in the Court's history where "improper rights were created." When Souter failed to name one, Grassley stepped in. "Well then, let me see if I can help you where you might think the Court improperly acted," said Grassley, and he referred to some of the landmark rulings of the Warren Court that greatly expanded the rights of criminal suspects.

But Souter refused to concede the point. The Warren Court rulings, he said, were a "pragmatic implementation" of the Bill of Rights. The problem with them was teaching law-enforcement officers how to protect the rights of suspects. "In the meantime," Souter said, "we have learned to live with a great deal [of the Warren Court rulings] and lived with them pretty well today."

After two days of that kind of testimony, Souter easily—and unsurprisingly—won over Senate Democrats. Biden went so far as to issue a report analyzing Souter's testimony and emphasizing the high stakes for the Court and the country. "No nominee in a quarter-century had come to this committee with less known about his constitutional philosophy than David Souter," Biden wrote. "And no nomination—at any time since the 1930s—had come before the Senate at a moment of such importance, in terms of setting the future direction of the Supreme Court." Souter's testimony was "reassuring" and "highly commendable," Biden wrote. "We believe that he clearly demonstrated himself not to be a doctrinaire legal conservative. He clearly distinguished himself from quite a broad school of legal conservatism—including some conservative positions not being taken by members of the current court." Biden concluded that Democrats should support Souter with a "hopeful heart."

Republicans, though concerned by Souter's seeming embrace of the liberal Warren Court ideology, could not abandon a man the White House had assured them was a reliable conservative. Some assumed

Souter was simply pandering to Democrats to get through the committee, and they refused to believe he meant what he said.

As a result, the reclusive New Hampshire judge, unknown to virtually everyone the day of his nomination, rode to confirmation by an overwhelming margin, 90–9. Incredibly, nine liberal Democrats opposed him, including two from neighboring Massachusetts, Ted Kennedy and John Kerry.

Once on the Court, Souter would quickly become one of its most liberal justices, ending for a time any hope of cementing a conservative majority. Over the years, Souter's nomination would come to be seen by conservatives as one of the single greatest failures of George H. W. Bush's presidency, and administration officials struggle today to understand how they so egregiously misjudged him. Some, like Luttig, have suggested that they never knew Souter's philosophy because Souter himself didn't know it. As a state court judge, he'd never grappled with the hard federal constitutional issues. Others have tried to erase it from memory. Liberman has called the experience the most painful in her life, and has said she wills herself not to think about.

One senior official summed up the administration's decision to nominate a cipher over the loyal Starr, waiting in the wings, this way: "There's the devil you know, and the one you don't," the official said. "We went with the one you don't."

5.

"THE YOUNGEST, CRUELEST JUSTICE"

Less than a year after William Brennan left the Court, his ideological ally, Thurgood Marshall, followed. The departure of the second of two liberal icons presented George H. W. Bush with another historic opportunity. Despite conservative misgivings, his first nominee, David Souter, finished his first term actually standing with Rehnquist. Now Bush would be given yet another chance to solidify the conservative majority. To accomplish that task he turned to the man he'd briefly considered the year before.

Clarence Thomas was well known in conservative circles. The former chairman of the Equal Employment Opportunity Commission, Thomas was a prominent black in the overwhelmingly white conservative world. He traveled the country giving speeches about the law and stressing personal responsibility. With top grades in college at Holy Cross and a law degree from Yale, Thomas had solid academic credentials as well as ideological ones. Bush put him on the D.C.-based federal appeals court in 1990. Conservatives expected that someday, Thomas would be heading to the Supreme Court.

George Bush paused only briefly before nominating the forty-three-year-old Thomas to replace Marshall, the Court's first African American. The president was nervous about the "optics," as he put it. He worried about how it would look, replacing one black justice with another, and he didn't like the idea of a quota seat. It's one reason he had suggested Thomas the year before, when his advisers had urged him to tap Souter. But politically, Thomas was compelling. His southern background and humble origins would trap southern Democrats into voting for him. "How could they vote against a favorite son?" one White House official asked.

No one—not the White House lawyers or the president—could have imagined that the serious conservative jurist would become the focus of one of the most lurid and personally explosive confirmation battles in Court history. Thomas would endure stinging attacks from senators and witnesses, many of which focused on personal charges that made the Bork hearings seem tame by comparison.

Reeling from the public humiliation of his confirmation hearings, Thomas joined a Supreme Court in flux. The third new justice in less than four years, he signified dramatic change. The shift from Marshall to Thomas represented the single most pronounced ideological turn in modern Court history.

Liberals who vowed to defeat Thomas by any means necessary felt sure the Bush appointee would hand right-wing interest groups the vote they had sought for more than a decade to overturn *Roe* and end affirmative action. Thomas's confirmation came just a year after Bush put Souter on the Court, and the pair joined Reagan appointees O'Connor, Scalia, and Kennedy, a new justice himself, as well as the firmly conservative Nixon appointee, Rehnquist, and Byron White, a Kennedy appointee who generally voted with conservatives. With a lineup of what appeared to be seven solid conservatives, few in the legal community—or in Republican circles—doubted that Thomas and his allies would do anything other than dismember the liberal legacy of the Warren Court.

But that conservative ruling coalition never materialized. Instead, in Thomas's first year the Court lurched dramatically and to many, inexplicably, to the left. The court rendered decisions that effectively upheld *Roe* and struck down the practice of offering prayers at public school graduation ceremonies. Those rulings, coupled with decisions in death penalty and other criminal cases, crushed conservative hopes that the Court Thomas joined would be more reliably conservative than the one Marshall had left.

Thomas's first year on the Supreme Court was a turbulent one, both for him and for the Court as a whole. The justices that year brought to life the old saying that a new justice makes a new Court. Thomas's entry onto the Court didn't merely change the vote of the liberal justice he replaced. It turned the chessboard around. Ideological alliances were rearranged. Thomas acted as a catalyst, spurring the other justices— O'Connor, in particular—to rethink their positions and realign themselves into new voting blocs on some of the most important issues of the day.

The term was well under way when a battered Thomas came on board in late October. He'd missed all the October arguments because he and the country were in thrall to the tawdry Senate Judiciary Committee hearings, reconvened after law professor Anita Hill alleged that Thomas had made lewd and pornographic comments in front of her. The bitterness of those hearings cast a pall over Thomas, whose every move was considered suspect, even his request for a simple swearing-in ceremony a week after his confirmation. Court officials had canceled Thomas's original ceremony because Rehnquist's beloved wife, Natalie, had died the week before. One of Thomas's new clerks, staring at a backlog of hundreds of cases and some twenty thousand pieces of mail, called Thomas at home in a panic. "Justice, they won't give me the briefs," the clerk said. "We can't get on the computers unless you get sworn in."

Thomas immediately called Rehnquist's assistant to set it up when the chief returned to work. The next morning, the day after Natalie Rehnquist's funeral, the aide reached Thomas in his old chambers at the

U.S. Court of Appeals for the D.C. Circuit. Rehnquist had come into the office, and he would be ready in forty-five minutes to swear in Thomas. Thomas called his wife, Virginia, and Senator John Danforth of Missouri, his friend and sponsor in the Senate, and the three rushed over to the Supreme Court. Rehnquist delivered the oath in the justices' conference room, with Virginia holding the Bible. He shook Thomas's hand and congratulated him as Danforth snapped a photograph with Thomas's camera. Rehnquist then turned and went back to his office. Thomas went to his new chambers.

To reporters, the simple swearing-in ceremony was suspicious and mysterious, even though it took place only two days later than originally planned.[1] "A secret," several called it in news stories.[2] Some had already speculated that the White House was trying to sneak Thomas onto the bench before journalists could unearth new allegations against him.[3]

Thomas greeted his young clerks, most of whom had clerked for him on the appeals court, with big hugs. He was gratified to see friendly faces. He spent that first week calling the other justices and stopping by their chambers to introduce himself. Blackmun, author of *Roe*, gave him a frosty reception at first. Kennedy, confirmed just three years earlier, had already developed an aura of pomposity, stressing the intellectual nature of the work and implying he was the Court's scholar. It was off-putting to Thomas, who told a close associate that he felt Kennedy was talking down to him. But other liberals were welcoming, including Marshall, the justice Thomas had replaced. Thomas is a gregarious man, and his conversation with Marshall, a renowned storyteller, stretched nearly three hours and ended with a piece of advice from the liberal legend. "I had to do what I had to do in my time," Marshall told Thomas. "You have to do what you have to do in your time."

Among the more liberal justices' young law clerks, however, Thomas was viewed with ill-disguised contempt. They openly questioned his qualifications and intellectual heft. The reliably liberal Blackmun even allowed his own clerks to refer condescendingly to Christopher Landau, one of Thomas's four clerks, as "Justice" or the guy who was really "running the show." It was a rude and glaring breach of protocol that implied that Thomas wasn't up to the job. Ironically, Blackmun's clerks exerted enormous influence over their own boss, which could explain why they assumed that Landau's experience as a former Scalia clerk meant Thomas would be casting his lot with Scalia as well.

Thomas spent those early days getting up to speed on the twenty cases the Court would tackle in November. But he was lonely and exhausted. Almost every afternoon, he went to a monastery near Catholic University to pray, and it was there that he came across the Litany of Humility, a prayer that asks Jesus for deliverance from "the desire of being loved, from the desire of being extolled, from the desire of being honored, from the desire of being praised . . . from the fear of being humiliated, from the fear of being despised, from the fear of suffering rebukes."

Thomas resolved that he would maintain the courage of his convictions. He would take hits for the things he believed. He would not change one word because of what others might say. His brutal confirmation hearing had made him impervious to criticism from the media and the liberal law professors. They had no credibility with him; he did not care whether they approved of him or not.

Thomas had barely a week to prepare for his first public session, when he joined his colleagues in the Court's marble courtroom and listened to arguments from lawyers presenting their clients' views. Thomas's first day in the courtroom was a busy one, with the justices hearing arguments in four cases. Such a heavy caseload would be the exception in coming years, with Rehnquist preferring to limit hearings to morning-only sessions.

On that November morning in 1991, all eyes were fixed on Thomas as the justices filed into the courtroom. That day, *People* magazine had just released its latest issue, featuring a cover story on Thomas and his wife, Virginia, who had agreed to an interview and several photographs at their home. The interview, in a magazine typically filled with celebrity news and features, struck some justices as inappropriate, as if it were beneath the dignity of a sitting justice to be profiled in such a mass-market periodical. It didn't help Thomas's cause with his new colleagues.

As the new justice, Thomas took his seat at the far end of the Court's long wooden bench, next to Kennedy. Ceremony and custom on the high court even extend to seat assignments for the justices. The nine seats are arranged by seniority, with the chief sitting in the middle, flanked by the most senior of the associate justices. The most junior justice sits on the very end of the bench on the right side, and with Thomas's arrival on the bench, Souter moved up a notch in seniority and over to the end seat on the left side.

The justices, who had put some of their work on hold as Thomas's hearings unfolded across the street, were curious how their new colleague would conduct himself. Blackmun took note of the occasion. "CT first on the bench," he wrote in his argument notes from the first case, which concerned an issue of immigration law. Midway through the second hour of arguments, Blackmun again took note of the new justice: "No questions yet from CT," he wrote on his argument papers. Thomas's silence was noteworthy because the other justices so frequently hammered lawyers with questions. Scalia was especially active and relished using the arguments as a chance to drive home his points by exposing weaknesses in a lawyer's position. From time to time, Rehnquist would admonish Scalia, directing him to let the lawyer respond or to stop interrupting other justices.

The justices heard from Thomas two days later, when all nine convened around the heavy wooden table in their conference room to discuss privately the arguments they had just heard. The justices gathered twice a week after oral arguments to discuss their views on the cases, but the conversation was no free-for-all. Rehnquist imposed tight rules. Each justice could speak once, in order of seniority. After that, they could make additional points, but Rehnquist discouraged it. The justices argued about the law in writing, in the draft opinions they would later circulate among the chambers.

Though quiet on the bench during the public sessions, Thomas wasted no time sharing his views in conference. Pundits and analysts would disparage Thomas as Scalia's intellectual understudy, but from the beginning that portrayal was grossly inaccurate. If either justice changed his mind to side with the other that year, it was Scalia joining Thomas, not the other way around. But journalists, not privy to the justices' behind-the-scenes discussions, assumed otherwise and wrote it as fact, creating a false impression that still lingers. Instead, from his first week, Thomas made clear that he was willing to be the solo dissenter, sending other justices a strong signal that he would not moderate his opinions for the sake of comity. By his second week on the Court, in his firm and ringing baritone, the rookie jurist was staking out bold positions in the justices' private conferences and urging them to rethink entire areas of criminal law he believed had been wrongly decided.

Thomas's approach was not well received by Blackmun or O'Connor, who believed the junior justice should be more deferential to his senior colleagues. The justices labor in solitude, separated from their peers. But they still define themselves very much in relation to one another. Those dynamics can be as much personal as professional, and they can attract or repel. The more senior justices like Blackmun were sensitive to interpersonal politics, especially among the three whose legal views were not well defined: O'Connor, Kennedy, and Souter. Blackmun was careful to compliment O'Connor for an opinion he found particularly well written, and he would sometimes compromise his position to get the result he wanted. In one controversial criminal case during Thomas's first year, Blackmun wrote a separate "upbeat affirmation" of O'Connor's majority opinion[4] that he "designed not to raise any hackles," as one of his clerks put it in a memo urging the same approach in another case.[5]

That was not Thomas's approach. He was the brash newcomer who believed there were right answers in the law. But the intensity of his views, coupled with wrongheaded media depictions of a rookie justice doing the bidding of his so-called mentor Scalia, helped create an internal dynamic that would prove costly to conservatives. By the end of Thomas's first year, O'Connor and Souter—and to a lesser extent Kennedy—had moved left, a shift that would ultimately prevent conservatives from undoing the liberal legacy of the Warren Court under Rehnquist's leadership.

Thomas's first private conference with the justices seemed routine enough. Justices have said they felt anxious or uneasy at their first conference, when they sat down with new colleagues—icons in the law—to share their own views. O'Connor remembers feeling nervous and determined to make a good impression in her first conference, but instead being completely rattled by a handshake from Justice Byron White. A former National Football League star, White crushed O'Connor's fingers in a viselike grip. Tears welled up in her eyes as she took her seat to become the first woman ever to sit at the Court's conference table. It was not how she envisioned getting things started.

At his first conference, Thomas spoke directly, but in the third case being reviewed, he capitulated to the power of unanimous group thinking. He immediately regretted his decision. The case concerned a thief's effort to get out of a Louisiana mental institution and the state's struggle to keep him there. Terry Foucha had been detained for four years in a state institution after a trial judge found him not guilty of burglary because he was insane.[6] After doctors determined that Foucha was no longer insane, he wanted out of the mental institution. But state officials refused. They pointed to a Louisiana law that allowed them to keep him institutionalized until he could prove he was no longer dangerous. Foucha contended that the law was unconstitutional, but a lower court rejected his arguments.

Rehnquist started the discussion by saying that he believed the lower court was wrong, and that Louisiana couldn't keep inmates who were no longer mentally ill locked up indefinitely by demanding they prove they weren't dangerous. The justices went around the table. All agreed with Rehnquist until the discussion turned to Thomas. He said he was "troubled" by the case. Under the Court's approach, the inmate would be kept in a mental institution for a shorter period of time than a sane prisoner, convicted of the same offense, would serve in jail. Grudgingly, however, Thomas said he too would rule for the inmate.

Thomas couldn't sleep that night as he pondered his vote at conference. The next morning, he went to Rehnquist. He had "thrown in the towel" the day before when he'd cast his vote with the rest of the justices in the case, he told the chief, but he realized he'd done the wrong thing. He wanted to change his vote. In only the third case he had considered, he would be the lone dissenter.

Thomas's dissent, when released months later, revealed none of his initial ambivalence at that first conference. He was sharply critical of the majority opinion written by White for unearthing a constitutional right where one simply did not, he believed, exist. Although it "may make eminent sense as a policy matter" to remove sane people like Foucha from mental institutions, he said, the Constitution "does not require the states to conform to the policy preference of federal judges." The Court's decision "invalidating this quite reasonable scheme is bad enough; even worse is the court's failure to explain precisely what is wrong with it."

As it turned out, Thomas was not alone for long. After he sent his dissent to the other justices, Rehnquist and Scalia sent notes to the justices that they too were changing their votes and would join his opinion. Kennedy declined to join Thomas's dissent, but he also changed his vote and wrote his own dissent, emphasizing the criminal nature of the case. The case was 5–4.

O'Connor did not go along with Thomas's thinking. She joined part of White's majority opinion, which criticized Thomas for his "importantly incomplete" descriptions of the law. In stirring language, White stressed that "freedom from bodily restraint has always been at the core of the liberty" protected by the Constitution. O'Connor would quote that language twelve years later in *Hamdi v. Rumsfeld,* in her opinion that enemy combatant Yaser Hamdi, an American citizen captured while fighting for the Taliban in Afghanistan, was entitled to a hearing to contest his detention.[7]

The *Foucha* case, coming as it did in the very first group of cases Thomas discussed with his new colleagues, showed the extraordinary immediate impact a new justice could have on his colleagues. It also foreshadowed how Thomas, willing to be the lone dissenter from the outset, would reshape the Court. His views persuaded three other justices to change their minds and take his side in the case. At the same time, O'Connor, who instinctively put herself in the middle of the Court, began to move away from Thomas and toward the more liberal justices.

Disagreements among the justices don't necessarily extend to their personal relations. White's opinion was sharply critical of Thomas's position, but the two men had developed a friendship. They shared similar outside interests—unlike the other justices, both preferred sports to opera. Both were big men, and law clerks joked that they were the only two justices who could shake each other's hands without imparting pain. Thomas had hired one of White's law clerks from the year before, and White encouraged Thomas to develop a system like his for running his chambers and reviewing cases. Thomas joked that he didn't have time to get a system, because he was "building my wagon as I was riding in it." After the *Foucha* case, White told Thomas he should not be intimidated. "Don't change your mind unless you're truly persuaded," White said.

When Thomas found himself alone again in his second week of arguments, he did not waver during conference. The case would be the most controversial Thomas tackled in his first term.[8] It stemmed from a lawsuit by Keith Hudson, an African American inmate at the state penitentiary in Angola, Louisiana. Prison guards beat Hudson while a supervisor watched, cautioning them not "to have too much fun." Hudson suffered a cracked lip, a broken dental plate, loosened teeth, and cuts and bruises, and he sued for damages, arguing that the beating was cruel and unusual punishment, in violation of the Eighth Amendment. A federal appeals court threw out Hudson's lawsuit because his injuries were only minor ones that required no medical attention. Hudson asked the Supreme Court to reverse that decision.

In the conference, Rehnquist outlined his problems with the lower court's decision. It shouldn't have focused on whether the inmate's injuries were serious, Rehnquist said. "Not every push or shove" is cruel and unusual punishment, Rehnquist said, but courts shouldn't have to draw those lines on whether the injury was significant. He believed a 1986 case was a better approach, focusing on whether the guards administered "unnecessary and wanton infliction of pain." Moreover, he said, Hudson's injuries were "not de minimis."

The other justices quickly began to fall in line. O'Connor agreed with Rehnquist, suggesting that courts instead should focus on whether the prison guards had been using force in a good faith effort to maintain or restore discipline, or whether they instead had been maliciously and sadistically trying to cause harm. Scalia said he was "less inclined to create a federal constitutional violation" but that he thought the lower court was wrong. Kennedy and Souter said they agreed with Rehnquist. All eight justices had voted to reverse the lower court when it was Thomas's turn to talk.

His analysis was blunt. Hudson's injuries, Thomas said, did not "rise to the 8th Amendment level" of cruel and unusual punishment. There should be an exception for minor injuries. The beating may have been a criminal assault by the guards, but it wasn't an unconstitutional punishment. He was voting to affirm the lower court and reject Hudson's lawsuit. Thomas's remarks jolted the unanimous dynamic of the group, a reality that again did not seem to unsettle Thomas in the slightest. In his notes from the conference, Blackmun punctuated Thomas's comments with an exclamation point, as if he could barely believe his position. "8–1" to reverse, Blackmun wrote on his notes.

Thomas staked out classic principles of judicial conservatism in his written dissent, accusing his colleagues of failing to recognize the limited role of federal courts and falling victim to the "pervasive view that the Federal Constitution must address all ills in our society." To Thomas, the conduct of the guards was "deplorable" and "properly evokes outrage and contempt." But that didn't mean it was unconstitutional, he said. "The Eighth Amendment is not, and should not be turned into, a National Code of Prison Regulation." That dissent was enough for Scalia. He changed his vote to join Thomas for the second time in less than a week.

O'Connor wrote the majority decision for the Court, and she delivered a harsh rebuke to Thomas. "To deny, as the dissent does, the difference between punching a prisoner in the face and serving him unappetizing food is to ignore the concepts of dignity, civilized standards, humanity, and decency that animate the Eighth Amendment," O'Connor wrote. Just weeks after joining the Court, Thomas was already sharply at odds with O'Connor.

Before the opinions were publicly released, one of Thomas's law clerks cautioned him that he was certain to be criticized. Thomas responded with a question to make his point. "But is it right?" Thomas asked.

"Yes," the clerk said, nodding in agreement.

"Well, you can't change it," Thomas said.

Prominent African Americans, editorial writers, and even Senator Arlen Specter, the Pennsylvania Republican who had so strongly supported Thomas during his confirmation hearings, blasted Thomas's decision. The *New York Times* said Thomas's position in the case revealed him to be "the youngest, cruelest justice."[9] A column in the *Washington Post* quoted a lawyer for the American Civil Liberties Union, who had represented Keith Hudson, saying that Thomas was Scalia's puppet,[10] even though Thomas had persuaded Scalia in the case.

Thomas didn't flinch. He didn't care about his reviews. Unlike Kennedy, who received harsh media coverage in his first few months on the bench after a vote in a race-discrimination case, public opinion would not sway him. Thomas believed the hydraulic pressure to move left, to be lauded by academia and the *New York Times,* was the opposite of judging. He loved Justice Harlan's dissent in *Plessy v. Ferguson,* the infamous 1896 case that upheld segregation. Harlan alone had dissented, emphasizing that the "Constitution is color-blind" and that the government couldn't punish people for wanting to use public facilities. "Can you imagine the hell he caught?" Thomas would ask clerks of Harlan. Thomas also thought often of the federal judges in the South, whose rulings in the 1960s against segregation came in the face of overwhelming public disapproval and cultural pressure.

"What if those federal judges worried about what would happen at the country club or what their neighbors would say or what they would say at the bar meetings?" Thomas would ask. "Where would I be? That has to be bled out of it. You're really required not to worry about these pressures."

Thomas's bruising confirmation hearing enforced his autonomy. He had offered his side of the story then, and no one had listened. With growing outrage, he had instead watched the press and the academics in the law schools, including at Yale, his alma mater, embrace a story he believed clearly and unequivocally to be false. From that point on, he did not care what they said about him—an attitude that persists to this day. Thomas, for example, is the only justice who rarely asks questions at oral arguments. He thinks his colleagues talk too much on the bench, and he isn't inclined to add to the chatter. But his notable silence is sometimes interpreted as a lack of interest, and friends have begged him to ask a few questions, just to dispel those suggestions. But Thomas won't. He doesn't care how his silence is perceived. "They have no credibility. I don't care what they think," Thomas would say of his critics. "I am free to live up to my oath."

Thomas found support in unusual places that first term. Despite their differences in style, he liked Souter, who was gracious and helpful, even though Souter himself was still learning his way after just a year on the Court. To aid his own transition, Souter had often sought counsel from Brennan, the justice he had replaced. Several months into the job, Thomas also dropped by Brennan's chambers to say hello. "Don't change your mind unless you're persuaded, and you'll do fine," Brennan told him, echoing White's earlier advice.

With Brennan and Marshall gone, the liberals lacked a voice to define their position. Thomas's insistent arguments, and Scalia's ready acquiescence, appeared to be shifting the Court's focus forcefully to the right. That unsettled O'Connor, who in many ways remained the former state legislator she had been before her nomination. She saw herself as a balanced person who offered the reasonable compromise in important cases. But when the balance of the Court began to shift to the right, O'Connor's line of compromise changed. With Thomas on the bench, she was not reacting to the liberals. She was pulling away from the conservatives.

Nothing better illustrated the intellectual fallout from Thomas's appointment than two cases argued in October, before Thomas joined the Court. The cases had split the justices 4–4, and they had agreed to hear them again so that Thomas, presumably, could cast the deciding vote. The practice is common when a justice joins the Court after the term is under way. When Kennedy joined the Court in January 1988, for instance, he cast the deciding vote in all four of the cases that were reargued for him. But that didn't happen with Thomas. Instead, after the 4–4 cases were reargued for him, Thomas found himself dissenting in both, because other justices, reexamining their own positions, changed their votes.[11]

One of those cases powerfully demonstrated the changing dynamics at the Court.[12] Souter switched sides to join the more liberal justices. Scalia flipped to join him, but then went back to join Thomas on the other side. And O'Connor backed further away from the new justice and closer to her colleagues on the Left. The case involved a Virginia man, Marc Doggett, who was indicted on a drug charge but was not arrested for almost nine years. He argued that the long delay violated his constitutional right to a speedy trial. Souter initially voted with Rehnquist, O'Connor, and Scalia to reject Doggett's claims. In conference, Stevens was adamant. "How can the defendant lose here?" he asked.

O'Connor was unconvinced. "I think I still" will vote against him again, she said. But not Scalia, who changed his mind and was siding with Doggett. The ardent conservative was persuaded that the lengthy delay rose to the level of a constitutional violation. Souter, too, changed course to side with the defendant. "Delay . . . becomes prejudicial," Souter told his colleagues. "Truth is placed at risk."

Thomas spoke last, after Souter. He was voting against Doggett. The votes in conference—with Souter and Scalia changing their minds and siding with Doggett—meant that only Rehnquist, O'Connor, and Thomas would be dissenting.

But the power of Thomas's argument, when he released his dissent, shuffled the pieces around again. He argued that the decision "will transform the courts of the land into boards of law enforcement supervision." The court had ordered the charges against Doggett dismissed, not because he suffered any harm by the delay, but "simply because the Government's efforts to catch him are found wanting." That wasn't the proper role of the federal courts, he said. "Our function . . . is not to slap the Government on the wrist for sloppy work or misplaced priorities, but to protect the legal rights of those individuals harmed thereby," Thomas wrote. "The Court positively invites the Nation's judges to indulge in ad hoc and result driven second guessing of the government's investigatory efforts. Our Constitution neither contemplates nor tolerates such a role."

O'Connor refused to sign Thomas's opinion. She still thought Doggett should lose, but believed Thomas had gone too far. She instead wrote a separate, one-paragraph dissent of her own that made the same legal point as Thomas had, but without his sweeping language about the proper role of the Court. That would become a pattern. When Thomas and O'Connor were on the same side that term, she typically wrote a separate opinion of her own and refused to join his. She did not join a single one of his dissents.

Thomas was, after all, in many ways O'Connor's opposite. Where he was urging the Court to rethink vast areas of the law, O'Connor wanted

to decide cases narrowly, one by one. She lacked a defined legal philosophy, and law clerks on both sides of the ideological spectrum grouped
her with Souter and Kennedy—both also seen as indecisive in 1991. In
a November immigration case, argued on Thomas's first day on the
Court, one of Blackmun's clerks told him that O'Connor "is, as usual,
on the fence." Without a clear legal framework for deciding cases,
O'Connor turned to instinct.

O'Connor was a cohesive presence at the Court, and the other justices viewed her warmly. She encouraged the justices to have lunch together almost daily when the Court was in session, and she organized
social events and dinners, often cooking one of her southwestern spe-
cialties. But on the law, she stood apart from the justices lined up on
the left and right. She was the independent cowgirl born with "an internal mechanism" to resist pressure.

In her first decade on the Court, O'Connor developed a close relationship with Lewis Powell, the soft-spoken moderate from Virginia.
Though she knew Rehnquist from their Stanford days, it was Powell who
helped her find her footing as a new justice. He also had warned her
early on to be wary of the charming—and notoriously persuasive—
liberal icon Brennan because he tended to include footnotes in his opinions that he would later argue were major points of law. O'Connor had
an unpleasant exchange with Brennan in her first term, and armed with
Powell's advice, she was always reluctant to join a Bill Brennan opinion.

Throughout the 1980s, with Brennan, Marshall, Blackmun, and
Stevens solidly anchoring the court's liberal wing, O'Connor more reliably sided with conservatives. Brennan's bold liberal positions were
like a force field keeping O'Connor away. But that barrier fell with
Brennan's retirement in 1990. When Thomas joined the Court a year
later, O'Connor had no shield to keep her from moving left, away from
his strong views. Brennan's reverse magnetism was gone.

But if O'Connor was backing away from Thomas, Scalia moved
closer. In the *Doggett* case, one of Blackmun's clerks told Thomas that
Scalia "might be tempted to join" his dissent—even though Scalia had

cast his vote with the other side during the conference. And Scalia did, immediately after he read Thomas's dissent.

From the beginning, Scalia found himself agreeing with Thomas's views on the law. After Thomas's very first conference, Scalia changed his mind to side with him in the *Foucha* case, and on several other occasions that term, Scalia switched his vote to join Thomas in dissent. But these maneuvers were unknown to outsiders and Court watchers.

Instead, journalists insultingly cast Thomas as Scalia's apprentice. When the Court announced a decision March 9 in a death penalty case that had split Scalia and Thomas,[13] they considered it newsworthy. Thomas was the only justice who voted to uphold the death sentence of a member of the Aryan Brotherhood, a racist prison gang. The *New York Times* solemnly noted that the decision marked the "first case that found Justices Thomas and Scalia on opposite sides." Thomas's lone dissent, the *Times* said, "was notable for the solitary position in which it placed him, without even the company of his apparent mentor, Justice Antonin Scalia."[14]

The clear implication was that after months of blindly following Scalia, Thomas had finally ventured out onto his own. But the *Times*'s stab at insight missed the mark, because Thomas and Scalia had parted ways in the case almost immediately after Thomas joined the Court. Although the case was publicly announced in early spring, the justices had heard arguments in the case—and cast their votes—the second week of November. In this case, as in others, Thomas acted independently of Scalia right from the start. He did agree with Scalia that term more than any of the other justices did, but no more frequently than Anthony Kennedy had in his first few of years on the Court. No one had accused Kennedy of trotting behind Scalia.

Thomas didn't reflexively take the conservative path, either. Thomas sided with liberals in a case argued his first week on the bench that involved a Nebraska farmer charged with possession of child pornography.[15] The farmer argued that federal agents lured him into ordering an obscene magazine that pictured boys engaged in sexual acts. The agents had come across his name in a separate investigation and spent two and a half years bombarding him with phony offers and solicitations, using fake names to trick him into buying the materials, until he relented. "This is entrapment," Thomas said during the conference. "The conduct was outrageous." Thomas later cast the key vote with liberals, and the Court reversed Keith Jacobson's conviction, in a 5–4 decision. Rehnquist, O'Connor, Scalia, and Kennedy dissented.

The next week in November, the Court took up a dispute in an obscure labor law case that gave O'Connor an opportunity to fire a warning shot across Thomas's bow. She made the most of it, with an opinion Thomas's clerks believed was designed to put the newcomer in his proper place as the junior justice.

The case, *Lechmere v. NLRB*, stemmed from the AFL-CIO's efforts to organize employees at a retail store in Newington, Connecticut.[16] A group of organizers, who didn't work at the store, started putting flyers on employees' car windshields in the store parking lot, but the storeowners kicked them off the property. Union officials thought the store was violating federal labor laws when it barred the organizers, so they filed a complaint with the National Labor Relations Board. The board had been sympathetic to unions on that issue in the past, and it promptly sided with the union in the Newington case. The storeowners challenged the board's decision, but a federal appeals court affirmed the ruling.

At their conference following the oral arguments, six of the justices thought the NLRB was wrong and had been too quick to side with the union. Stevens, Blackmun, and White sided with the union. Stevens argued that deferring to the board's judgment "makes sense," especially because the union had trouble contacting the two hundred store employees when it first tried to get names and addresses through their license plates. But the other justices believed the store could bar the union organizers from the private parking lot. The union had other ways of getting its message across. They thought the NLRB had been misinterpreting a thirty-five-year-old Supreme Court decision and was applying the wrong test to determine when union organizers could go onto private property in their efforts to organize.

Rehnquist was adamant; O'Connor, less so. The case was "close," she said, but she concluded that the board had used the wrong test. Scalia said he was "entirely with Sandra" on the issue and emphasized that the union organizers were seeking access to private, not public, property. Kennedy said he too was with O'Connor and Scalia, and that he also believed the case was "close." Thomas, who did not discuss the case at length, also said he would reverse the NLRB's decision.

Rehnquist assigned the opinion to Thomas to write, and he issued his draft less than a month later, in mid-December. Although several of the justices believed the case was a close call, Thomas had no reservations. He attached a note that said he had become convinced the NLRB was so far off base it made no sense for the Court to send the case back for further study.

Instead, he proposed clarifying the proper test for determining when union organizers can go onto private property and apply it in the case. By doing that, the Court could just reverse the decision below outright, handing a victory to the storeowners, instead of sending it back to the lower court to rethink the issue and apply the proper standard. "The conference vote in this case was to reverse and remand. In the writing, however, I became convinced that outright reversal was warranted," Thomas told the justices in his short note. "I hope this resolution of the case will prove agreeable to those who voted at Conference (as I did) to reverse and remand."

But it wasn't Thomas's note about flatly reversing the case that stopped several of the justices short. It was one paragraph, in the middle of the opinion, in which Thomas accused the NLRB of ignoring the directives of the Supreme Court. Thomas quoted *Marbury v. Madison*, the landmark 1803 case in which the Supreme Court established its power to strike down acts of Congress as unconstitutional, to boldly remind all: "We say what the law is." The Court had definitively explained "what the law is" before, Thomas said. Employers are required only in limited circumstances to allow such union organizers onto their property, and those circumstances weren't remotely present. The NLRB just blew it, in Thomas's view.

"Phew! Real conservatism," Blackmun wrote on the first page of Thomas's draft opinion. As he read through the opinion, Blackmun inserted exclamation points in the margins, in response to the points Thomas made. The boldest mark, as if Blackmun had a visceral reaction to Thomas's words, appears next to the paragraph quoting *Marbury v. Madison*.

The next day, O'Connor wrote Thomas a terse note, sending copies to the other justices, saying that she would not sign on to his decision circulated the day before in the union case. She, like Blackmun, disliked Thomas's raw characterization of the Court's decision-making power and believed he had been much too hard on the NLRB. To O'Connor, the rules weren't so clear, and she was offended that Thomas was "taking the National Labor Relations Board to task" for no good reason. "I have some reservations about your draft in this case and will either await additional writing or write something myself spelling out my concerns," she told him.

It took just a week. In pointed language days before Christmas, O'Connor circulated an opinion calling Thomas's opinion "troublesome" and "troubling." Even a "cursory reading" of the case law would show that the board had tried to follow the Supreme Court's decisions, she said. She believed the case law was unclear, and she suggested Thomas had not been "forthright" in acknowledging that. "The Board was more faithful to our cases than the court admits," she wrote. When Blackmun read her opinion, he was pleased to see her reprimand Thomas. "Well, good for her," he wrote on the first page of her draft concurring opinion.

Thomas hadn't understood how his strong language would be received, and after reading O'Connor's concurrence, he agreed to delete the offending paragraph completely. "The changes you have made satisfy the substance of my concerns," O'Connor told Thomas. "I now join your opinion and withdraw my concurrence." Her separate concurring opinion was never publicly released.

Still, the bold punches from Thomas kept coming. In December, while the justices were still digesting his opinion in the union case, he circulated a note about a criminal case involving a sexual assault on a four-year-old girl.[17] The girl had been too distraught to testify at trial, and the judge allowed her babysitter, mother, and medical personnel to testify about what the young girl told them immediately after the assault. The defendant, Randall White, argued that the adults' testimony was inadmissible. He challenged his conviction on the grounds that it violated the Sixth Amendment's confrontation clause, which guarantees a criminal defendant the right "to be confronted with the witnesses against him."

The justices agreed that the Constitution did not prohibit adults from testifying about their conversations with the girl. But Thomas, in his note to the other justices, said he was planning to write separately, to suggest that in future cases the Court should reexamine its decisions under the Constitution's confrontation clause. He believed the Court had been too friendly to criminal defendants in the past. "Curious letter from a new junior," Blackmun wrote at the bottom of Thomas's note.

While Thomas's opinions were causing O'Connor to back away, Scalia was in the process of alienating Souter. Souter had joined the Court only the year before, and he was distressed at times by the burden of his responsibilities. He'd never authored a federal court opinion, and he insisted on writing his own first drafts. In his first term, he was so overwhelmed by his opinion assignments that most were released late in the year. He wrote only two dissents. His struggle to reach decisions prompted even O'Connor to privately mock him for frequently complaining that a decision was "very difficult" or that his vote was merely "tentative."

If Thomas's forcefulness came through in his opinions, the charming and expansive Scalia was equally blunt in his notes to the justices.

He frequently demanded changes in opinions before he would agree to offer his support, often assailing fellow justices with pointed language in matters seemingly as rudimentary as vocabulary usage. An example was a full-page memo directed at O'Connor in April 1992 to complain about her use of the word "implausible" instead of "improbable" in one of her opinions.[18] He listed the definition in *Webster's Second* and included a passage from *Roget's Thesaurus*. In the same memo in the case, he also asked whether O'Connor would be willing to write "irrational or incredible" instead of merely "irrational." "I apologize," Scalia wrote, "if these suggestions seem rather picky."

"They do," wrote Blackmun on his copy of the memo. Blackmun, ironically, was himself such a stickler for proper grammar and punctuation that he had made similar demands and would instinctively edit memos, letters, and notes from clerks and other justices as he read through them.

Scalia and Souter had clashed in two cases the term before, but their conflicts became more evident as the 1991 term progressed. Scalia was particularly put off by Souter's decision in a case challenging the prison sentence of a sixteen-year-old boy.[19] After a night of heavy drinking, the boy had a car wreck on a Minnesota Indian reservation that killed a two-year-old girl. A judge sentenced the boy to three years in a juvenile detention facility, but an appeals court said the judge didn't properly consider the federal sentencing guidelines. Under the guidelines, the boy's sentence would be cut in half. The government, wanting the longer sentence, then took the case up to the Supreme Court.

At their conference, the justices voted 7–2 to side with the boy and uphold the appeals court's more lenient sentence. Souter and Scalia were in the majority, and Rehnquist assigned the opinion to Souter. But when Souter circulated his opinion the next month, Scalia reacted bluntly. He accused Souter of writing an opinion that "goes out of its way, it seems to me, to establish a proposition I do not agree with." Souter thought the Court needed to look back to the committee reports and floor statements when Congress passed the sentencing provisions for guidance on which of the two sentences to impose. But Scalia thought that kind of legislative history had no place in criminal sentencing.

Many conservatives like Scalia believe that courts should not look to the legislative history—the debate and pronouncements about a law when the legislature approved it—when they are trying to discern its meaning years down the road. Scalia and others believe that legislative history is irrelevant and misleading, and that the words of a handful of the most vocal legislators shouldn't carry the day. To some extent, this view is grounded in the practical consideration that the views of legislators are sometimes entered into the "record" well after the fact or at the behest of interest groups and don't reflect the views of Congress. More fundamentally, Scalia and others believe that the Constitution is very specific about the steps needed to make statutory "law." A law needs not only the vote of both houses of Congress but also the endorsement of the president. Scalia believes that relying on legislative history undermines the law-making scheme.

Other justices sharply disagree, believing the legislative record can be useful when the statute's words are unclear, as they often are. So pronounced are the divisions that those justices sometimes make light of Scalia's determined views during oral arguments, playfully warning lawyers who dare to suggest that a statute's legislative history is illuminating to be prepared for an earful from Scalia.

Scalia's enmity toward legislative history is strongest in cases involving criminal statutes. Criminal laws are supposed to be clear, and most justices accept that when laws are unclear, the criminal defendant should get the benefit of the doubt, since he may not have known his conduct was wrong. In the teenager's case, Scalia was adamant that legislative history could never be used to justify a harsher criminal sentence against a defendant. As Scalia saw it, most people wouldn't know about any random comments by the legislators who debated the bill and therefore wouldn't have fair warning of a crime's punishment. If the law was unclear, or two provisions conflicted, Scalia believed the more lenient criminal punishment must apply. "Happily for this defendant," as Scalia said of the teenager, the legislative history happened to support the more lenient sentence. He wrote a separate opinion, concurring with the result, but sharply disagreeing with Souter's reasoning.

Thomas also wrote a separate concurring opinion. Courts have always held that ignorance of the law is no excuse for a crime, he said. But floor statements and committee reports aren't the law, Thomas explained, and courts can't expect people to know about them. O'Connor refused to go along. She sided instead with a dissenting Blackmun, who thought the harsher sentence was the right one.

In January, the justices announced they would take up the case liberals dreaded and conservatives wanted: *Planned Parenthood of Southeastern Pennsylvania v. Casey,* a frontal assault on *Roe v. Wade.* Blackmun and his clerks were particularly anxious, as they believed the Court was on the verge of reversing *Roe* and permitting states to ban abortion entirely. Tensions were rising to intemperate levels among the law clerks, several of whom nearly came to blows.

Law clerks were particularly suspicious of Thomas, whose own clerks would rebuff their efforts to inquire about his views on cases "for the usual unfounded secrecy grounds that attach to everything in [those] chambers," as one of Blackmun's clerks complained near the end of the term. That was in marked contrast to clerks in other chambers, including those of O'Connor, Kennedy, Souter, and White. Those clerks frequently shared information about their justices' views on cases, and they used it to supplement what the justice had communicated in writing to the other members of the Court. It was a way of getting a more complete picture of a justice's position.

The tension between the liberal-leaning justices and their new colleague bubbled to the surface in late January, in a highly technical case that barely merited a mention deep inside the financial sections of most newspapers.[20] The controversy erupted in a complex bankruptcy dispute that asked when a federal appeals courts could step in and rule on interim issues in the middle of bankruptcy proceedings.

The justices discussed the case in conference January 24, and initially voted 7–2. The case did not track along ideological lines, with the conservative White and liberal Blackmun in dissent. The discussion was brief, and Rehnquist later assigned the opinion to Thomas.

But the near unanimity of the conference evaporated a month later, when Thomas's draft hit the other justices' desks. To the more liberal justices, including ones originally on his side, Thomas was trying to use "the most boring case possible," as one clerk put it, to sneakily shift the law in a more conservative direction. Blackmun and Stevens were certain Thomas was using the case to shore up Scalia's views on legislative history and on the proper way for courts to figure out the meaning of statutes.

In his opinion, Thomas focused solely on the words of the statutes to reach his conclusion. But then, in two short paragraphs at the end of his brief, eleven-paragraph opinion, Thomas flatly rejected the use of legislative history to support the outcome. "We have stated time and again that courts must presume that a legislature says in a statute what it means and means in a statute what it says there," Thomas wrote.

To some of the other justices, that discussion had no place in the opinion. Although it reflected the ardent views of Scalia, it certainly did not mirror their own. Blackmun and his clerks reacted with alarm. In a technical case with broad consensus, Thomas had taken "the opportunity to make Justice Scalia's view of legislative history a required approach to statutory construction," one of Blackmun's clerks told him. Dripping with disdain, the clerk also took Thomas to task for the cases he used to support his views. "Apparently to show how really learned he is, his support comes from cases in 1842, 1810, 1897 and 1819," she told Blackmun. "Apparently, ever since the turn of the century the Court just hasn't gotten statutory interpretation right." In a note to Blackmun, the clerk said, "My only strong recommendation is not to join this attempt to transform a mundane decision into a victory for the radical right."

Blackmun immediately fired off a letter to Thomas that is notable for its bluntness. Typically, the justices who plan to dissent just say so, or remain silent if they have already made their views known at conference. But Blackmun felt he had to make clear that Thomas could not pull a fast one on the Court. "You appear to have adopted in this opinion some of the flat rules Nino proposes for statutory construction. I do not agree with that rigid approach, and I, therefore, cannot join your opinion. I shall wait for the other writings in this case," Blackmun said in the note, which he also sent to the other justices.

Stevens also planned to write "a little something" to criticize Thomas's approach. When Stevens circulated his concurrence days later, he minced no words. "Whenever there is some uncertainty about the meaning of a statute, it is prudent to examine its legislative history," Stevens began, before quoting a 1915 decision from the esteemed Judge Learned Hand that statutes should be construed "not as theorems of Euclid, but with some imagination of the purposes behind them."

Blackmun had already concluded that the case was not particularly significant. He and White were prepared to switch their votes. Both joined O'Connor, who continued her practice that term of joining Thomas's opinions as infrequently as possible. She wrote another terse one-paragraph concurrence that would reverse the appeals court on narrow grounds, sending a pointed message to Thomas to hold back.

O'Connor's most blistering assault on Thomas came in a case argued in late March, involving Frank Robert West, a Virginia man who was convicted of burglary.[21] Police investigating a recent home invasion had found stolen television sets and electronic goods in his home. West had no luck challenging his conviction in state courts, so he moved to federal courts and filed a constitutional claim, invoking a procedure called habeas corpus.

Habeas corpus is a hoary procedure derived from English law going back at least a thousand years and mentioned in the Magna Carta. The phrase is Latin for "produce the body," and at its core it gives a prisoner the right to petition a court to demand that his captor justify why he is being held. It was used historically to test the legality of arbitrary executive detention. Traditionally, it wasn't much use for state conflicts. When called upon to justify the detention, state officers could simply point out that the prisoner was being held in the ordinary course, after a jury trial and appeals.

But over the years, particularly in the 1950s and 1960s, the liberal Supreme Court expanded habeas corpus to create essentially another round of appeals for prisoners. It said a prisoner could turn to federal court and challenge his conviction by arguing that the trial judge hadn't properly adjudicated his federal defenses. Many conservatives viewed the expansion of federal corpus jurisdiction with great dismay. They believed it was a typical excess of the Warren Court and that it belittled state sovereignty. Rolling back habeas review of state criminal convictions became an important tenet of the conservative "federalism revolution," and Rehnquist, as an associate justice, began active attempts to curb it in the late 1970s. O'Connor also viewed the task as an important aspect of restoring the dignity that she believed had been stripped from sovereign states. In a 1991 case, in which the Court approved the execution of a death-row inmate whose lawyers filed his state-court papers a few days too late, O'Connor began her opinion for the Court with the statement: "This is a case about Federalism."[22]

With Thomas's arrival, conservatives believed that the Court would finally turn its back on the Warren Court's habeas precedents once and for all. In West's case, a federal court of appeals had reexamined the evidence that persuaded the jury to convict him and concluded that the evidence was insufficient. Once the case got to the Supreme Court, the Bush administration urged the Court to take dramatic steps to curb the review of state convictions. The government's brief was signed by the top conservative lawyers in the Bush administration—including Solicitor General Ken Starr and future chief justice John Roberts—and the case was argued by Maureen Mahoney, another conservative luminary who would frequently be mentioned as a likely Supreme Court appointee during George W. Bush's administration.

At conference, all nine justices believed the federal appeals court was wrong; there was sufficient evidence to support the conviction. Rehnquist assigned the opinion to Thomas. But when the justices saw Thomas's draft opinion, all but Rehnquist and Scalia backed away.

To resolve the case, Thomas engaged in a lengthy historical analysis of the law of habeas corpus, outlining earlier cases and describing when federal courts can hear state prisoners' constitutional arguments. Then he rejected West's claim, writing that there was more than enough evidence to convict him.

O'Connor had written extensively in the area, including in her first cases as a justice. In fact, it was a habeas issue that had caused the rift between Brennan and O'Connor in her very first term. When she saw Thomas's opinion, she was furious. She believed he wrongly described the Court's previous cases—including one of her own opinions two years earlier. In a separate concurrence, joined by Blackmun and Stevens, she eviscerated Thomas, mentioning him by name eighteen times. Rarely do justices repeatedly single out an author by name, and certainly not with that startling frequency. Instead, they often name the justice in a footnote or merely refer to the "majority opinion" or the "dissent."

But O'Connor was brutal, paragraph after paragraph. She didn't disagree with Thomas on the outcome, but she delivered a stinging lecture on how he'd summarized the law. Justice Thomas errs in describing the history of habeas corpus law, she said. Justice Thomas quotes Justice Powell's opinion out of context, she said. Justice Thomas errs in characterizing a 1953 case. Justice Thomas understates that case's holding. Justice Thomas incorrectly states that we have never considered one of the issues before the Court. Justice Thomas fails to accurately describe a 1979 case. Justice Thomas mischaracterizes two 1989 cases. On and on, eighteen times.

"You are so right," Stevens wrote O'Connor as soon as he saw her opinion in the case. He and Blackmun quickly joined it.

Thomas, however, hadn't proposed a sweeping overhaul of the law or pulled new theories out of thin air. In fact, he had specifically refused to embrace the tougher standard for reviewing West's claim that lawyers for the Bush administration had proposed. Thomas said there was no need to address such "far reaching issues" as the administration proposed.

Years later, Thomas acknowledged that he was taken aback by O'Connor's opinion. "At first I thought, 'Whoa, she's a tough cookie,'" he said. "But they had been working on these problems for years and I come marching in like this," energetically pumping his arms back and forth to demonstrate his point. "I was the new kid on the block. I was brash. I just took it like the rookie football player who gets clobbered by the linebacker: 'Welcome to the NFL.' "[23]

The case was publicly announced in June, and the outcome remained 9–0, with all the justices agreeing that the prisoner should lose. But Thomas had lost his majority. Six of the justices refused to sign his opinion. Only Rehnquist and Scalia went along. As such, his opinion was considered a "plurality," which does not have precedent-setting value or bind the lower courts. Souter, Kennedy, O'Connor, and White all wrote separately, saying they agreed with the result, but not with Thomas's approach.

With the strains between the justices now in open view, the Court in late April heard arguments in *Planned Parenthood of Southeastern Pennsylvania v. Casey,* the most explosive case to reach the Court in more than a decade. It gave the Court a direct opportunity to overrule *Roe.* With Thomas on board, a perceived sixth conservative vote, many inside and outside the Court feared that was inevitable.

But outsiders didn't know about a surprising development in another controversial case. Kennedy had dramatically reversed course to join the Court's more liberal justices in a battle over school prayer. The result would outrage conservatives, including some of his fellow justices.

6.

CHANGE OF HEART

Amonth after the *New York Times* pronounced Clarence Thomas the "youngest, cruelest justice,"[1] Anthony Kennedy found himself in a quandary.

Kennedy had been struggling to write an opinion for the Court's conservatives in one of the term's most contentious cases.[2] A Rhode Island man named Daniel Weisman had asked the Supreme Court to prohibit prayer at public school graduation ceremonies because he didn't think his daughter should be subjected to what he believed to be a religious exercise. He argued that the prayer violated the First Amendment's establishment clause, which says that government cannot make laws "respecting an establishment of religion." Kennedy had disagreed with Weisman's arguments at first. But now, in March, his views were changing.

In the three years since Kennedy had joined the Court, he had surprised his right-wing detractors in the Reagan administration by developing a solidly conservative reputation. He'd voted consistently with

Rehnquist and Scalia on the culturally divisive issues, and in some cases had written opinions even more conservative than they'd hoped.

By 1991, conservative expectations for Kennedy were high. The Court was under close scrutiny that term, not only because Clarence Thomas was new to the bench, but because the Court's docket was once again packed with cases on social issues. If Kennedy's first year on the Court in 1988 had been controversial, the 1991 term promised to be no less so, with cases on civil rights, religion, and, of paramount importance to the Right, the most significant challenge to *Roe v. Wade* since it became the law of the land in 1973.

The justices dove into the tough cases right away, hearing arguments on the prayer case during Thomas's first week on the bench in November. The school district argued that asking a rabbi to lead students in a bland generic prayer about tolerance and freedom hardly rose to the level of religious coercion. The lawyers for the school district were so optimistic about their chances with the newly constituted court that they took an unusually aggressive position in the case. They argued that the Court had gone overboard through the years in excluding religion from public life, and they wanted the justices to use young Deborah Weisman's case to rewrite an entire area of constitutional law.

Those lawyers weren't neophytes, and they had good reason to think they would get their way with the new conservative Court. Chuck Cooper, who represented the school district, was a former Rehnquist clerk who had headed up the Justice Department's Office of Legal Counsel in the Reagan administration. There Cooper had played a key role in judicial selection and fought against Kennedy's nomination to the Supreme Court. Ken Starr, the Bush administration's solicitor general who had once been at the top of the short list for the Court himself, joined Cooper in the case. Their proposal—a wholesale revision of Supreme Court doctrine—was an unusually risky strategy. But Cooper and Starr were optimistic. They felt they were merely accepting an invitation the Court's four most conservative members had extended in Kennedy's first term, in a hotly disputed case over religious displays during the winter holiday season. In that 1989 case, the American Civil Liberties Union had sued to dismantle two public displays in Allegheny County, Pennsylvania. One featured a menorah displayed outside a government building; the other, a nativity scene in a courthouse. The case produced bitter divisions among the justices.[3]

The religion clauses in the Constitution's First Amendment had preoccupied conservatives since the 1950s, when the liberal Warren Court enforced a stricter separation between church and state. One clause prohibits the "establishment" of religion. The other guarantees "the free exercise thereof." Many conservatives believed that the Court's existing establishment clause case law went too far in driving religion from the public square. They thought the Court's insistence on neutrality between religion and nonreligion came at the expense of the people's right to "free[ly] exercise" their religion as guaranteed by the Constitution.

In the Allegheny County case, the Court, in an opinion by Blackmun, permitted the menorah, which stood alongside a Christmas tree and a sign about religious freedom. The Court concluded that the display conveyed an overall message of tolerance and diversity rather than an endorsement of a particular religion. But at the same time the justices rejected the nativity scene by the grand staircase inside the Allegheny County courthouse. Because it stood alone in a place of prominence, an observer might reasonably conclude that the government was endorsing the celebration of Christmas, Blackmun wrote.

In reaching his conclusions, Blackmun relied primarily on a 1984 case involving a nativity display in Pawtucket, Rhode Island.[4] The Court had narrowly upheld that display—with the newly appointed Justice O'Connor providing the decisive fifth vote—because the display had been surrounded by secular symbols (such as reindeer) that, in O'Connor's view, negated any religious "message." The 1984 Rhode Island decision had been derided by academics as ad hoc decision making, and it produced not a few snickers from conservatives who believed it was the jurisprudence not of the Constitution, but of interior decorating.

Not surprisingly, O'Connor again provided the margin of victory for Blackmun's opinion in 1989. Equally unsurprising, conservatives remained unpersuaded. The conservative position in the Allegheny case was forcefully articulated in a four-justice dissent that rejected the Court's overall approach to the establishment clause. The dissent's combination of wit, brio, and gleeful-poke-in-the-eye derision appeared to be vintage Scalia. But its author was none other than junior Justice Kennedy. He swept aside Blackmun's arguments, blasting his senior colleague for showing "hostility" and "callous indifference" toward religion. Kennedy accused him of creating a ridiculous rule that would allow religious displays in public spaces only if they were surrounded by "Santas, talking wishing wells, [and] reindeer."

Then Kennedy extended the invitation: "Substantial revision of our Establishment Clause doctrine may be in order." Perhaps the Court should discard its existing standards for interpreting the establishment clause, Kennedy wrote, and ask instead whether the government's action either involved "coercion," like a tax or mandatory participation in a religious exercise, or was an "exhortation to religiosity" so extreme that it amounted to proselytizing.

The prickly Blackmun fired back. He said the new justice's accusations were "as offensive as they are absurd." Kennedy had failed to recognize the "bedrock" principle that "regardless of history, government may not demonstrate a preference for a particular faith," Blackmun wrote. Adopting Kennedy's proposal, he said, would "gut the core of the Establishment Clause." The battle lines on religion cases had been drawn.

Three years later, conservatives interested in making wholesale changes to establishment clause doctrine thought their position on the Court had gotten only stronger since Kennedy fired the warning shot with his dissent. David Souter and Clarence Thomas had replaced liberal giants William Brennan and Thurgood Marshall, and although neither new justice had decided an establishment clause case, conservatives assumed they would be less strict than their predecessors when it came to separating church and state.

In Souter's first term on the Court, he'd given them little reason to think otherwise. He'd voted with Rehnquist more than 80 percent of the time, including in a case that prohibited federally funded clinics from engaging in abortion counseling. Those voting patterns, coupled with his eccentrically old-fashioned personal habits, offered the impression that he was a traditional conservative, just as the Bush administration had insisted when it appointed him. In Souter's first couple of months on the Court, clerks for the conservative justices believed he shared their approach to the law. After having lunch with Souter early in the new justice's first year, one of the law clerks for another justice sent a fellow clerk an approving message on the computer: "This guy is very conservative."

Thomas was better known, having worked in the Reagan and Bush administrations, where he'd established a solid conservative reputation through his decisions and the numerous speeches he delivered on law and responsibility to colleges and other outside organizations. He'd also served for a longer period—though still only just over a year—as a federal appeals court judge than Souter.

With Souter on board and Thomas taking Marshall's seat, conservatives were confident they had at least five votes. One of the new Bush appointees—if not both—would surely allow the graduation prayer.

In Cooper's opening brief in the school prayer case, he cited Kennedy's dissent in the nativity scene case nine times, and he took a particularly aggressive position during the arguments. It's easy to suggest in hindsight that Cooper overplayed his hand, especially in light of his earlier reservations about Kennedy. But it was a hand he believed Anthony Kennedy had dealt him with his 1989 dissent.

At the argument, Kennedy sounded surprisingly skeptical of Cooper's arguments, but Cooper pressed on. At one point, O'Connor asked him whether he thought a state legislature could adopt an offi-

cial religion, "just like they might pass a resolution saying the bolo tie
is the state necktie?" The question seemed designed to force Cooper to
admit he'd gone too far, and the spectators laughed at the absurdity of
the prospect.

But Cooper's response was yes, so long as the government didn't co-
erce anyone to participate in the religion, that would be fine. Cooper
thought he was simply following Kennedy's road map to its logical des-
tination, but he had gone too far. Sensing some hesitation by conservatives, Solicitor General Starr backed off slightly from Cooper's
position when it was his turn; he recognized that the Court's conservatives were cooler to their argument than they had hoped.

Two days later, the justices gathered around the table in their private
conference room to discuss the case and cast their votes. The spotlight
had been especially harsh that week. Just the day before, Congress had
delivered a sharp rebuke to the Court when it overwhelmingly passed
the landmark Civil Rights Act of 1991. The legislation, which President Bush had already announced he would sign into law, reversed at
least three of the Supreme Court's race-discrimination rulings from
Kennedy's first full term. It came after a two-year political battle in
which legislators denounced the justices as hostile to women and minorities and accused them of setting back the cause of civil rights.
Not only had the press beaten up on the Court and its newest justice,
now the Congress and Republican president George H. W. Bush were
piling on.

Kennedy had been shocked by the outcry from the civil rights community when the justices took up those race cases in 1988. In scaling
back the kind of discrimination lawsuits people could file, he had
thought the Court was merely addressing a law that, as he later would
put it, "we thought was broken." He quickly saw it was more than that,
a pointed lesson for a new justice.

Some years later Kennedy said in an interview that he had failed "to
recognize the super importance of our precedents in the area." As a
new justice, he would quickly come to factor that into his decision mak-

ing. Even his memos to other justices in the years after those civil rights decisions sometimes mention concerns about the public's reaction to their decisions.

With the justices besieged from all sides, it was probably not the ideal time for Chuck Cooper to press for a complete overhaul of establishment clause doctrine.

In the conference to discuss the case, the chief justice began the conversation on the prayer case forcefully. "This is not an establishment of religion," Rehnquist said. He looked back at history and said the Constitution's framers "did not believe" they were excising all references to God from public discourse. Besides, it was hard to see how any real harm could be done by such a bland and noncoercive invocation. White, a Kennedy appointee who often voted with the conservatives, spoke next. He had been one of the four dissenters in the Allegheny County case, and he readily agreed with Rehnquist.

Blackmun, who followed White, was adamantly opposed to the prayer, and Stevens weighed in with an impassioned, lengthy warning that "to rely on history is a dangerous policy." Stevens pointed to the Holy Wars and talked about how America had evolved from a Christian nation to a Judeo-Christian country to one that now has "expanded" its tolerance of other religions. "This is a very important case," Stevens stressed.

"It is a very important case," said O'Connor, speaking next. "I share the concerns of Harry and John." The nation has "evolved over time to protect other religions," she said. "This is state-sponsored prayer."

Scalia was next. Since the justices speak in order of seniority, he spoke immediately after O'Connor. "I respect evolving traditions," Scalia said, "but this is not remotely establishment" of religion. He would allow the prayer. If the prayer was deemed unconstitutional, the principle would necessarily extend to any invocation of God at any public event, like the presidential inauguration or the opening of Congress or the beginning of a school day with the Pledge of Allegiance to "one nation, under God." Forbidding people to publicly acknowledge their Creator was nothing less than "social engineering," Scalia said. But he added that he didn't think the Court needed to go as far as Kennedy had suggested three years earlier in the nativity scene case, when he suggested a wholesale revision of existing law.

Blackmun had been taking detailed notes of the discussion, and in the middle of Scalia's remarks he tallied up the vote. "Gets down to K-D-T!" he wrote. Blackmun recognized that the Court's three newest members, Kennedy, David Souter, and Thomas, would decide the case.

When Kennedy spoke, he sounded very much like the justice who'd written the dissent three years earlier that accused the Court of "hostility" to religion in banning a nativity scene from the courthouse. "Freedom means not being afraid of ideas," Kennedy said. The prayer did not improperly influence students or compel participation. He would allow it.

Then it was Souter's turn. As far as outsiders knew, the New England jurist was a reliable conservative. But he had struggled in his first year as he tried to make the transition from New Hampshire judge to Supreme Court justice. His first opinion took nearly all term to write, even though it had appeared to be a relatively simple case that the justices had decided unanimously in their conference in October. When he finally did circulate his opinion, he lost his unanimous Court. The justices suggested countless changes, and only Rehnquist, White, and O'Connor wound up joining it. Three justices, Scalia, Kennedy, and Stevens, wrote separate opinions taking issue with parts of Souter's effort.

Signs of dithering by Souter were emerging. The *New York Times* wrote in May that lawyers referred to Souter's chambers as "a black hole from which nothing emerges."[5] *Newsweek* accused Souter of being "slow off the mark," and said law clerks blamed him for causing gridlock in the Court's work.[6] On ABC's *World News Tonight* later that month, Supreme Court correspondent Tim O'Brien reported that Rehnquist had stopped assigning Souter opinions.[7]

Liberals who'd hoped Souter would be a moderate expressed disap-

The Rehnquist Court, which served together longer than any court in modern history. Over an eleven-year span, from 1994 to 2005, the Court would prove disappointing to conservatives who had hoped for a reversal of liberal rulings, including *Roe v. Wade*. From left: Justices Clarence Thomas, Antonin Scalia, Sandra Day O'Connor, Anthony Kennedy, David Souter, Stephen Breyer, and John Paul Stevens, Chief Justice William Rehnquist, and Justice Ruth Bader Ginsburg. AP IMAGES

Two old friends from the West: Sandra Day O'Connor, in a 1950 Stanford University yearbook photo, and William Rehnquist, in a 1948 Stanford yearbook picture. Rehnquist would lead the Court for nineteen years, but O'Connor would dictate its direction. AP IMAGES

Ronald Reagan introduces his first Supreme Court nominee to the press in the Rose Garden. O'Connor's "heart sank" when Reagan offered her the job and she thought of the pressures ahead. AP IMAGES

President Reagan presides over a birthday luncheon for William Rehnquist in 1982. Four years later, Reagan would tap him as chief justice. AP IMAGES

Reagan's next two nominees, Chief Justice William Rehnquist and Justice Antonin Scalia, while staunch conservatives, would not change the direction of the Court. AP IMAGES

Former president Gerald Ford, who nominated the surprisingly liberal maverick John Paul Stevens to the Court in 1975, praises Reagan nominee Robert Bork as "uniquely qualified" as Bork's Senate Judiciary Committee hearings get under way. A series of White House missteps surrounding the Bork nomination would doom Reagan's chances of remaking the Court. AP IMAGES

With the nomination of federal appeals court judge Anthony Kennedy, Reagan's third choice to replace Lewis Powell, Reagan's opportunity to change the Court had passed. AP IMAGES

Conservatives consider George H. W. Bush's nomination of David Souter, a reliable liberal vote, one of the biggest presidential mistakes in the twentieth century. Souter is signing documents in the Court's conference room, where the justices meet privately to discuss cases. He soon would be considered as liberal as William Brennan, the justice he replaced. AP IMAGES

Clarence Thomas takes the constitutional oath to become a justice as President George H. W. Bush looks on. Thomas replaced liberal icon Thurgood Marshall, who had followed his friend and former colleague William Brennan into retirement a year later.
AP IMAGES

Justice Clarence Thomas would prove to be a solid conservative, but his strong views about the law would affect the Court in unexpected ways and cause Justice O'Connor to move to the left. AP IMAGES

A dying Rehnquist leaves his home in suburban Virginia. Rehnquist surprised the nation when he declined to retire in 2005, encouraging his old friend O'Connor to leave the Court first. © *CHICAGO TRIBUNE*. PHOTO BY PETE SOUZA

White House advisers Dan Bartlett, Scooter Libby, Harriet Miers, and Vice President Dick Cheney listen to President Bush make remarks in the Rose Garden about O'Connor's decision to retire. O'Connor's pivotal position on the Court gave Bush a historic opportunity to change its direction. © *CHICAGO TRIBUNE.* PHOTO BY PETE SOUZA

White House Counsel Harriet Miers and Deputy Counsel William Kelley escort John Roberts into the White House to meet with President Bush before his nomination to the Supreme Court. Later that night, Bush would nominate Roberts to take O'Connor's place on the Court. AP IMAGES

President Bush and John Roberts walk past a portrait of Ronald Reagan minutes before Bush introduces his first Court nominee to the nation. Roberts had worked as a lawyer in the Reagan administration and believed in Reagan's goals of judicial conservatism. AP IMAGES

The battle over the Court's future is at a fever pitch, as reporters pore through files of John Roberts from his time as a lawyer in the Reagan administration. They would find no smoking guns, but plenty of evidence that Roberts was a staunch judicial conservative who believed courts should have a limited role in society.
© *CHICAGO TRIBUNE.* PHOTO BY PETE SOUZA

The divisive issue of abortion takes on outsized importance during confirmation hearings. The 1973 landmark decision *Roe v. Wade* forever changed the tone of judicial nominations and confirmations. © *CHICAGO TRIBUNE*. PHOTO BY PETE SOUZA

Pallbearers, including John Roberts, carry Rehnquist's coffin into the Supreme Court for a memorial service. The day before, Bush announced he was nominating Roberts to be chief justice. Roberts, a former Rehnquist clerk, is second from right; David Leitch, another Rehnquist clerk and the former deputy White House counsel who supported Roberts's nomination, is in front of Roberts. © *CHICAGO TRIBUNE*. PHOTO BY PETE SOUZA

John Roberts and the other pallbearers walk up the steps and past the Supreme Court justices as they take Rehnquist's coffin into the Court's Great Hall, where his body would lie in repose until his funeral the next day. © *CHICAGO TRIBUNE*. PHOTO BY PETE SOUZA

In order of seniority, the eight associate justices walk down the steps of the Supreme Court just before Rehnquist's casket is brought out of the Great Hall and taken to St. Matthew's Cathedral for his funeral. © *CHICAGO TRIBUNE.* PHOTO BY PETE SOUZA

John Roberts and his son, Jack, moments before the Senate Judiciary Committee begins confirmation hearings on his nomination to be chief justice of the United States. © *CHICAGO TRIBUNE.* PHOTO BY PETE SOUZA

Justice John Paul Stevens, the Court's oldest member, swears in John Roberts as chief justice, as Roberts's wife, Jane, and President Bush applaud. © *CHICAGO TRIBUNE.*
PHOTO BY PETE SOUZA

Justice Sandra Day O'Connor swears in Alberto Gonzales as attorney general.
Conservatives worried Bush would tap Gonzales, his longtime adviser, as the nation's
first Hispanic Supreme Court justice. They waged a persistent campaign against his
nomination to the Court, fearing he lacked solid conservative credentials and, once
confirmed, would drift to the left like Souter and Kennedy. But in the end, when
Bush passed him by, Gonzales sided with conservatives as the only high-level official
to urge the president not to nominate Harriet Miers to replace O'Connor.
AP IMAGES

White House counsel and new
Court nominee Harriet Miers
listens as Senate minority leader
Harry Reid of Nevada speaks
during a news conference after
Bush announced Miers's
nomination. Reid told Bush that
Miers would start out with 56
votes—those of the 55 Senate
Republicans and his own.
AP IMAGES

Senator Arlen Specter, the powerful chairman of the Senate Judiciary Committee, meets with new Court nominee Harriet Miers. Later, Miers would accuse Specter of misinterpreting her remarks, angering the maverick Republican and alienating a key ally. © *CHICAGO TRIBUNE*. PHOTO BY PETE SOUZA

After Harriet Miers withdrew, Bush nominated experienced federal appeals court judge Samuel Alito, who had been Miers's choice from the beginning. Immediately upon his nomination, the reserved Alito stepped into a media maelstrom and began visiting with senators, including Patrick Leahy, the leading Democrat on the Senate Judiciary Committee. Leahy ultimately would vote against Alito. © *CHICAGO TRIBUNE*. PHOTO BY PETE SOUZA

Sam Alito's low-key manner during his confirmation hearings made it difficult for Democrats to gain traction in their questioning.
© *CHICAGO TRIBUNE.* PHOTO BY PETE SOUZA

Democratic senators Chuck Schumer of New York and Dick Durbin of Illinois listen to Alito testify during his hearings before the Senate Judiciary Committee. Schumer and Durbin aggressively questioned Alito and would vote against his nomination.
© *CHICAGO TRIBUNE.* PHOTO BY PETE SOUZA

The Roberts Court. With new chief justice John Roberts in the center seat and associate justice Samuel Alito replacing Sandra Day O'Connor, the newly constituted Supreme Court is poised to go in a more conservative direction. President Bush succeeded, where previous presidents had failed, in placing on the Court two leading exponents of judicial conservatism. Front row, from left: Anthony Kennedy, John Paul Stevens, Roberts, Antonin Scalia, and David Souter. Back row: Stephen Breyer, Clarence Thomas, Ruth Bader Ginsburg, and Alito.

pointment after seeing his votes in those early cases, particularly in a case involving federally funded family-planning clinics. Souter agonized over the case until Rehnquist finally told him, "You've got to decide." Souter cast his vote with Rehnquist in the dispute over federal grants to abortion clinics, declining to take a more moderate approach favored by O'Connor.

Harvard Law School professor Laurence Tribe, who had argued the case for the abortion clinics, told the *Boston Globe* there was "far less basis now" than during Souter's confirmation hearings for believing he would "play an important centrist role."[8]

Souter often sought counsel from William Brennan, the justice he spoke so admiringly of in his confirmation hearings. He visited Brennan's chambers on the Court's third floor, and he occasionally would invite the retired justice to lunch. Late that spring, he tapped another liberal adviser when he hired one of Tribe's assistants, Peter Rubin, to clerk for him the next term. Rubin had just finished helping Tribe with a book that was strongly in favor of abortion rights. Rubin's intellect was matched by his insistent personality.

By November of his second year on the Court, Souter was sounding more like the justice Senator Warren Rudman had privately assured liberals he would be. In the justices' conference to discuss the school prayer case, Souter showed no hesitation. "Attendance at graduation is not fully voluntary," Souter said. A prayer during the ceremony would make a child feel as if he had to participate. He agreed with the liberals.

The case now was 4–4. Thomas, as the junior justice, spoke last. He didn't think it was necessary to make wholesale changes to the Court's establishment clause doctrine; he believed the prayer was constitutional under the existing framework. He would allow it.

The more conservative justices had narrowly prevailed by a vote of 5–4. Since Rehnquist was in the majority, he got to assign the opinion. He gave it to Kennedy, who had been so forceful in dissent in the nativity scene case during his first full year on the Court.

But Kennedy didn't have a clear mandate for how to write the prayer case. There didn't appear to be much support for a dramatic revision of the Court's doctrine, as he'd suggested three years earlier. Moreover, Kennedy himself was backing away from that forceful dissent.

As O'Connor knew, and Souter would come to learn, any justice in his first years can be overwhelmed by the work and, as a result, rely more heavily on law clerks, who do research and draft opinions. In Kennedy's first year as a justice, his supporters at the Justice Department, worried that he wouldn't be as conservative as they'd hoped, helped him hire his clerks. Not surprisingly, they selected bright conservatives who had excelled at their elite law schools. Miguel Estrada, who would later be a potential Supreme Court pick, was one. Peter Keisler, who, like Estrada, would be tapped for a seat on the prestigious D.C.-based federal appeals court, was another. Thomas Hungar, who would go on to work in the solicitor general's office and dazzle the justices with his arguments, was a third. Hungar had drafted the opinion in the nativity scene case from Kennedy's first term.

But after a few years on the Court, Kennedy had started to settle in. His clerks weren't uniformly conservative. In the 1991 term, he hired another Laurence Tribe protégé, Michael Dorf, who'd just helped the professor write a book on the Constitution.

Kennedy, who taught constitutional law part-time throughout his career, adopted a professorial approach to thinking through cases with his clerks. He put a whiteboard in the corner of his office, and he would outline cases with his law clerks gathered before him. Kennedy liked to try out a number of legal positions. Other justices, like Scalia, would identify the critical principle and follow that to its logical conclusion. O'Connor, too, would give her clerks clear directions. Not so with Kennedy.

Sometimes he would take one position in discussions with his clerks, then take another after a day or two of thinking it through, until he settled on his legal conclusion. It drove his law clerks crazy, especially if they'd already started writing the draft opinion. They'd have to stop and take another approach. At the end of the term, his departing law clerks started explaining to the new crop that they would "just have to roll" with Kennedy's unusual decision-making style.

In the spring of 1992, four months after Rehnquist assigned him the decision in the graduation prayer case, Kennedy still hadn't circulated a decision. He couldn't make the conservative position fit his evolving view. Finally, toward the end of March, he gave up. After grappling with the issues and writing draft after draft, he concluded that he couldn't do it. The conservatives, he'd come to believe, were wrong.

Kennedy left his chambers and walked down the hall to see Rehnquist. Apologetic and embarrassed, Kennedy delivered the news. In writing the opinion for the majority to allow the prayer, Kennedy had changed his mind about the result. He'd written a decision ruling instead that the prayer was unconstitutional.

It's not unusual for a justice to change his mind after he casts his vote in a case, especially if he was wavering from the beginning. The justices sometimes think about a case differently when they read the proposed opinion or see a dissent. But it's less common for a justice who's writing the majority opinion to do so. And it's rarer still when that justice was the pivotal vote in the outcome of the case.

But that was the position Kennedy found himself in. The case had deeply divided the Court along ideological lines. Kennedy's change of heart meant that conservatives would lose. There was nothing Rehnquist could do. He recognized that Kennedy was the swing vote, so he advised him to go ahead and circulate his draft opinion.

After talking to Rehnquist, Kennedy went back to his chambers and wrote privately to Blackmun, who was supposed to be writing a dissent. He extended an olive branch, in light of the harsh words they had exchanged three years earlier in their clashing opinions in the nativity scene case. "After the barbs in [the nativity case], many between the two of us, I thought it most important to write something that you and I and the others who voted this way can join," Kennedy told Blackmun. "That is why this took me longer than it should have and, of course, I will be most attentive to your criticisms." Kennedy then circulated his draft opinion holding that the prayers were unconstitutional. The flip angered the Court's conservative justices and stunned their clerks.

With Kennedy's change of heart on prayer, Blackmun was now the senior justice in the majority, so he could either reassign the opinion to another justice or try to work with his new ally. The next day, Blackmun's clerk suggested that he work with Kennedy, even if the opinion wasn't exactly what he wanted. "Getting Justice Kennedy's vote and winning this case is the greatest victory of the year," the clerk wrote. "If I were you, I would take an imperfect opinion and assign it to [Kennedy]. I might condition that assignment on changes you suggest, if that is ever done."

Blackmun agreed. Two weeks later, he wrote Kennedy a note. "I have read your draft opinion with interest," Blackmun said. "As you indicated in your note to me, we have disagreed on the proper approach to the Establishment Clause in the past, but you have done good work in finding common ground in this case. With some changes, it will be an opinion I could join."

Kennedy, anxious about his switch in the case, wrote back the next day. He could accommodate some of Blackmun's suggestions, but not all. He insisted on keeping one paragraph Blackmun resisted. Kennedy wanted to stress that the decision was narrow, that it did not address questions of religion in "a myriad of other contexts in the public schools and public education." Kennedy told Blackmun he wrote the paragraph because he was worried about how the public would interpret the ruling. "I believe it is important for the court, in a decision which is likely to be quite unpopular, to state that the court in striking down graduation prayers is not expressing any hostility to religion or religious persons," he wrote Blackmun.

Just one week later, with the Court's conservatives angry and upset by Kennedy and his turnaround, the justices heard oral arguments in the most explosive case of the term, *Planned Parenthood of Southeastern Pennsylvania v. Casey.*[9] The case was a constitutional challenge to a

Pennsylvania law regulating abortion, but the stakes were much higher than one state's restrictions. The justices could use the case to overturn *Roe v. Wade.*

Again, conservatives had every reason to hope the Court would strike down *Roe* and send the issue of abortion back to the states, where legislatures could ban it outright if they so desired. Just three years before, during Kennedy's first term when the Court had decided a challenge to a Missouri abortion law, Kennedy had joined conservatives in suggesting that the Court overhaul the decision.[10]

O'Connor, the fifth vote in that case, had written separately to articulate her own test for challenges to laws that restrict abortion—what became known as the "undue burden" test. Her view appeared to recognize that women had a constitutional right to abortion, but not an unfettered one; the government could restrict access to an abortion so long as the restriction did not "unduly burden" a woman's right to end the pregnancy. In light of that approach, it was far from clear that O'Connor would side with the conservatives in a wholesale repudiation of *Roe* when the Court took up the *Casey* case. But conservatives believed that at this point, her vote wasn't as important. With Souter and Thomas now on board, conservatives reasoned, the Court surely would have the five votes it needed to overturn *Roe*.

Planned Parenthood had challenged a number of the law's provisions, including a twenty-four-hour waiting period for women seeking abortions, as well as a requirement that married women tell their spouses before having the procedure. The law also required minors to get their parents' consent. The Philadelphia-based federal appeals court had upheld all the law's provisions except the one requiring spousal notification. A dissenting judge, Samuel Alito, believed that provision was constitutional, as well.

At oral argument, Planned Parenthood's lawyer, Kathryn Kolbert, went straight to the point: So long as *Roe* was the law, all of Pennsylvania's restrictions were illegal. The Court must either strike down the Pennsylvania statute or admit it was overruling *Roe v. Wade.* The Court couldn't simply abandon *Roe*'s standards for deciding the constitutionality of abortion regulations, no matter how "politically expedient" that approach might be.

After Kolbert spoke for several minutes, a plainly piqued O'Connor broke in. "Ms. Kolbert, you're arguing the case as though all we have before us is whether to apply stare decisis and preserve *Roe v. Wade* in all its aspects. Nevertheless, we granted certiorari on some specific questions in this case. Do you plan to address any of those in your argument?"

Kolbert discussed the specific provisions, especially the spousal-notification requirement, but she continued to devote most of her time to the more general issue of *Roe* as the law of the land. With a presidential election looming, it was an all-or-nothing strategy intended to make the Court do almost anything other than what it had done back in 1989 in *Webster*, which was to make changes to *Roe* while pretending to leave its fate for another day.

When Pennsylvania's attorney general, Ernest Preate, rose to defend the restrictions, O'Connor questioned him extensively on the spousal-notification requirement. "It's a curious sort of a provision, isn't it?" she observed. Why not provide notice to all fathers? "Would you say that the state could similarly require a woman to notify anyone with whom she had intercourse that she planned to use some means of birth control after the intercourse that operates, let's say, as an abortifacient? Could the state do that? I mean, it would be the same state interest."

It seemed clear from O'Connor's tone that she was unpersuaded by Preate's argument that the spousal-notification requirement didn't amount to an "undue burden." That standard was her own invention, after all, and she believed it would be an undue burden on women if they had to tell their husbands before getting an abortion.

Solicitor General Ken Starr spoke after Preate, urging the Court to adopt Rehnquist's approach in the *Webster* case. Souter's question was pointed: Would a legislature have the authority, under that approach, to prohibit all abortions not necessary to preserve the life of the mother?

Starr said he would rather not answer a question like that "in the abstract."

"Well, I'll grant you that," Souter responded, "but you're asking the Court to adopt a standard and I think we ought to know where the standard would take us."

In the conference after the oral argument, Rehnquist voted to uphold the statute in its entirety. He acknowledged that the Court "would have to overrule" two earlier cases, but perhaps it wouldn't be necessary to overrule *Roe,* he said. White, the next to speak, said he agreed with the chief.

The next justice was Blackmun, who elected to "pass" although there could have been no doubt regarding his views. Stevens, speaking next, said he thought the waiting periods were an "insult to women" and clearly unconstitutional, as was the spousal-notification provision, which he called "outrageous."

Next came O'Connor. The lower court had gotten it mostly right, she said. Like the lower court, she would uphold everything but the spousal-notification requirement.

Scalia said he would uphold the law. He had long been on record in favor of overruling *Roe.* He thought courts should permit state laws restricting abortion as long as the legislature could offer a rational reason for enacting them.

Kennedy, as the justices expected after the *Webster* decision, agreed with Rehnquist. All the provisions were constitutional, he said, but the Court would need to overrule parts of the two earlier decisions, as Rehnquist had indicated, to clarify its position.

Souter spoke next. He had refused to address the issue in his recent confirmation hearings and had never publicly discussed his views on *Roe v. Wade.* Women's groups had opposed Souter's nomination because they were afraid he would overturn *Roe,* but they had warmed to him after listening to him testify at his confirmation hearings. The groups had been devastated by his vote with conservatives in the abortion counseling case the year before.

But now, in the conference on *Casey,* Souter cast his lot with his more liberal colleagues to strike down part of the law. Souter objected to the spousal-notification provision and like O'Connor thought the Court should develop a different standard for approaching abortion cases. He approved of O'Connor's suggestion that the Court allow restrictions, so long as they did not impose an "undue burden" on a woman's right to an abortion.

As in the graduation prayer case, the court was divided 4–4 when it was Thomas's turn to speak. Like Souter, Thomas had refused to answer questions about *Roe* during his hearings. He said he'd never discussed the case, not even in private. When it finally came time to talk about it with his new colleagues, Thomas voted with conservatives. He would uphold the law.

Rehnquist had been careful not to raise the issue directly at conference, but it appeared clear he had five votes to overturn *Roe v. Wade.* He assigned the opinion to himself. It was one he had waited eighteen years to write, and he circulated his draft to the other justices barely a month later, on May 27.

"Wow!" *Roe*'s author, Blackmun, wrote on the first page of his copy. "Pretty extreme!"

Rehnquist never explicitly said the Court was overturning *Roe,* but his opinion did just that. *Roe* had said the right to an abortion was a fundamental one, like the right to marriage, procreation, or contraception. But Rehnquist said the Court in *Roe* was wrong to put abortion in that class of cases. Unlike marriage, procreation, or contraception, which the Court had held were liberty interests protected by the Constitution, abortion involves the "purposeful termination of potential life," he wrote. "One cannot ignore the fact that a woman is not isolated in her pregnancy, and that the decision to abort necessarily involves the destruction of a fetus." The Court in *Roe* "reached too far" when it analogized the right to abort a fetus to the rights involved in those cases. The sort of "constitutionally imposed abortion code" the

Court had developed in the years since *Roe* had no basis in constitutional law.

Instead, he continued, the approach in his *Webster* opinion was the right one. That approach was one that four justices, including Kennedy, had embraced in the 1989 case. "We therefore hold that each of the challenged provisions of the Pennsylvania statute is consistent with the Constitution," Rehnquist concluded. "Whether each of them embodies wise social policy is of course not for us, but for the people of Pennsylvania, to decide."

But two days after Rehnquist circulated his opinion, Kennedy sent Blackmun a private, handwritten note.

> *Dear Harry,*
>
> *I need to see you as soon as you have a few free moments. I want to tell you about some developments in Planned Parenthood v. Casey, and at least part of what I say should come as welcome news.*
>
> *If today is not convenient, I will be here tomorrow. Please give me a call when you are free.*
>
> *Yours,*
> *Tony*

Rehnquist and the other conservatives were getting the sense that Kennedy was wavering—a real concern after his flip in the graduation prayer case. After Rehnquist circulated his majority opinion effectively overturning *Roe,* Scalia went home from the Court and called Kennedy. Could he come over and take a walk? Scalia asked. Kennedy agreed, and the two justices—who live blocks away from each other on the same street in McLean, Virginia—spent an hour walking around their neighborhood and talking about the case. By the end of the walk, Scalia felt confident Kennedy was a solid vote. He went home thinking the five would stand together.

But within a day, an opinion jointly written by Kennedy, O'Connor, and Souter sat on Scalia's desk. It was the "welcome news" Kennedy had told Blackmun he wanted to share. He hadn't said a word about it during his walk with Scalia.

O'Connor, Kennedy, and Souter had developed the opinion privately over the course of several weeks, with each justice writing parts of it. The three justices plowed over most of *Roe v. Wade*, substituting a new framework for analyzing abortion decisions, as Rehnquist had done. But their standard was entirely different. The three had adopted O'Connor's proposal, which would allow abortion regulations that did not impose an "undue burden" on a woman's right to the procedure. They upheld all the provisions of the statute except the spousal-notification requirement.

They then went out of their way to "reaffirm" *Roe v. Wade* repeatedly and at great length. They loaded the opinion with praise for the doctrine of stare decisis and ponderous philosophical musings on the liberty interests of women and on pregnancy itself. "The mother who carries a child to full term is subject to anxieties, to physical constraints, to pain that only she must bear," the three wrote. "That these sacrifices have from the beginning of the human race been endured by woman with a pride that ennobles her in the eyes of others and gives to the infant a bond of love cannot alone be grounds for the State to insist she make the sacrifice.

"Her suffering is too intimate and personal for the State to insist, without more, upon its own vision of the woman's role, however dominant that vision has been in the course of our history and our culture," they continued. "The destiny of the woman must be shaped to a large extent on her own conception of her spiritual imperatives and her place in society."

The analysis was as preposterous to conservatives as Blackmun's manifesto on abortion and pregnancy in *Roe v. Wade*. It was too much for Scalia, especially coming from Kennedy, whose vote he thought he had secured in their conversation before the draft opinion was circulated.

Just as he had in the graduation prayer case, Kennedy had switched his vote. Again, the Reagan appointee had abandoned a position he'd taken only three years before. Again, he'd not only refused to abandon liberal rulings that incensed conservatives, but he'd put the principles on more solid footing than ever before.

Scalia hadn't finished writing his dissent in the school prayer case when the trio circulated their opinion in the abortion case. Scalia decided to open fire. Kennedy, he concluded, was a lost cause. There was no point in holding back now.

Scalia's dissent in the graduation prayer case slapped Kennedy right in the face. He began by quoting extensively from the opinion Kennedy had written three years before. That opinion had stressed the history and purpose of the establishment clause and emphasized that government policies accommodating and supporting religion were an accepted part of the nation's political and cultural heritage. That three-year-old decision, Scalia wrote, had stressed that the meaning of the establishment clause was to be "determined by reference to historical practices and understandings." The views in that three-year-old decision, Scalia said, "of course prevent me from joining today's opinion, which is conspicuously bereft of any reference to history."

But taunting Kennedy with his own words was nothing compared to the way Scalia ridiculed the new position Kennedy had adopted. He repeated comments he'd made back in the Court's November conference. The Court, Scalia wrote, was doing nothing more than "social engineering."

Kennedy was stung by the forcefulness of the attack, but downplayed it to Blackmun, Stevens, O'Connor, and Souter. "Nino's dissent does not, in my view, require any adjustment or response in the majority opinion," he wrote in a June 18 note. That said, Kennedy was proposing a new draft with some "minor revisions." The changes included an additional paragraph looking back at the traditions and history of the First Amendment. "I thought the original opinion was somewhat incomplete without it," Kennedy told the four justices, not mentioning that Scalia's dissent laid bare the inconsistencies in his analysis in the two cases. The new paragraph was an obvious attempt to counter Scalia's criticism.

"The lessons of the First Amendment are as urgent in the modern world as in the 18th Century when it was written," Kennedy wrote. "One timeless lesson is that if citizens are subjected to state-sponsored religious exercises, the state disavows its own duty to guard and respect that sphere of inviolable conscience and belief which is the mark of a free people." To compromise that belief, Kennedy summed up, "would deny our own tradition."

The justices took the bench the morning of June 24 to announce opinions. They had put off the most controversial ones until the end, as always, since those are the most divisive and take longest to write. The courtroom was full, as spectators gathered to see which of the block-buster cases the justices would decide. When Rehnquist announced that Kennedy had written the opinion in the school prayer case, con-servatives in the courtroom breathed a sigh of relief. But as Kennedy began to speak, it was evident immediately that Starr and Cooper were on the wrong side of a rout.

A few days later, the law clerks staged their annual skit for the jus-tices, a tradition at the Court at the end of the term. When the law clerk playing Anthony Kennedy appeared before the crowd, the others played the theme song from *Flipper*, a popular 1960s television show whose main character was a dolphin.

On June 29, the justices again took the bench to announce the re-maining decisions of the term, including the biggest of them all, *Planned Parenthood of Southeastern Pennsylvania v. Casey*. Hundreds of protesters, carrying signs and singing, had gathered outside of the court. Photographers and television cameras jostled to record them.

Early that morning, before the justices went to the courtroom, Kennedy met in his chambers with a reporter from *California Lawyer* magazine who was working on a profile of the home-state justice. Kennedy's office has soaring windows that overlook the marble plaza in front of the Court and beautifully frame the dome of the Capitol across the street. As he stood by the window in his office, looking at the protesters marching below, he told the reporter of his struggles. "Sometimes you don't know if you're Caesar about to cross the Rubicon or Captain Queeg cutting your own tow line," Kennedy said just before he went downstairs to the packed courtroom to announce the decision that would redefine him as a justice.[11]

Conservatives still sneer at Kennedy's comparison of himself with Julius Caesar, but the joke was oddly predictive of how they would come to regard his opinion in *Casey*. To "cross the Rubicon" means to make a bold decision from which there is no turning back, but in Caesar's case it was an act of treason, and it triggered a civil war that put Caesar in power and effectively ended republican government. It thus fit nicely with the conservative story line that Kennedy was an imperialist bent on making decisions himself that were best left to legislatures. "Cutting your own tow line" refers to an act of inattentive incompetence by Captain Queeg in Herman Wouk's Pulitzer Prize–winning novel, *The Caine Mutiny*. Captain Queeg cuts his own towline because he is so preoccupied with lecturing an enlisted man on the importance of wearing shirttails tucked in that he fails to see his ship is moving in a circle, cutting the towline that trails behind it. That story fit well with the other conservative theme, which is that Kennedy voted to reaffirm *Roe* for the sake of public appearances, but at considerable expense to the institution he served. He was lost either way.

The mood in the packed courtroom was somber. Everyone knew the stakes. Kennedy's decision in the school prayer case five days before had given liberals some hope that the Court wasn't as solidly conservative as they had thought. Maybe it wouldn't be so eager to overturn *Roe*.

O'Connor, Kennedy, and Souter each took a turn announcing parts of the opinion. Kennedy's rhetoric conveyed his lofty view of the Court and its role in American life. "At the heart of liberty is the right to define one's own concept of existence, of meaning, of the universe, and of the mystery of human life," Kennedy had written in his section of the decision. That passage infuriated conservatives such as Scalia, who scoffs at what he calls the "sweet mystery of life" passage. It was contrary to how he saw his role as a justice charged with the limited task of interpreting the Constitution. Kennedy, on the other hand, appeared to have visions of grandeur and a taste for the rhetorical high life.

Scalia then read from his dissent, which ripped into the Court's opinion point by point, mocked its grand assertions, and insisted that the Court's role in protecting liberties should be limited to those identified either in the Constitution or by societal tradition. Never one to mince words, he charged: "The Imperial Judiciary lives."

Scalia's dissent showed once again why he is regarded as the Court's preeminent master at the art of burning bridges. In his own undiplomatic words, he'd drawn a bead on what conservatives would view as Kennedy's biggest failing.

Strict judicial conservatives, like Scalia and Thomas, think courts should stay away from the hard social questions unless the Constitution clearly compels them to intervene. Kennedy, in contrast, takes a more expansive view of courts' role in public life, and some of his opinions seem to rest on moral and political foundations, rather than simply legal ones.

Even Kennedy's newly decorated chambers reflected his attitude about his role. When justices join the Court, they get to decorate their chambers in any style, and their choices can be revealing about their personalities. O'Connor, for example, used the warm colors and fabrics of her beloved Southwest, even turning large Indian drums into coffee tables. Thomas and Stevens were more basic, with little adornment beyond the original rich wood paneling and bookcases and large fireplace. Scalia's is similar, but he has mounted by his desk an enormous buck he refers to as "Leroy." Ginsburg's is more modernist, as befits the New York intellectual that she is. Breyer's has a more European feel, with books stacked all around and a roaring fire in the fireplace.

But Kennedy decorated his in a grand style. He chose a deep red paint for the walls and lined them with dark wood bookshelves. He also selected a red carpet with a repeating pattern of large gold stars that is identical to the carpet in the Old Senate Chambers in the Capitol, where the Court heard oral argument from 1860 to 1935. The aesthetic speaks of governmental authority and power, as well as a fondness for the pomp and splendor that went with it in the past.

More than O'Connor and Souter, two other Republican appointees who let them down, Kennedy has been accused by conservatives of buckling under pressure from the cultural and media elite. They complain that he's a victim of the "Greenhouse Effect," a coinage first used by columnist Thomas Sovell, then by Judge Laurence Silberman, to describe the temptation a justice faces to drift left to appeal to the press, and to veteran *New York Times* Supreme Court reporter Linda Greenhouse in particular. Kennedy, they suspect, understood and possibly agreed with the conservative position on issues like abortion and school prayer, but he refused to see them through to their logical, if politically unpalatable, conclusion.

The question of cultural drift on the Supreme Court has been a frustrating one for conservatives, and there are dramatically different versions of it. Kennedy would say that what conservatives see as a drift to the left is instead nothing more than the manifestation of the weighty responsibilities a justice assumes when he arrives at the Court. It's insulting to suggest that he's become more liberal because of pressure from the cultural and media elite, Kennedy would say: he's trying to conscientiously work through difficult legal questions, many of which have no clear answers.

But conservatives see a justice who's moved to a more liberal point of view and believe he's been influenced by Washington's legal and social culture. The legal conferences and embassy parties and European trips and flattery from academics and powerful editorial pages can lead all but the most firmly rooted justices to drift away from their moorings. Kennedy's change of heart in *Casey* and *Lee v. Weisman* are seen as obvious examples of the phenomenon.

That's one reason why so many conservatives cast Kennedy in the role of traitor. Even though he is more conservative than either O'Connor or Souter, he nonetheless is subjected to far harsher criticism than O'Connor, who was beloved by her clerks and seen as a trailblazing woman entitled to some slack, or Souter, who conservatives see as simply a mistake by George H. W. Bush, and so never a turncoat.

Bush's advisers were flat-out wrong in thinking Souter would follow in Scalia's footsteps. He'd done nothing as a judge in New Hampshire—and had no experience in Washington in a Republican administration—to suggest he would be a reliable conservative vote. Even his own chief Senate sponsor, Warren Rudman, believed he would leave *Roe* alone and privately assured liberals they needn't be concerned. Moreover, Souter's hard turn to the left came so quickly that conservatives never looked to him with hope. He didn't string them along; he broke up with them right away.

Kennedy was different. He wasn't completely comfortable in either camp, and justices who hoped to get his vote, whether liberal or conservative, were bound to be disappointed some of the time. He raised conservatives' hopes in his first few years, and he later came through on major cases. From the 1992 term until the end of the Rehnquist Court, he voted with Rehnquist as often as any other justice on the Court. He supported limits on affirmative action in college admissions,[12] and although he refused to overturn *Roe,* he would allow bans on certain abortion procedures.[13] He endorsed an approach that would permit more religion in public life.[14] He provided a pivotal vote to hand the presidency to George Bush in *Bush v. Gore.*[15] Even so, Kennedy continued to side with the more liberal wing on some of the other divisive cases, and his grandiose writing style made his decisions in those cases even more grating for conservatives. He reversed course on the death penalty, writing that the government couldn't execute juveniles or those with mental retardation.[16] In both cases, he had previously joined Court majorities going the other way. He also wrote two decisions giving gays and lesbians greater rights than ever before.[17] He has urged courts to look abroad and consider international law when making decisions.[18]

Kennedy's drift away from the right—and Souter's swift landing on the left—were stinging ideological defeats for conservatives wanting justices with clear conservative philosophies. They had a Supreme Court with seven Republican appointees, but they still were unable to overturn *Roe v. Wade* or a host of liberal precedents set down by the Warren and Burger Courts. Their disappointment was profound.

7.

THE CLINTON WAY

For twelve years, the Reagan Revolution gripped Washington and transformed the world, but it did little to realize the goals of movement conservatives or evangelical activists who had done so much to carry Reagan's party to power. Ronald Reagan aligned himself with social conservatives and vowed to nominate justices who would overturn *Roe v. Wade*, allow school prayer, and scale back the rights of criminal defendants. But despite four appointments, Reagan left office with a Supreme Court almost as liberal as it was when he moved into the Oval Office.[1]

Reagan's first nominee was historic. Sandra Day O'Connor became the first female justice, but she was not the reliable conservative vote right-wing opinion leaders had sought. She prevented the Court from overturning *Roe v. Wade*, and she favored a much stricter separation of church and state than did the Religious Right. Reagan's next selections, William Rehnquist for chief justice and Antonin Scalia as associate, remained firmly planted in the conservative camp throughout their judicial careers. But those nominations had little impact on the Court's direction because they both replaced solid conservatives. Reagan's nomination of fellow Californian Anthony Kennedy proved to be another dismal choice for movement conservatives.

George H. W. Bush, who conservatives thought would be the standard-bearer for what they hoped would be, in essence, Reagan's third term, also failed to dramatically move the Supreme Court, despite being given the historic opportunity to replace two liberal icons, William Brennan and Thurgood Marshall. David Souter was an unmitigated disaster for Reagan conservatives and the prolife movement, and while Clarence Thomas became one of the Right's most reliable votes, the forcefulness of his views affected the Court in unexpected ways. His arrival on the Court actually pushed moderates like O'Connor further to the left.

All told, twelve years of Republican control over the executive branch brought little of the desired change that conservatives had clamored for since Earl Warren first donned a black robe. Reagan and his successor nominated five justices to the Court in a dozen years, and three of the five moved to the left to embrace a more expansive role for the Court and the Constitution. Few would argue that the Rehnquist Court was more liberal than the Courts before it, but the justices' steady march to the political center was not enough for right-wing activists and politicians. They wanted an outright victory, with the Court changing course on the excesses of the Warren and Burger Courts, and Reagan and Bush had failed to deliver.

And now, Bill Clinton had been elected president.

President Clinton's approach to Supreme Court nominations was different from that of any other president before or since. He was a lawyer and former law professor himself, a graduate of Yale Law School, and he possessed a deep and abiding respect for the Supreme Court. When Byron White announced in March 1993 that he would retire at the end of the term, Clinton embarked on a long, public, and, at times, agonizing search. The process to replace White, a Kennedy nominee who voted with conservatives, was disorganized and messy. White House counsel Bernard Nussbaum gave Clinton a list of about fifty possible nominees. Clinton himself helped winnow it down.

Clinton had wanted to look outside the federal bench and nominate a politician with life experience and a "big heart." He had his own heart set on New York governor Mario Cuomo, but Cuomo turned Clinton down. The administration continued to sift through other contenders, but there were rampant leaks, as officials floated names and even publicly discussed whom they had interviewed. The experience left some prospects feeling sandbagged when they fell off the list.

Throughout the first part of 1993, as he searched for a nominee, Bill Clinton's popularity plummeted. The young president made so many political missteps in his first year that he soon earned the distinction as the least popular newly elected president in the history of polling. Finally, in the first week in June, the White House appeared settled on Interior Secretary Bruce Babbitt as Clinton's first nominee. But the weakened president was forced to reconsider when environmentalists urged him to keep Babbitt in place. When Republican senators raised protests of their own to Babbitt's potential nomination, Bill Clinton backed down.

That week, White House lawyers contacted two federal appeals court judges, including Ruth Bader Ginsburg, a diminutive intellectual powerhouse who had been a crusader for women's rights when she worked as a lawyer for the American Civil Liberties Union. Clinton had first met Ginsburg in the 1980s, when she gave a speech at the University of Arkansas Law School at Little Rock while he was governor. About halfway through her talk, Clinton and his wife, Hillary, walked into the auditorium, and Clinton introduced himself afterward. Ginsburg remembers being impressed by the young governor's charm.

Clinton hadn't spoken to Ginsburg since, but she had impressed him as a trailblazer who'd literally written the book on gender inequality when she taught at Columbia Law School. She proffered theories that were inclusive, eschewing an "us versus them" approach, and Clinton thought the fractured Supreme Court would benefit from such a personality.

Like O'Connor, Ginsburg had been the victim of discrimination herself, having earned a clerkship with Supreme Court justice Felix Frankfurter only to see it pulled away when he learned she was married with a five-year-old daughter. Ginsburg, a sixty-year-old grandmother, had the life experience and that "big heart" Clinton wanted, and the intellect and legal skills to match her remarkable personal history.

And Ginsburg was no bomb thrower. In her twelve years on the D.C.-based federal appeals court, she developed a reputation as a careful, measured judge and was widely respected by conservatives and liberals as a skillful technician. Even those who disagreed with her respected her approach. She also didn't let ideology get in the way of her relationships with her colleagues: Antonin Scalia had become a good friend when they served together on the appellate court, and they remained close, even regularly celebrating New Year's Eves together with their spouses. When Clinton consulted Senator Orrin Hatch, the Utah Republican and influential member of the Senate Judiciary Committee, he quickly signed off on her.

Clinton's aides contacted Ginsburg about a week before the nomination, when she was at a federal judicial conference in Maryland. Several times that week, Nussbaum called her, asking questions about her background and then about her upcoming travel schedule, which Ginsburg took as a positive sign. He wanted to know where she would be that weekend. She was supposed to attend a wedding in Vermont, she said. Nussbaum told her she shouldn't go; she should plan to be in Washington.

But then he called back. "It's okay to go," he told her.

Ginsburg assumed the White House had moved on. That Friday, Clinton interviewed Boston-based federal appeals court judge Stephen Breyer, who had strong support on Capitol Hill, having worked there as chief counsel for the Democratic-controlled Senate Judiciary Committee when Ted Kennedy was chairman. The meeting quickly leaked to the press, and White House Secretary Dee Dee Myers confirmed the interview.

But Breyer, a Harvard Law School professor, hadn't been at the top of his game. He'd just left the hospital with bruised ribs and a collapsed lung, which he'd suffered in a bicycle accident. His injuries prevented him from flying to Washington from Boston, so he was driven to New York and took the train down from there. He stayed in Washington after his lunch with President Clinton, waiting to get the nomination.

Clinton wasn't sold on Breyer. He decided not to offer him the nomination and asked to meet with Ginsburg. Saturday, shortly after she and her husband arrived in Vermont, Nussbaum called her again. "We need you to come back."

Ginsburg didn't want to leave abruptly and arouse suspicion, so they agreed that she would attend the wedding and leave first thing the next morning. Nussbaum picked her up at the airport and took her directly to the White House. He'd assured her she was dressed fine, in the comfortable pants she'd worn on the plane, since Clinton would be coming from the golf course. Instead, when she met President Clinton, he was wearing a suit and tie, having just come from church.

The conversation lasted just over an hour. It was her first and only interview for the Supreme Court. Clinton was deeply engaged in the discussion, almost excited to talk about the law and the Court. He had plans of starting annual dinners with the justices at the White House. He asked Ginsburg about the women's movement in the 1970s, and the two discussed constitutional law. Ginsburg thought it was a wonderful conversation, and she found herself once again impressed by Clinton and his enthusiasm.

When she arrived back home, a fleet of White House lawyers was going through her tax information to make sure everything was in order. It was. "What would you expect?" one commented. "Marty Ginsburg is a tax lawyer."

Ruth Bader Ginsburg didn't correct him, but her husband didn't handle the Social Security taxes and other matters that the lawyers focused on. She had done that from day one.

Marty Ginsburg made lunch for everyone, including Deputy White House Counsel Vincent Foster. Ruth Ginsburg was struck by how sad and remote Foster seemed, how quiet he was. A month later, he killed himself.

Later that night, Nussbaum called Ginsburg at home and told her not to go to sleep because Clinton wanted to talk to her. Clinton called at 11:33 p.m., after he finished watching an NBA finals game. He'd been unable to get the telephone switchboard to place the call, so he made it himself from the kitchen in the residence. He offered Ginsburg the nomination and said he planned to make a few remarks the next day in the Rose Garden.

There was never a doubt Ginsburg would be confirmed to replace the more conservative Byron White. Clinton had told advisers back in March that he wanted to take his time and hit a "home run" with the nomination. Whether by accident or design or a combination of both, Clinton had done just that.

Ruth Bader Ginsburg spent the first week meeting senators, none of whom offered up opposition. The next week, she went through private tutorials with law professors. She picked people to lead her through various subjects she expected to discuss in her hearings. Kathleen Sullivan, the respected dean of Stanford Law School, led Ginsburg through the religion clauses. Robert Gorman, of the University of Pennsylvania Law School, took her through labor law, and on and on.

Ginsburg spent the third week in mock practice sessions. The White House legal team had given her two videotapes of past confirmation hearings. One was David Souter's. "That's the way to do it," a White House lawyer told her. The other was Robert Bork's. Ginsburg couldn't bear to watch Bork, her old colleague on the federal appeals court, suffer through his contentious hearings. She knew him too well and liked him too much.

The White House was worried about questions from Republicans over Ginsburg's membership on the board of the American Civil Liberties Union, and in the mock sessions, when lawyers were pretending to be the senators, they repeatedly pressed her to defend various ACLU positions. Finally, Ginsburg had had enough. "Stop it," she said. "There's nothing you can do to make me bad-mouth the ACLU."

In her hearings a few weeks later, not one Republican asked her a single question about her work with the ACLU and its position on issues. Senators treated her politely, deferring to her when she declined to respond to questions about specific cases or legal issues. Ginsburg's arrival at the Court would mean dramatic change: Her taking over the more conservative White's seat meant the Right would need both Kennedy and O'Connor to prevail in divisive cases on social issues— at times an impossible task. Yet Ginsburg was confirmed 96–3.

Breyer would get a second shot at the Court nine months later, when Harry Blackmun announced his retirement. This time President Clinton took just over a month to decide. He looked at a full list of nominees, including Bruce Babbitt and federal appeals court judge Richard Arnold of Arkansas. But he went back to Breyer, whose fourteen years of judicial experience and even temperament, Clinton believed, would make him an effective justice on the Court.

Clinton was right. The Senate confirmed Breyer 87–9 to replace Blackmun, but it was no even trade. Blackmun hadn't been a particularly likable colleague, and Breyer, like Ginsburg, brought collegiality to the group. As Breyer said after President Clinton announced his nomination in the Rose Garden, the law should bring people "together in a way that is more harmonious, that is better, so that they can work productively together."

By the time Breyer joined the Court in the fall of 1994, conservatives had lost their battle to remake it. In Ginsburg's first term, the conservatives lost their majority in a number of controversial cases, when O'Connor and Kennedy sided with the Court's more liberal wing. It wasn't Rehnquist leading the day. It was Souter, Stevens, Blackmun, and Ginsburg, typically joined by O'Connor and Kennedy. At the end of the 1993 term, Souter's influence had grown to the point that he was comfortable mocking Scalia in a religion case as a "gladiator" who lunged "at lions of his own imagining."[2]

Souter was taking Scalia head-on, countering his historical analysis and disputing that Scalia understood what the framers intended. In the religion case, Scalia wrote a twenty-three-page dissent blasting Souter for his "facile conclusions" and "manipulation of the facts." Souter replied calmly. He said Scalia's position would be more acceptable if it "had prevailed with the framers and with this court over the years." Souter had the majority opinion, with O'Connor and Kennedy on board.

When Breyer moved into his chambers that fall, the justices knew the prospects of a Rehnquist Revolution were dead. Journalists and law professors had tapped Souter as the liberal leader. Breyer thought he could help move the Court even further away from the right.

Breyer is very much like the classic absentminded professor, but with a twist. When he arrived at the Supreme Court, employees noticed that he muttered to himself when he walked the hallways. He talked about his "umbrella jokes," which were so obscure they were over most people's heads. But he also brought infectious, almost boyish, enthusiasm to his discussions about the Court's work. He liked to talk, to hash things over. He joined the Court with high hopes of swaying O'Connor, a centrist he believed he could help guide a bit further left.

But Breyer's vision of a new progressive majority met with crushing disappointment his first term, when the Court issued its opening volley in a possibly revolutionary case that went to the very balance of power between the federal government and the states. The justices, in a 5–4 vote, ruled that Congress exceeded its powers when it passed a law prohibiting guns near schools.

The Constitution only gives Congress certain powers, such as collecting taxes, declaring war, and regulating commerce. It leaves the rest to the states. The Supreme Court in the twentieth century had watched passively as Congress passed more and more laws in areas of traditional state concerns. Typically, Congress justified these laws under its power to regulate interstate commerce, under the theory that almost anything, in some way, affected it. Toward the end of Breyer's first term, the Court sat up and said no more. In the spring of 1995, Rehnquist led the more conservative justices to strike down part of the Gun-Free School Zones Act.[3] The Court said Congress had stretched its power to regulate commerce beyond recognition when it passed the law. The decision, *United States v. Lopez,* marked the beginning of what many believed would amount to a "federalism revolution," as the five more conservative justices began imposing limits on Congress's power to bend states to its will. Although the Court would eventually stop short of revolution, some commentators feared that the justices were poised to dramatically overhaul the entire federal system.

After the justices discussed the gun case in their conference, it was clear to Breyer and others that the conservatives would demand a new approach. Breyer was despondent as he walked back to his chambers from the conference room on the first floor. When he walked into his office, his law clerks, seeing his expression, knew how the vote had gone. One began quietly singing a song by the popular band R.E.M., "It's the End of the World As We Know It."

Some of the news coverage of the Court's decision was nearly as dramatic. "The High Court Loses Restraint," read the headline on the *New York Times*'s editorial.[4] "Top Court Ruling on Guns Slams Brakes on Congress," proclaimed the *Washington Post.*[5] But during the next ten years, as the Court struggled over the issue of when to insist that the federal government take a backseat to the states, the world would not end. And neither would the steady march of congressional intervention into topics previously within the bailiwick of the states.

Breyer was a seasoned judge and professor when he joined the Court, but new pressures astonished him. He jokes that Rehnquist would always say justices spend their first five years wondering how they got to the Supreme Court. They spend the rest of their Court tenure wondering how their colleagues got there.

As Breyer settled into the work, he achieved little success trying to persuade the independent O'Connor. Like Rehnquist, O'Connor preferred to do her give-and-take through the exchange of written drafts and memos. But some of the justices liked to talk things out, and Breyer would find a receptive ear in Kennedy. The two have offices right next door, and they talk often. Kennedy describes Breyer as "so inventive, such a fine lawyer," adding, "I love to go into his office and say, 'You know, I'm working on this.' "

Breyer's engagement was especially evident in *Bush v. Gore,* when the Court stopped the recount of ballots in Florida during the disputed 2000 presidential election, essentially handing the presidency to George Bush.[6] Outraged Democrats and liberal law professors saw it as a purely political move, but Breyer was behind its muddled outcome.

The bitterly contested case evolved from events unraveling the night of November 7, 2000, when networks declared George W. Bush the winner of the 2000 presidential election. The margin of victory for Bush came in Florida, where the Texas governor initially pulled in about 1,700 more votes than then–vice president Al Gore, who saw the narrow margin and refused to concede defeat. Under state law, Gore sought hand recounts in four counties that were Democratic strongholds. Gore would eventually sue in a Florida circuit court to contest the election results, and the Florida Supreme Court took his side and ordered a recount. It was George W. Bush's appeal of that decision that would set the stage for a case that would shake the political world and deeply damage the Supreme Court's reputation for years to come.

The case, the Court's second pass at the issue, was decided under intense time pressure. Midday on Saturday, December 9, the Court voted 5–4 to stop the recounts until it decided the issues in the case. It got briefs from both sides on Sunday afternoon. It heard arguments on Monday, and it announced its decision the next evening, December 12, which was the official deadline for certifying electoral college votes. The liberal and conservative justices agree today on one thing: If only they had had more time, they would have produced a better decision.

"The problem with *Bush v. Gore* was that it came so fast, it had to be decided so fast," Kennedy said in an interview. "I think that conceptually, it was a case of medium difficulty." Said O'Connor: "I don't think what emerged in the last opinion was the Court's best effort. It was operating under a very short time frame, to say the least. Given more time, I think we probably would've done better."

At conference after the arguments on Monday, the Court's five most conservative justices agreed that the Florida Supreme Court was wrong to order the recounts. Rehnquist circulated an opinion based on Bush's leading argument, which focused on a narrow provision in the federal Constitution. The provision, a part of Article II of the Constitution, provides that each state's "electors"—the people who represent the state in the electoral college and actually elect the president—must be chosen "in such manner as the legislature thereof may direct." Bush argued that the Florida Supreme Court had essentially rewritten or ignored multiple provisions of the state's election statutes. The result was that courts, not the Florida legislature, were prescribing the manner of choosing Florida's electors, in direct defiance of Article II of the Constitution. Gore argued that the state court wasn't rewriting the law, but interpreting it. He said there was nothing wrong with allowing state courts to "interpret" election statutes and implement the state legislature's will. The question essentially became whether the Florida Supreme Court had so twisted the words of the election laws that it had gone beyond any reasonable view of "interpretation" to "rewriting."

Bush argued—and the conservative justices appeared to agree—that the Florida Supreme Court violated the federal Constitution when it changed various procedures and deadlines set out in state law for counting votes. By ignoring the statutory deadline, the Florida court was making a new law, and the Constitution said the state legislatures—not courts—were supposed to do that. The argument was simple, defensible, and highly specific.

But Breyer and Souter, believing they could sway Kennedy, had begun championing a theory that the Florida Supreme Court violated equal-protection concerns because it didn't require uniform standards in the recount. As a result, some counties in the state were counting the ballots one way, and some were counting it another. Bush's lawyers made this argument, but they put it third in their legal briefs.

The two liberals were willing to agree that the Florida Supreme Court was wrong on those grounds. But, unlike conservatives, they didn't think the recount should stop. They thought the answer was to provide clear standards. They believed they could pry Kennedy away from the conservatives with that approach: The Florida Supreme Court was wrong, but they could bring clarity to the crisis by allowing the recounts to continue if done properly.

They were right on one count. Kennedy was amenable to the equal-protection argument. He refused to sign Rehnquist's opinion and began working with them on an alternative opinion. O'Connor, who liked the idea of having liberals sign on to that reasoning, agreed to go along. Eventually, so too did Rehnquist, Scalia, and Thomas. The Court's most conservative justices felt that they had no other choice; the next president would be determined by Kennedy's vote. They worried that if they didn't sign on to Kennedy's handiwork, he would change his mind, as he had in the past. Conservatives had long believed that landmark cases brought out the worst in Kennedy; his change of heart on abortion, affirmative action, and school prayer had doomed right-wing efforts to change legal history.

At the end of the day, Kennedy would not go along with Breyer and Souter on the remedy. Kennedy would later explain that the outcome had to do with bringing a renegade court to heel. The recounts, Kennedy thought, had to stop because of a looming deadline to certify Florida's electoral votes. Although many legal scholars would agree with Kennedy's negative assessment of the Florida Supreme Court's decision, the justices' negotiating back and forth left his own court with a mess. The Rehnquist Court had effectively handed the presidency to George W. Bush on the basis of an unsigned majority opinion resting on equal-protection grounds. Dissenting justices eviscerated the conservatives, accusing them of hypocrisy and political bias, pointing out that they didn't typically embrace novel claims under the equal-protection clause. They said conservatives had irrevocably damaged the Court and its reputation.

Rehnquist's opinion garnered votes from only Scalia and Thomas.

In the years since, Breyer and Souter have said they continue to believe they could have swayed Kennedy, if they'd only had more time. "Just one more day," Souter reportedly has said.

But other liberal justices never thought it was possible. The case was over, they believed, that Saturday, December 9, when conservatives voted 5–4 to stop the recount.

Kennedy now scoffs at the suggestion he was on the fence. "I think he's wrong," Kennedy said of Souter's remarks. "I think with one more day, I might have persuaded him."

The struggle over Kennedy's vote was a familiar one over the eleven-year period the Rehnquist Court was intact. Both he and O'Connor came to wield the most power—not because of their influence on the law or on the other justices, but because their votes were so frequently in play. They weren't the most influential justices; they had the most power. They became must-have votes if their conservative brethren wanted to carry the day. The liberal justices had an easier task: They needed to get just one of their votes. Sometimes O'Connor and Kennedy sided with liberals and sometimes with conservatives. Their decisions would dictate how the Court resolved the case. They soon were called "swing votes," a term they both intensely disliked. O'Connor repeatedly insisted she wasn't the deciding vote, but just one of nine. "I don't think I'm a swing vote. The cases swing; the justices don't," Kennedy said. "There's a connotation of inconsistency, of change, but I think it's just the opposite. I think it's the cases that change, not the law."

Kennedy was more conservative than O'Connor on race, religion, and abortion, and over the years he became increasingly frustrated with her legal positions. A common criticism of O'Connor was that she adopted malleable standards that she could manipulate in a future case to get a desired result. Kennedy, her fellow justice in the middle, was subjected to some of the same criticisms, but he saw himself differently. He shared some of the frustration that conservatives express over O'Connor's approach to the law. Although he also took a pragmatic approach to things, he thought O'Connor was simply more willing to walk away from positions she'd taken in earlier cases. "I think I may adhere somewhat more closely to whatever standard I come up with," Kennedy said in an interview. "I mean, if I say something, I want to stick with it."

The Court's decision in a controversial abortion case in 2000 was a good example. In that case, *Stenberg v. Carhart,* the justices asked whether states could ban a certain type of abortion procedure commonly referred to as "partial-birth abortion."[7] More than thirty states had banned the procedure, including Nebraska. But abortion-rights groups argued that the state laws were unconstitutional, under the Supreme Court's 1992 ruling in *Planned Parenthood of Southeastern Pennsylvania v. Casey.*

Conservatives had been furious at Kennedy for switching sides in *Casey,* but eight years later it was Kennedy who felt betrayed, and he lashed out at O'Connor and Souter for taking *Casey* in a direction he had never intended. O'Connor and Souter insisted that the *Casey* decision made clear that states could not ban the partial-birth abortion procedures. They joined the liberals in voting to strike down the laws. The decision was 5–4.

Kennedy felt had. That was not what he thought the three of them had agreed to in the *Casey* decision. While reaffirming the basic holding of *Roe v. Wade,* Kennedy believed, *Casey* had also emphasized that states have an important role in regulating abortion. States are entitled to make moral choices to protect and promote the life of the unborn child—including banning certain procedures, Kennedy believed—so long as they didn't make it all but impossible for a woman to get one. In Kennedy's view, the Nebraska law banning partial-birth abortion reflected the state's decision that the procedure was morally wrong, and that was a decision the state was entitled to make under *Casey.*

Kennedy wrote a bitter dissent, accusing the majority of repudiating "this understanding" and distorting *Casey* to get the result they wanted in the partial-birth abortion case. *Casey,* he wrote, "is premised on the States having an important constitutional role" in the abortion debate. States can take sides in the abortion debate and come down on the side of life. Kennedy wrote: "Through their law the people of Nebraska were forthright in confronting an issue of immense moral consequence. The State chose to forbid a procedure many decent and civilized people find so abhorrent as to be among the most serious of crimes against human life, while the State still protected the woman's autonomous right of choice as reaffirmed in *Casey.* The Court closes its eyes to these profound concerns."

Years later, Kennedy remained steadfast. "I thought the *Casey* standard was one in which we said that the states do have a role, and that was not followed in *Stenberg,*" he said.

A divided Court is living proof that reasonable minds can differ. Constitutional cases are particularly prone to divide the Court because the document is so much more vague and open-ended than laws passed by Congress. What is a "cruel and unusual" punishment? What is an "establishment of religion"? The justices look to different sources for answers. There are the Court's previous cases and the writings by the founding fathers. There's societal tradition, and even the occasional dictionary. Still, no matter how many sources they examine, the constitutional questions don't, as a rule, yield a clear answer.

So what's a justice to do? Scalia and Thomas find clear answers in the doctrine of originalism. They look to the language of the Constitution and the way it was originally understood. More than the other justices, Scalia and Thomas will decline to recognize new constitutional rights. Their approach is appealing, in the sense that it helps narrow a justice's discretion. But it doesn't eliminate all discretion.

The First Amendment, for example, protects "freedom of speech." Scalia has ruled that it protects a person's right to burn a flag in protest. But his fellow originalist, Robert Bork, cites the flag-burning decision as an example of "judicial revisionism" where the Court abandoned the Constitution's original meaning.[8]

None of the other Republican appointees on the Rehnquist Court saw the law as Scalia and Thomas did. Rehnquist himself became more result-oriented at the end of his career, disappointing Scalia, Thomas, and other conservatives who saw him take inconsistent positions in the law. And Scalia and Thomas didn't always share the same approach. Thomas sometimes looked in different places than Scalia for the answers, such as to the Declaration of Independence and its promise of equality.

Stevens was a maverick who didn't ascribe to a particular theory. He was fiercely independent in his writings and actions. When the justices donned their robes before taking the bench, Stevens was the only one who refused assistance from the aides in the robing room. He always insisted on putting on his own robe. He took his own path in his opinions, too.

Souter looked to history and the more flexible traditions of the common law—that is, the law the Court itself makes when it creates, adapts, and follows precedent. His decisions were anchored in the eighteenth century, back in the "roots" of the law. But his analysis often produced a liberal result.

Kennedy was not an originalist, despite his conservative instincts. He was willing to recognize a right to engage in homosexual sodomy, to have an abortion—rights that would have baffled the framers of the Constitution. Kennedy's approach, of course, infuriated justices like Scalia and Thomas, who thought he was too quick to substitute his own policy views for the will of the people.

There's no question that Kennedy has conservative instincts, and liberal justices who try to get his vote will be disappointed more often than not. He is more conservative than O'Connor was, especially on abortion and affirmative action. But Kennedy doesn't think about the law in the same way as Thomas and Scalia.

When Kennedy first joined the Court, he visited the University of Chicago Law School, and dean Geoffrey Stone told him he believed it was harder to be a Kennedy than a Scalia or a Brennan. Kennedy thought Stone was wrong at the time, but he says he's come to see his point. The clear legal philosophy of Scalia and Brennan "does seem to yield them an answer a little more quickly," Kennedy said. "I try to accommodate more of the precedents in a more case-by-case approach than does, say, Nino or Bill Brennan. That doesn't mean there's less consistency."

Talking about his approach to judging, Kennedy can sound more like his liberal colleague Stephen Breyer.

The philosopher Isaiah Berlin wrote a celebrated essay called "The Hedgehog and the Fox," in which he drew a distinction between "hedgehogs," who know "one big thing," and "foxes," who know lots of small things.[9] It's a distinction that applies to the personalities on the Supreme Court. Foxes and hedgehogs bring different skills and perspectives to the Court. The foxes understand compromise and consensus. They strive to maintain the Court's role as a guardian of constitutional tradition, while at the same time serving as a referee in debates that are sometimes inescapably political. Sometimes, they reach compromise and consensus only by papering over real differences, as the justices did in *Casey.*

The hedgehogs, on the other hand, don't place much value on compromise and consensus. They think there are right answers in the law, and their clear vision helps keep the Court honest by pointing out when its reasoning is inconsistent or unprincipled. Scalia is a classic hedgehog who is guided by an overarching theory and assesses cases in light of it. For a hedgehog like Scalia, the 1992 *Casey* decision is institutional cowardice in the face of political pressure.

Breyer, in contrast, is a fox, a one-case-at-a-time pragmatist without a grand global theory. In his book *Active Liberty,* he tried to describe what he referred to as an "attitude" for weighing principles and inter-preting the Constitution.[10] Not surprisingly, prominent academic hedgehogs attacked the book, arguing that an attitude could never pro-vide the principled consistency of a theory.

Kennedy, like Breyer, is a fox. He pays attention to the social and po-litical fallout from the Court's work, and he frequently winds up in the middle, looking for that elusive compromise position that will resolve the most divisive either-or cases. The fox in Kennedy leads him to join in a political compromise like *Casey,* believing compromise may be a source of strength and legitimacy. There are times, however, when Kennedy seems to wish he were a hedgehog. But Kennedy is no Scalia, and when he tries to write with sweep and scope, he reaches for grand phrases and philosophical musings—the "sweet mystery of life" stuff that drives conservatives bananas.

When Clinton nominated Breyer, some liberal Democrats were dis-appointed; they'd wanted him to nominate a more forceful progressive voice, a William Brennan for the twenty-first century. But Breyer, who is a moderate liberal on criminal-law issues, has probably been more ef-fective on the Court than a bolder liberal would have been. The justices can influence others, even in subtle ways. Breyer's approach to judging has helped Kennedy defend his own style. The fact that Breyer—a re-spected academic, published author, and heralded thinker—doesn't have a particularly clear philosophy or framework has given Kennedy a safe haven from the withering criticism that he is too inconsistent or case-by-case.

With Breyer's nomination, Bill Clinton's contribution to the Court was over. Clinton had succeeded—though an often chaotic process—where Republican presidents had failed. His two nominees were im-pressive intellectuals with obvious liberal credentials and long paper trails, yet both were easily confirmed. And both Ginsburg and Breyer had a combination of gravitas and deft political skills that would make them respected and, more important, effective on the Supreme Court. The liberal equivalent of Antonin Scalia, Harvard's Larry Tribe, for example, could have ended up pushing Kennedy over to the embrace of conservatives—just as Brennan did with O'Connor. Instead, Breyer's ingratiating style kept open dialogues that would be important in close cases.

The Republican leadership came to terms with the Supreme Court's less than conservative makeup; it had no choice. After Breyer's confirmation, conservative activists would have to wait a staggering eleven years—the longest period in history that a court with nine justices went without a vacancy—before a Republican president would once again have the chance to continue the conservative movement's ideological crusade to move the Supreme Court to the right. In that eleven-year period, the Court would shoot down restrictions on abortion,[11] extend broader constitutional rights to gays and lesbians,[12] scale back the use of the death penalty,[13] order the Ten Commandments out of courthouses,[14] limit presidential power in wartime,[15] and give criminal defendants more protection under the federal sentencing guidelines.[16]

O'Connor's retirement would give conservatives a chance to go in a different direction. And they were going to make damn sure that this Bush did not follow in his father's footsteps.

8.

THE NATURAL

About a month after a dying Rehnquist swore in President Bush to a second term, David Leitch, one of Bush's senior advisers, packed up his office in the West Wing. Leitch had worked two years as the deputy White House counsel, and he was heading off to the more lucrative private sector to be the general counsel at Ford Motor Company. But before he left the White House for good, Leitch needed one more meeting with Karl Rove. He wanted to share his insight on possible candidates to replace Rehnquist when he retired, as most expected, in June.

Leitch was uniquely positioned to give Rove authoritative advice. He had worked with all of the top contenders and knew them personally. He'd clerked for federal appeals court judge J. Harvie Wilkinson after law school. He'd gone on to work in the Justice Department for J. Michael Luttig, and he later became law partners with John G. Roberts in the Washington-based firm of Hogan & Hartson. For the past two years, Leitch had worked directly with White House Counsel Alberto Gonzales. He also understood what the job of chief justice entailed.

Leitch had clerked for Rehnquist on the Supreme Court just a few years after Roberts did.

Leitch sent Rove an e-mail in late February, asking for a meeting to talk about the Supreme Court. Several days later, on Leitch's last day in the White House, the two sat down together for breakfast. Rove listened intently as Leitch went through the possible nominees. Leitch said they all had their strengths, even Gonzales, whom conservatives vociferously opposed. "They're all great," Leitch emphasized to Rove.

But one stood out. Roberts.

"If the president picks Roberts, you can sell him as the nominee who was selected purely on the merits—the quality candidate," Leitch told Rove. "He's the best Supreme Court advocate of his generation. Democrats can't attack him. Enough Republicans know him, and know he's not David Souter. He's going to be reliable. People will love him. The president will love him."

Rove did not disagree. John Roberts was widely considered one of the top lawyers to argue before the Supreme Court, an assessment shared by Democrats and Republicans alike, as well as by liberal justices like Ruth Bader Ginsburg. An honors graduate of Harvard Law School, he'd come to Washington in 1980 to clerk for then–associate justice William Rehnquist. He stayed to work as a lawyer in the Ronald Reagan and George H. W. Bush administrations. As deputy solicitor general for the elder Bush, Roberts represented the administration's position in the Supreme Court. He was poised to become a judge in 1992, when Bush nominated him to the D.C.-based federal appeals court. But Roberts's nomination, coming at the end of Bush's term, languished in the Democrat-controlled Judiciary Committee and died when Bill Clinton was elected. With a Democrat in the White House, Roberts left government service and moved to Hogan & Hartson, where he quickly became one of the nation's top appellate lawyers and was regularly called upon to argue before the Supreme Court. Before he left the practice of law in 2003, he had argued thirty-nine cases before the high court—a remarkable number for an institution that hears only eighty or so a year.

Nine years after Roberts was first nominated to the D.C.-based federal appeals court, George W. Bush tapped him again for the same post in 2001. When Republicans gained control of the Senate, Roberts finally got his Judiciary Committee hearing. Democratic senators grumbled that he refused to answer their questions, but they conceded his brilliance. "By all accounts, you are one of the most accomplished lawyers in the country and one of the most knowledgeable about our legal system," Senator Dick Durbin, the liberal Illinois Democrat, said when questioning Roberts. The Senate confirmed him by unanimous consent.

At fifty, Roberts was a decade younger than Wilkinson. In a sense, his short stint on the federal bench was positive, because he was seen as less partisan and divisive than the more experienced Luttig, who'd left the Justice Department to become a federal judge and had made some enemies in his fourteen years on the bench. Rove worried initially about whether Roberts was conservative enough, but he also was no Souter. He demonstrated solid enough conservative views as a lawyer in the Reagan and Bush administrations to pacify conservatives fearful of another disastrous appointment. That set him apart from Gonzales, who conservatives believed was not one of them.

"Look," Leitch said to Rove. "We sell him as the nominee picked solely on the basis of qualifications. If this president stood up and said, 'John Roberts is the best person in America for the job,' people would say, 'That's right.' "

After Rehnquist announced his illness in late October, the White House had narrowed down a list of finalists to replace him. They'd kept an evolving list of candidates since 2001, and most observers had fully expected Bush to make a nomination in his first term. Some right wingers, in fact, were miffed that Rehnquist had refused to retire before the 2004 presidential race. They believed a more loyal conservative, someone like Warren Burger, would never have gambled on Bush winning reelection. But this time, they were certain Rehnquist would retire at the end of the Court's term in June, if he lived that long.

By midspring, Rehnquist had not revealed his plans, but his health was clearly in decline. He was so gaunt that his clothes hung on his frame. His skin was grayish, and his trips to the doctor were more frequent. No one in the White House imagined he'd try to serve another year. Unknown to outsiders, including Rehnquist himself, the administration was preparing to interview possible replacements. Advisers wanted to be able to quickly recommend a handful to Bush so he could interview them personally and make his decision.

In late March, Gonzales asked Roberts to come by his office in the Justice Department. Gonzales had left the White House to be the attorney general, but he remained deeply involved in finding Rehnquist's replacement. Harriet Miers, an old friend of the president's from Texas, had taken his job as White House counsel and was still learning her way. Gonzales took the lead in the search.

Gonzales was considered a potential nominee himself. Bush had long suggested he would like to name the first Hispanic to the Supreme Court, and Gonzales seemed the obvious choice. He was an experienced lawyer and judge—he'd been a justice on the Texas Supreme Court before he moved to Washington to work for the president. Bush knew him and trusted him. But the conservative groups did not. They'd spent the past nine months making the case against him in discussions with Rove and, now, with Miers and her deputy, William Kelley. They believed his opinions on the Texas Supreme Court, particularly one in an abortion case, showed he wasn't a solid judicial conservative.

Gonzales told Roberts he just wanted to get together for an informal discussion, and the meeting—on April Fools' Day—was brief and cordial. Gonzales was familiar with Roberts's views on the law, having recommended his nomination to the D.C.-based federal appeals court in 2001.

Gonzales also was impressed with his intellect and skillful advocacy. Roberts's arguments had a crackle that most others lacked, even among top Supreme Court advocates. He would spend more than a month preparing, jotting down hundreds of possible questions in a notebook and practicing his responses aloud in his home or car or office. For one case, Roberts came up with more than five hundred questions, and if he stumbled over a word while practicing his response, he would change it to another. During his arguments in court, the justices were quick to engage him, peppering him with questions and then eagerly awaiting his response. For lesser advocates, the justices are more inclined to sit silently. They're not as interested in what the lawyer has to say, so they lean back in their chairs and let him speak without interruption. That is not what a John Roberts argument was like.

About a month after meeting with Gonzales, the White House asked Roberts to meet with a selection team made up of the president's most powerful advisers, including Vice President Dick Cheney. Roberts had some idea what to expect. He had gone through the process as an appeals court nominee, and he'd been on the other side as a government lawyer, asking prospective judicial candidates the questions himself. Roberts had spent his entire legal career thinking about the proper role of the courts. He ardently believed that courts should be modest and restrained, and that judges were not supposed to try to solve society's problems. He disdained the more liberal point of view that judges should be more willing to step in and try to improve things.

A long-ago conversation between two legal titans of the twentieth century illustrates the different perspectives. Justice Oliver Wendell Holmes, a leading proponent of judicial restraint, had just had lunch with Judge Learned Hand. As they said good-bye, Hand told Holmes, "Do justice sir, do justice." Holmes responded swiftly: "That is not my job. It is my job to apply the law."[1] John Roberts admired Holmes's approach to judicial restraint.

As a young lawyer in the Reagan administration, Roberts tested his theories when he interviewed judicial candidates for the lower federal courts. He framed his questions to get a sense of how the prospective nominee viewed the Constitution and how broadly he saw his role as a judge. One of Roberts's favorite questions focused on how the candidate would handle a lawsuit over a badly run prison, where the grim conditions actually constituted a violation of the Constitution's ban on cruel and unusual punishment. Some prospects told Roberts they would appoint an administrator to come in and take over the prison. That was the wrong answer, as far as Roberts was concerned. He wanted to hear a more modest view of a judge's role in the system. Judges don't know how to run prisons, and, in his view, they have no business trying to do so. They're supposed to maintain the law. Instead of stepping in and taking over the operations of a jail, Roberts believed, judges should hold the officials accountable. One way would be to hold them in contempt of court until they improved conditions.

The morning of his interview with President Bush's selection team, Roberts went to work in his courthouse chambers downtown as usual. Later that day, he drove himself back up Massachusetts Avenue, past the big embassies that line the street, to Cheney's residence in northwest Washington. He got there forty-five minutes early, so he sat in his car until it was time to go in.

Roberts was ushered into a study outside the conference room where he would meet the selection team. Again, he waited. He read through every title on the bookshelves in the small room as the advisers gathered on the other side of the door. Roberts was struck that most of the books were on trout fishing.

When the door finally opened and Roberts walked inside, Rove greeted him warmly. Gonzales and Miers were there, as well as Cheney and Scooter Libby, Cheney's chief of staff. Rove tried to put Roberts at ease with a joke as he pulled back a chair for him. "Here," Rove said, smiling, "sit in the hot-wired seat."

As the others took their seats, Cheney looked to Gonzales. "Well, you're the lawyer," Cheney said to the attorney general. "Let's get things started."

Gonzales, not Miers, took the lead, guiding Roberts through a series of broad questions focusing on his judicial philosophy. Gonzales appeared troubled by a series of exchanges Roberts had had in 2003 with two of the most aggressive and vocal Democrats on the Senate Judiciary Committee, which was then considering his nomination to the D.C.-based federal appeals court. Both Senators Chuck Schumer of New York and Dick Durbin of Illinois asked whether Roberts saw himself as a "strict constructionist." That phrase refers to a judge who interprets the Constitution by closely adhering to the exact words of the document and what the framers intended when they wrote it. It's generally considered a conservative approach, similar to one used by Thomas and Scalia.

In his appeals court hearings, Roberts had refused to say whether he was like Scalia or Thomas. Instead, he told Schumer that he didn't have an "overarching" judicial philosophy and that he didn't think an "all-encompassing approach" to interpreting the Constitution was particularly desirable. "I don't know if that's a flaw for a judicial nominee or not, not to have a comprehensive philosophy about constitutional interpretation," Roberts told Durbin during his hearings. "I just don't feel comfortable with any of those particular labels."

Gonzales and Bush's other advisers wanted to make sure Roberts did, in fact, have a conservative legal philosophy. They believed that previous Supreme Court nominations showed all too well that if a nominee lacked a conservative legal framework, he or she would drift to the left once on the Court and facing pressure from elite liberals in the media and in the law schools. O'Connor and Kennedy, for example, had conservative instincts when they were nominated, but they lacked a legal framework or philosophy that emphasized the restrained role of the courts in society. Souter, they would quickly learn, had neither conservative instinct nor philosophy.

A number of the more outspoken legal conservatives were worried about Roberts. Even when he worked in Republican administrations, or socialized with conservative lawyers, Roberts kept his personal views so close that his friends laughed that they didn't know his opinions. Some found his caution bewildering or, even, frustrating. Others said it reflected his careful temperament.

Kenneth Starr, who'd worked with Roberts in the Justice Department in the 1980s, spoke for many when he ribbed Roberts in 2002 about his tight-lipped reputation. Both men were on a panel at a conference at Brigham Young University that featured top lawyers from several different administrations who had worked in the solicitor general's office. Starr had been the solicitor general during the elder Bush's administration, and Roberts had been his principal deputy. When an attorney asked about the dynamics in the office over the years, Starr tossed the question to Roberts. "John will probably choose not to comment," said Starr, "because I think John has no views on any subject. But, John, would you care to comment?"

Said Roberts, laughing along with Starr: "No, but of course."

Those stories were trickling out into the conservative legal community, and some didn't know what to make of the brilliant lawyer-turned-judge whose closest friends included liberals. Roberts's response to Schumer and Durbin that he didn't have an overarching judicial philosophy needed more explanation. Gonzales pressed him on it during the interview with the selection team. "What," Gonzales asked Roberts, "did you mean by that?"

Roberts tried to elaborate carefully on his response in the hearings, when he said the justices themselves don't always apply a consistent approach to interpreting the Constitution. Some of the Court's more liberal justices were, at times, strict constructionists. Justice Hugo Black, one of the court's greatest defenders of free speech, took a strict-constructionist view when he interpreted the First Amendment's provision that "Congress shall make no law . . . abridging the freedom of speech, or of the press." To Black, "no law meant no law," Roberts said. On the other hand, Scalia and Thomas are considered strict constructionists, but they don't always take that approach. That's particularly evident in a series of decisions about federal power. The Court's conservatives have joined together to rule that the Constitution limits lawsuits against state governments for violating federal laws. But the words of the Constitution don't speak so broadly to that issue. The label of "strict constructionist" isn't always that revealing.

The interview was brief and awkward. The team, warned by Gonzales and Miers that it was verboten to talk about specific cases, seemed unsure of what questions to ask. Roberts, so accustomed to making eloquent arguments as an advocate before the Supreme Court, answered with short, almost clipped sentences. He left feeling he hadn't done particularly well with this group.

Roberts had read the group correctly. His performance was considered underwhelming enough that the advisers initially weren't inclined to put him on the short list of candidates who would meet with Bush. Some, like Miers and Rove, were suspicious of his conservative stripes because he'd kept his opinions to himself for so long. But Miers's deputy, William Kelley, made an impassioned plea. "I promise you the president will love John Roberts," Kelley argued, with urgency in his voice. "You have to bring him back."

Kelley, a highly regarded conservative legal scholar from the University of Notre Dame Law School, had joined the counsel's office when Miers took over. He was serious and sincere and, rare in Washington, lacking in the kind of driven ambition that causes high achievers to continually push for the next ring. He, his wife, and their five children were happy in South Bend, Indiana, and they fully expected to return when his time in the White House was up. He had no desire to move up to the upper-echelon schools like Yale or Harvard or Chicago, though he surely could have with his résumé. After law school at Harvard, Kelley had moved to Washington to clerk for Starr on the D.C.-based federal appeals court, then on to a clerkship with retired chief justice Warren Burger and Scalia. He later joined the solicitor general's office, where he argued before the Supreme Court and got to know Roberts.

No one knew it when Kelley started at the White House, but he shared Leitch's views that Roberts was the ideal nominee. After Bush was declared the winner of the 2004 presidential election, Kelley had turned to a colleague on the Notre Dame law faculty and said with enthusiasm, "This means we can get John Roberts on the Supreme Court." Miers, who had been in her office only a few months when O'Connor retired, trusted Kelley's judgment. She backed him up on Roberts, and the group finally agreed to put him on the short list. Roberts would get an interview with the president.

Roberts realized he was still under consideration for the expected vacancy when Miers called him a few weeks later to get information for a background check. The two spoke a couple of times in June as White House lawyers went through his financial dealings, and Roberts gave them information about his background and other personal details.

As June wore on, Roberts began to think Rehnquist would not retire. He'd given no indication he planned to step down, and Roberts and other clerks saw Rehnquist as a man who very much lived his life day by day. He was not indecisive, but fatalistic—the kind of man who would think, "If I can do my job today, I'm going to do it." All through June, every weekday, Rehnquist was going to work in his chambers at the Court.

That was an entirely different outlook than Rehnquist had once had. Two decades earlier, Rehnquist would shake his head and tell clerks he "never can understand why justices stay so long." Several of his older law clerks, at their annual reunion months before he learned he had thyroid cancer, reminded Rehnquist that he once was puzzled about why some justices insisted on saying on the Court past their prime. "It turns out you look at it differently when you're looking at it from this perspective," he responded.

O'Connor's July 1 bombshell exploded everyone's expectations— especially at the White House. Instead of nominating a new chief to lead the Court, they would be replacing the Court's first female justice.

Roberts and other prospective nominees for Rehnquist's seat, including Luttig and Wilkinson, assumed their chances of getting the nomination had dropped precipitately. The equation changed, and White House lawyers turned their focus to women or minority candidates. Roberts's mother called him from her home in Maryland after reading a newspaper story speculating on who would replace O'Connor. "The list has changed!" she told her son. "The short list used to be short. Now it's big."

Beyond the new diversity issues created by O'Connor's retirement, the position of associate justice also was a different one, and that affected the list of names. Luttig, for example, believed the White House was interested in him as chief justice, not as an associate justice. He could wait. Because of his age and experience, Wilkinson, too, was seen by some in the administration as a better nominee for chief justice.

Then there was O'Connor's philosophical position on the Court. As a moderate, she had provided liberals with a critical fifth vote on key social issues like abortion, affirmative action, and religion. Replacing Rehnquist with a staunch conservative like Luttig was one thing, because that wouldn't change the balance of the Court. But tapping a hard-liner to take O'Connor's place would mean a historic rightward shift, as both sides knew all too well. Her seat was the ball game.

In early July, Lally Weymouth hosted her annual summer bash in the Hamptons, an exclusive soiree her late mother, the *Washington Post*'s Katharine Graham, had started decades before. The party was the must-attend event of the summer season for the New York and Washington elite, attracting top figures in politics, business, and law. That night, O'Connor's retirement was a frequent topic of conversation among governors, senators, and industry leaders.

"What does this mean, Justice O'Connor before Chief Justice Rehnquist?" New York governor George Pataki asked over dinner. His tablemates included two men on opposite sides of the looming battle: Chuck Schumer, one of the most effective Democrats opposing Bush on the Senate Judiciary Committee, and former White House counsel C. Boyden Gray, the leading outside spokesman supporting Bush's judicial nominees.

Schumer and Gray responded almost in unison. "It means John Roberts," they speculated, "not Mike Luttig."

Roberts certainly wasn't getting that message from the White House. He had agreed back in April to teach a two-week class at University College in London, as part of Georgetown University Law Center's summer program, and he was scheduled to leave Saturday, July 9. The White House didn't seem at all concerned that Roberts was leaving the country, which Roberts took as another negative sign.

Roberts got to London on Sunday morning and spent the next two days settling in, dealing with paperwork, and getting ready to teach. The first class was Tuesday, and he outlined the course for his students. The very next day, Roberts got a telephone call from Bill Kelley.

Kelley asked Roberts to return to the United States for an interview with Bush. He implied that Bush was interviewing other people as well, and he told Roberts to keep the entire trip completely confidential. In Washington, reporters were frantically trying to determine whom the White House was considering. Some news reports were suggesting Bush was delaying a nomination until Rehnquist retired, so he could make both replacements at once—giving the administration flexibility to nominate a hard-line conservative to replace Rehnquist and a more moderate woman or minority to replace O'Connor.

That was not the plan, and the administration did not want any leaks that it was close to making a decision on the O'Connor vacancy. Kelley suggested that Roberts come up with an excuse for canceling his class and not, under any circumstances, divulge that he was jetting off to Washington for a day or so.

Roberts, who had gone to London by himself, took a cab to Heathrow Airport Thursday. He was waiting on his flight when, to his dismay, he saw a familiar face. "John! What are you doing here?" former attorney general Dick Thornburgh exclaimed, rushing over to pump Roberts's hand enthusiastically, exaggerating the friendship in the way people do when they unexpectedly see acquaintances in foreign places.

Roberts recovered quickly. "I've been teaching a class for Georgetown," he said, offering nothing more than a smile.

"Oh," Thornburgh responded. "When did that start?"

Roberts did not want to say Tuesday. He was certain Thornburgh, who'd been through the Souter and Thomas nominations when he was attorney general under the elder Bush, would make the connection if Roberts said the class had begun just two days before. "Oh, a little while ago," Roberts answered, before hurriedly saying good-bye.

On his flight back to Washington, Roberts thought about what he would say to Bush. As he did when preparing for a Supreme Court argument, he anticipated possible questions. The president isn't a lawyer, so Roberts mulled over how he could best explain his thoughts on the law and his views about the Supreme Court's role in society. He knew Bush would also be interested in him as a person, and he spent time thinking about what he could say about his life and how his experiences had shaped him. In preparing for an argument in the Supreme Court, Roberts had always believed it was best to use specific examples to make his points, and that's what he hoped to do with Bush. He could talk about growing up in Indiana, for example, to show how he appreciated what he considered midwestern values—straightforwardness, honesty, hopefulness, and a lack of guile.

As Roberts was arriving back in Washington later Thursday afternoon, Bush was meeting with another prospective nominee, J. Harvie Wilkinson, a judge on the U.S. Court of Appeals for the Fourth Circuit in Richmond, Virginia. Wilkinson had driven up to Washington from his home in Charlottesville earlier in the day to meet with Bush. The selection team had winnowed the list to five contenders, all of them federal appeals court judges. Four were white men.

At the time, outsiders assumed Bush would nominate another woman to replace O'Connor, but his advisers hadn't dramatically changed their list over the past three weeks. They'd cast a wide net but found no ideal woman or minority candidate. Some were too inexperienced. Some were too old. Some had ethical or personal issues. Others weren't considered conservative enough.

Two prospects who would have been serious contenders—and quite possibly the eventual nominee—said they didn't want the job because of personal reasons. Maura Corrigan was a respected Michigan Supreme Court justice who had wowed Kelley and others with her intellect and strength of character, but she flatly refused to be considered. She didn't want to go through the process.

Neither did Miguel Estrada, the brilliant young appellate lawyer who'd immigrated to the United States from Honduras as a teenager, speaking little English, and who'd gone on to the Ivy League and top jobs in government and at a private law firm. Bush nominated him to the D.C.-based federal appeals court in 2001 at the same time he tapped Roberts, but Democrats considered Estrada unacceptably conservative and feared he would be the first Hispanic nominated to the Supreme Court. Though he answered the same questions Roberts did, Democrats accused him of stonewalling and blocked his appeals court nomination in 2003—marking the first time in history an appellate court nominee was defeated by a filibuster. Throughout July, Miers made repeated entreaties to Estrada. She even enlisted conservative senators like Mitch McConnell of Kentucky to attest that they would go to the mat for him in the Senate this time. But Estrada had suffered a tragic personal loss the Thanksgiving before, when his wife died in an accidental drug overdose after taking medication for her severe back pain. Estrada was firm. He would not go through the confirmation process again. "I'd hate to say no to President Bush if I were asked," Estrada told Miers, "but I would."

Having come up short, the White House concluded it would put questions of race and gender aside and focus solely on judicial philosophy. That was made easier because Bush and his advisers knew he was certain to get another nomination. Rehnquist would retire or die on the bench, and they could add to the Court's diversity at that point.

After initially deferring to Gonzales when she first moved into his old office, Miers had assumed control of the process. By the time O'Connor retired, Miers was directing the nominations strategy, searching for potential candidates, talking with them in person or by phone and reviewing their records. She relied on Kelley for his legal analysis. Though also new to the office, he quickly made his presence felt, putting in Miers-like fifteen-hour days and digesting thousands of opinions by prospective nominees.

Kelley left no stone unturned. He closely examined opinions for clues on whether a prospective nominee was, as Bush had requested, like Thomas or Scalia. With some, it took one bad opinion to knock them out. Denver-based federal appeals court judge Michael McConnell was a favorite of some conservatives, but he'd written a decision earlier in the spring that would have subjected police officers to sweeping liability for actions while on the job.[2] That was enough for Kelley. Like those Justice Department lawyers twenty years earlier who were disturbed by then-judge Kennedy's decisions, Kelley thought the opinions revealed how a judge saw the law and his role—and reflected the kind of justice he would be. But unlike those Justice Department lawyers who warned the Reagan White House against Kennedy, Kelley had an attentive audience in Miers. She trusted his judgment.

If the president focused solely on philosophy, the favorite choice among movement conservatives was Mike Luttig, whose vociferous opposition had helped to damn Kenneth Starr's nomination to the Supreme Court in 1990. The elder Bush put Luttig on the same Richmond-based federal appeals court as Wilkinson in 1991, after Luttig had helped shepherd through the Souter and Thomas nominations. Luttig had spent several years in the Justice Department, working with Dick Thornburgh and Bill Barr, but he felt he had grown up at the Supreme Court: He started working there as a new college graduate, and he developed a close and lasting relationship with Chief Justice Burger, who encouraged him to go to law school at the University of Virginia. He later clerked for then-judge Scalia on the D.C.-based federal appeals court and for Burger. As a federal appellate judge, Luttig maintained close ties to the Supreme Court, especially through his friendships with Thomas and Scalia. His law clerks revered him as a teacher, and he sent the overwhelming majority of them on to clerkships with Supreme

Court justices. Many had taken jobs in the Bush administration, where they were lobbying for his nomination.

But Luttig was explosive and controversial. Democrats openly said they would try to block his confirmation, and more than a few conservatives opposed him as well. Luttig pursued a different strategy than Roberts, who had carefully cultivated an accommodating image that would help him get through a confirmation battle. Luttig had concentrated on getting nominated. He was openly ambitious, and critics came to suspect that some of his opinions were written to get attention for himself. He created a cultlike atmosphere with his law clerks, and he implicitly encouraged them to fight for him—and against his competitors, especially Wilkinson.

Some conservatives were put off by Luttig's biting criticism of Wilkinson in a series of published appellate court opinions. Luttig saw Wilkinson as "squishy" and analytically undisciplined, and he did not hesitate to express his views. He openly mocked Wilkinson's legal writings, much as he had privately discounted Kenneth Starr when he was under consideration for the Supreme Court in the elder Bush's administration. At the same time, Luttig also had a falling out with Laurence Silberman, the established D.C.-based federal appeals court judge who counted Vice President Cheney as a close friend. Silberman and Luttig competed for the same law clerks, and Silberman thought the younger Luttig was unprincipled and lacking in character because of his tactics in recruiting top contenders. Luttig thought Silberman was mad because he was getting old and finding it harder to get the top clerks. Regardless, Luttig had enemies, and his enemies had friends in high places.

Bush also met with Samuel Alito, a fifteen-year veteran of the U.S. Court of Appeals for the Third Circuit in Philadelphia. He was Luttig's opposite. Alito was quiet, almost shy. He spoke softly, mumbling at times, and he certainly had no enemies. Unlike Luttig, Alito hired liberal law clerks as well as conservatives. Some of Luttig's supporters snidely took to calling Alito the "Invisible Man," suggesting he hadn't truly established himself as a prominent conservative voice. But Kelley, who had analyzed all of Alito's opinions, told Miers he could not find one he disagreed with. Alito also had worked with Chuck Cooper and Doug Kmiec in the Justice Department in the 1980s and was well known and regarded by other high-ranking officials there, including Mike Carvin and Ken Starr. They knew Alito to be a careful and conservative legal thinker. Carvin, who had so strongly opposed Kennedy's nomination in 1987, had always said Alito would be his first choice.

The fifth contender was a largely unknown judge from Louisiana, Edith Brown Clement. Bush had put her on the U.S. Court of Appeals for the Fifth Circuit in New Orleans in 2001, after she'd served ten years as a federal trial court judge. But the conservative groups that lined up to offer immediate support for Bush's nominee flat-out refused to believe Clement was a serious prospect. Her star was dim compared to the other prospects, who had sparkling academic credentials and had held elite legal jobs, either at prestigious firms or in the highest-level positions in government. Clement had no major opinions in her tenure on the court, and she wasn't seen as particularly intellectual. She hadn't clerked on a federal appeals court, much less for a prominent judge or a Supreme Court justice, like the other contenders. Everyone assumed she was on the list because Bush wanted to see a woman's name there.

Of the group, the decorous and gentlemanly Wilkinson had once been considered the favorite. He had defenders in the administration who believed Luttig had picked fights with him over the years to enhance his own Supreme Court prospects. But other administration lawyers sided with Luttig, even those who didn't particularly like his brash style. They thought Wilkinson was too malleable, too much like his mentor, the moderate Lewis Powell. But Wilkinson had a bigger problem: At sixty, his age was creeping up on him.

President Bush found himself liking Wilkinson a great deal as their conversation unfolded late that Thursday afternoon. He'd spoken briefly to Wilkinson in February, when the judge came to Washington to swear in John Snow to be treasury secretary, so the discussion this time felt friendly and relaxed. They talked generally about the law, since questions about specific cases or rulings in a particular area were off limits.

"What does federalism mean to you?" Bush asked, referring to the balance of power between the federal government and the states, an issue that captivated the Rehnquist Court.

Wilkinson responded, "It means Texas and Rhode Island can do different things."

The interview also focused on personal questions. Bush asked Wilkinson about his biggest disappointment in life, and Wilkinson talked of the rejection he'd felt when he lost a campaign for political office when he was in his twenties. They discussed exercise. Wilkinson is a runner who takes his young law clerks on outings with him. After talking for about an hour, Bush gave Wilkinson a twenty-minute tour of the White House. Wilkinson left for his home in Charlottesville that night thrilled by the entire experience. "At no point did anyone, never once, even indirectly, ask about how I might rule in a particular area," Wilkinson said, almost marveling at the process. "I was never pushed."

As Bush was conducting the secret interviews to find O'Connor's replacement, the media spotlight remained on Rehnquist. Photographers and television cameras camped in front of his Virginia town house recorded his every arrival and departure. The week before, CNN had reported that Rehnquist's retirement was imminent. Bush was returning from the G8 summit in Scotland, and he would receive a letter from Rehnquist after Air Force One landed, one syndicated columnist reported with confidence. But the letter never came. A producer for Fox News saw Rehnquist getting into a car outside his house and asked when he would be retiring. "That's for me to know," Rehnquist growled, "and you to find out."

That Thursday, as Bush was kicking off his interviews and Roberts was landing in the United States, Rehnquist checked out of the Virginia Hospital Center. He'd spent two days there battling a fever, and a crush of cameras and journalists greeted him when he arrived home. It was too much for his children, who wanted the photographers gone and the retirement speculation ended. Without involving the Court's public information office, Rehnquist and his family released a personal statement later that night. Rumors of his imminent retirement, Rehnquist said, were unfounded. He was, he said flatly, "not about to announce my retirement."

The statement worked. The photographers and television cameramen left their perch in front of Rehnquist's home the next morning. It was just about the same time that Roberts was arriving at the White House to meet with the president. Luttig also was there that day, and the staff had to carefully coordinate the visits so the two men, once close friends, didn't run into each other.

Bush arrived at the White House on Marine One and interviewed Luttig first. Despite his high-level government service, his years of experience on the bench, and his close friendships with Justices Scalia and Thomas, Luttig found himself feeling nervous when he greeted Bush. The ambitions of fifteen years came crashing down on him as he struggled to get through the interview. Bush was asking only the most general questions about the law, but Luttig responded awkwardly. His voice was almost strained as he talked. Unlike Roberts, Luttig had done well when he met with the group of advisers in the spring in Cheney's residence. He had spoken smoothly and confidently then, articulating his views on the law and where the judges went off the rails when they tried to do too much.

On this day in the White House, Luttig and Roberts traded places. Roberts went forward.

After Luttig left the White House, Bush greeted Roberts warmly, trying to convey that the interview wasn't a make-or-break session. "I know you don't do this every day," Bush told Roberts with a smile, seeking to put him at ease. As with the other contenders, Bush asked Roberts personal questions about his life and his family. He then shifted to

Roberts's general views on the law and on the proper role of a judge—
two topics Roberts had spent his entire legal career thinking about. It
was less an interview than a conversation.

Roberts left feeling good about it, though he wasn't particularly optimistic about his chances to get the nomination. He summed up his
thoughts to his wife, Jane, when he got home: "Whatever happens," he
said, "I was glad to have had the chance to have done that."

With no word from the White House, Roberts flew back to London
Saturday afternoon, and he arrived early on Sunday morning. He spoke
with Kelley a couple of times that day on his cell phone. "Who would
oppose you?" Kelley asked Roberts. "Do you have any enemies?"

Later that night, about 2 a.m. London time, Kelley called again. "We
want you to come back," Kelley said. "But there are no promises."

Roberts thought Bush had probably narrowed his decision to two
people, as his father had with Souter and Edith Jones and as Reagan had
done with Kennedy and Doug Ginsburg. Kelley did not tell Roberts
whether he was the actual nominee or just a finalist, but he suggested
that things were promising. "It's very exciting," he told Roberts in one
of their final conversations.

Roberts packed up his things on Monday and prepared to leave London early the next morning. He concluded that he wouldn't be returning, regardless of what happened. His class ended Friday, and it seemed
pointless to try to fly back to teach one more day. He turned the course
over to an assistant.

Roberts rose about 3 a.m. Tuesday to head for Heathrow Airport. He
lugged his suitcases outside, only to find a deserted and darkened London street. His hotel was near the site of a subway bombing the week
before, and traffic was blocked off. He trudged several blocks to hail
a taxi.

About the same time, back in Washington, the president and first
lady were hosting an official dinner for the prime minister of India.
Andy Card, Bush's chief of staff, spotted Justice Thomas and his wife,
Ginni, in the grand dining room. Card knew he couldn't divulge a

name, but he wanted to tell Thomas something, to at least give a hint. "You're going to be happy with the choice," Card told Thomas.

Bush had made his decision.

As Kelley had predicted, Roberts was the president's clear favorite. Bush was impressed with Roberts's intellect and experience, telling advisers his credentials "just jumped off the page." Bush also liked Roberts's personal style and smooth, easygoing manner. Bush had emphasized to his lawyers in the counsel's office that he wanted to nominate a "good colleague." Roberts, Bush believed, had all the right qualities. He wouldn't alienate other justices or push them away. He was fair, and he would listen to others' views. But Roberts also had strong views of his own. Bush thought Roberts's service in the Reagan and Bush senior administrations showed he didn't worry about unpopular decisions. Like Thomas and Scalia, he would be able to stand up to the heat.

Roberts knew none of that. When he finally arrived at Heathrow Airport early Tuesday morning for his flight to Washington, carrying his bags and laptop computer, he noticed a long line snaking through the terminal. "Why are those poor fools in that line?" he thought to himself as he walked by. Just then, he heard an announcement that the computers for the airline he was flying had, in an unfortunate choice of words at an airport, "crashed." As he turned around, he quickly realized he was going to be another poor fool in that long line. It took nearly two hours to check in, and Roberts began worrying he wasn't going to make it back. He found himself thinking that Bush would just go down the list to the next nominee if he got stranded in London.

Roberts's flight arrived at Washington's Dulles International Airport about an hour late. When his plane was at the gate, he turned on his BlackBerry, but he hadn't received any updates or instructions on what to do next. As he walked through Customs, he received an urgent e-mail. It was from Kelley, and the message was brief. "Call immediately," Kelley wrote.

Roberts looked around him as he waited to clear Customs. Signs were posted everywhere: Cell Phone Use Prohibited.

His cell phone reception was scratchy when he finally made it through Customs and reached Kelley. "You need to be home at 12:30 for a phone call," Kelley said. He didn't disclose to Roberts why or who would be calling.

Roberts rushed outside and got into a cab, giving the driver his home address in the Washington suburb of Chevy Chase, Maryland. The driver turned around and looked at Roberts in the backseat. "Where is this place, Chevy Chase?" the driver asked. "This is my first day driving a cab. You have to help me."

When the cab pulled up in front of Roberts's house, he shoved money at the driver—British pounds, American dollars—and ran inside, throwing his laptop computer and suitcase on the chair. The phone started ringing as he closed the door, and when he picked it up, Miers was on the line. Roberts's heart dropped. She wouldn't be offering the job. She would be making the consolation calls.

"How was your flight?" Miers asked, making polite small talk. She then asked Roberts if she could put him on hold. Roberts waited, holding the phone to his ear, for several long minutes. The next voice he heard was that of President Bush.

Roberts's wife, Jane, arrived from her downtown law office as Roberts was saying good-bye to Bush. He hung up the phone and sat stunned in a wing chair. "The president has just said he would like to nominate me," Roberts said.

Bush went back to his lunch with the first lady and Australian prime minister John Howard and his wife. As he sat down at the table, he told the group he'd made a call about the vacancy on the Supreme Court. "I just offered the job to a great, smart, fifty-year-old lawyer who has agreed to serve on the bench," Bush said to those gathered around the table.

Roberts had barely had time to tell his wife about the conversation with Bush when Kelley arrived to take him downtown. Roberts rushed to take a shower and pull out a clean suit before jumping into the waiting car. In the White House, Kelley took Roberts to an empty office by the Oval Office, where he met with Rove and counselor Dan Bartlett. Bush's advisers didn't want Roberts wandering around the West Wing where anyone could see him, so they told him to stay put. He had told no one other than his wife where he would be, not even his parents.

Outside the White House, journalists had all but crowned Clement the nominee. Camera crews had rushed to Washington's Reagan National Airport to await her expected arrival from New Orleans. Television screens flashed her photograph and biography. The Clement frenzy had begun earlier that morning, after Leonard Leo, the former head of the Federalist Society, had told conservative lawyers and legal scholars in a conference call that Clement was the likely pick. No one in the White House had said so, but Leo knew Bush had interviewed Clement the previous Saturday, and he believed that the president wanted to nominate a woman.

Several of the lawyers on the conference call erupted. Wendy Long, a former Thomas clerk who had left a partnership at a major New York law firm to help with the confirmation battle, groaned aloud. With the Court in the balance and history on the line, Bush could not squander his choice with a less-than-stellar nominee who only had conservative instincts. They wanted an intellectual leader who could forcefully articulate conservative legal philosophies of judicial restraint, someone who would help return the Court to its modest role in the democratic system. They saw Clement as falling far short of this standard.

Long had confronted Leo over the weekend about Clement, asking him how the conservative groups could possibly support her. At Leo's request, Lee Liberman Otis, the former White House lawyer who had signed off on David Souter, had read Clement's opinions, and she'd found them lacking. Otis thought Long was right. Though a perfectly acceptable federal appeals court judge, Clement was no intellectual powerhouse on a par with Roberts or Luttig.

Leo tried to reassure the conservatives on the line that Clement would be a solid choice. Boyden Gray, the former White House counsel under the elder Bush, groused that her record was "thin." Gray had spent the past year working tirelessly as the main outside spokesman, defending Bush's appellate court nominees and laying the groundwork for the Supreme Court fight. He couldn't believe that the White House would tap Clement for the history-making pick.

But late that afternoon, Clement was seen in her chambers in New Orleans. The conservative lawyers ready to do battle were relieved but not surprised. They had expected more from Bush. When he'd said he would appoint a justice in the mold of Thomas and Scalia, they'd taken that to mean a justice with a clearly defined conservative legal philosophy. It wasn't enough that the nominee was considered conservative in her hometown. The White House, they thought, evidently understood that.

With the maelstrom swirling around Clement, Roberts was cloistered in a quiet office off the Oval Office. One of Bush's advisers suggested that he be prepared to make brief remarks when Bush introduced him to the nation later that night. The White House had scheduled an unusual prime-time announcement, and all the networks planned to broadcast it live. Roberts also talked to Bush in the White House, and he thanked the president again for the honor of the nomination.

That afternoon, Roberts's wife, Jane, pulled out her children's Easter clothes, gave the children a bath, and rushed to get ready herself. An accomplished lawyer, Jane Roberts has an energetic confidence about her, especially when she starts speaking in her Bronx-Irish brogue, which reflects the neighborhood she grew up in and her mother's Irish roots. She was supposed to be at the White House for dinner at 6:45 p.m., and the children would arrive later with their nanny. But even for Jane Roberts, it was all hard to process. She hurried out the door and into her PT Cruiser, but the air-conditioning was broken, and traffic was horrible, making the sticky Washington heat even more stifling. As she saw the clock creep closer to 6:45, she felt her face shine and her hair frizz. She was getting very stressed, thinking about being late for dinner with the president on the night her husband was going to be nominated to the Supreme Court. Despite that, she pulled into the White House gate almost on time, only to be told she didn't have clearance and would have to wait. She did.

When Jane was finally in the living quarters, the first lady and she had champagne before dinner, and Bush asked about Roberts's mother. "Does your mother know?" Bush asked. Jane had called her earlier that afternoon and told her to be sure to watch the news, without divulging why, so Bush picked up the telephone. "Hello, Mrs. Roberts. This is the president," Bush said. "I just wanted to let you know I'm going to be nominating your son tonight."

At about 7:30, Andy Card brought Bush a telephone and dialed the Republican and Democratic leaders in the Senate so Bush could tell them he planned to nominate Roberts. Then Jane's cell phone began to ring, after Bush had just told them how much he hates cell phones and that he had recently taken someone to task in a cabinet meeting. Jane had left it on because she was worried that the children wouldn't be cleared into the White House, but when she rushed to answer it, it was her sister-in-law's father. "It's John!" he said, having just heard a news flash. Minutes later, the phone rang again, but this time it was her real estate agent. "Jane, I just can't believe it!" she exclaimed. Finally, Josie and Jack, both four years old, came running in. The president never complained about the cell phone. Bush and Roberts left the room to prepare for the announcement, leaving the family behind with the first lady. But no one told Jane Roberts what they had planned for them, and as she walked down the hall with Laura Bush and the children, it wasn't clear until the last moment that Josie and Jack were expected to stand beside her. So they waited a few moments in front of the assembled cameras for the president and Roberts.

The two men strode down the Cross Hall in the White House just after 9 p.m. Bush stood in front of the podium, with Roberts at his right side, and he began by talking about the magnitude of the moment. "One of the most consequential decisions a president makes is his appointment of a justice to the Supreme Court," Bush said. "When a president chooses a justice, he's placing in human hands the authority and majesty of the law." A nominee must have "superb credentials and the highest integrity," be "a person who will faithfully apply the Constitution and keep our founding promise of equal justice under law," Bush continued. "I have found such a person in Judge John Roberts."

Jane Roberts and the children stood off to the side. It was late for the children, and she hadn't had a chance to prepare them for what to expect. Josie stood solemnly, wide-eyed and serious, as the president spoke. But joyous Jack careened around, pretending he was Spider-Man. Jane Roberts didn't hear a word Bush said. She didn't want to create more commotion, so she was afraid to silence him and risk causing a scene. But she was worried that Jack would walk over to the president and try his favorite trick: untying people's shoes. When it became evident that Jack had that in mind, she carefully pulled him over. Bush, too, found it incredibly distracting; he told a small group of supporters days later, "I kept hoping his mom would yank him out of there."

Roberts then took over. He'd been awake more than twenty-four hours, having gotten up the night before in London for his rushed flight back to Washington and the phone call from the president. His eyes were red, almost bloodshot. His words were few. "Before I became a judge, my law practice consisted largely of arguing cases before the Court. That experience left me with a profound appreciation for the role of the Court in our constitutional democracy and a deep regard for the Court as an institution," he said, looking out at the reporters gathered in the room.

"I always got a lump in my throat whenever I walked up those marble steps to argue a case before the Court," Roberts said. His voice started to break, and he paused momentarily; his friends watching on television tensed, worried he was about to cry. But then he continued. "And I don't think it was just from the nerves. I am very grateful for the confidence the president has shown in nominating me. And I look forward to the next step in the process before the United States Senate."

Two days later, an ebullient Bush attended a fund-raiser at Wind Falls, the ten-acre Virginia estate of construction mogul Dwight Schar,

the finance chairman of the Republican National Committee. Gray
was there, and he greeted Bush in the receiving line. Bush immediately
thanked Gray for his work on judicial nominations, then turned the
conversation to his new Supreme Court pick. "I checked this man out.
I checked this man out," Bush told Gray and others nearby, with enthusiasm. "I just hope he's the same twenty years from now as he is
today."

9.

"EXCEPT HE'S NOT A WOMAN"

Sandra Day O'Connor heard about Roberts's nomination after a day of fly-fishing in Idaho. Her first reaction was enthusiastic. "That's fabulous!" she said. Roberts was a "brilliant legal mind, a straight shooter, articulate, and he should not have trouble being confirmed by October."[1] But then came this qualifier. "He's good in every way," O'Connor said, "except he's not a woman."[2]

As the news began to sink in, O'Connor felt disappointed. She had said publicly she hoped a woman would take her place. First Lady Laura Bush had said so, too. But now, with Roberts taking her seat, O'Connor saw a court of eight men together well into the future. She was almost certain Bush wouldn't nominate a woman to replace Rehnquist as chief justice. "So that almost assures there won't be a woman appointed to the court at this time," she concluded.[3]

She was mystified, and not a little annoyed, that Bush would replace her with a man. She could think of a number of women judges she believed would have been fine justices. That Bush instead turned to a man suggested that the White House failed to appreciate the significance of more than one female voice on the bench. It wasn't that she thought women saw the law in a different way because of their gender. O'Connor never believed that. But women had different life experiences, to be sure, and that influenced their thinking. "There was not enough feeling that my replacement should be a woman," O'Connor said in an interview many months later. "I was very sad about that. I was so sad it didn't happen."

As the Court's first woman, O'Connor keenly felt she'd been a symbol, a role model for millions of young professional women over the years. "It did open doors for women on a scale never before seen in this country," O'Connor said. "I was very conscious of that. That's important for me." And while it was fine to be the first, she said, you don't want to be the last—especially when it was so hard to be first.

Looking back, O'Connor said, Reagan was right to seek out a woman for the job. People want to have trust and faith in government, she said, and having institutions that reflect the population matters. "It seems to me for women to see some women in these important public offices matters to the voter, to the citizens of our country," said O'Connor, slipping into the language of a legislator. "Women have different life experiences than men do. Everyone brings to a collegial institution like an appellate court a lifetime of experience and problems that help shape your views about how things should be."

Unlike Ginsburg, a longtime advocate for women's rights before becoming a judge, O'Connor was not an outspoken feminist. Growing up on the Lazy B ranch, she was treated like one of the boys, driving tractors and rounding cattle and changing flat tires. But her gender came to make a difference in the Court's cases, especially in those that involved women. Abortion was an obvious example. But even in cases that didn't directly involve women's issues, her questions in the Court's argument sessions sometimes focused on problems that the men didn't imagine. There is no better example than a routine case the justices heard in the late 1990s on the privacy rights of automobile passengers.[4]

The argument showcased O'Connor's empathy for the vulnerable and her visceral dislike of clear rules—the two characteristics that most prominently distinguished her from her more conservative male colleagues. The Court was supposed to decide whether the police could order a passenger out of the car after officers had pulled over the driver for a traffic violation. Police officers said they needed the authority for their own safety, since a passenger could be dangerous. But during arguments in the case, Maryland's attorney general, Joseph Curran, took a logical leap. He said the police should also be able to detain a passenger, suspected of no wrongdoing, right there on the roadway for ten or twenty minutes while the officer wrote out the driver's ticket. It would be only a "very diminished intrusion" into the passenger's privacy, Curran argued.

O'Connor looked as if she would bolt from her seat. "Well, not necessarily," she interjected sharply. "Suppose it's a driving snowstorm, or a blinding rainstorm, the passenger is a mother with a very young baby, and the officer automatically can order her out of the car, to put the baby down outside where he can see the baby and raise her hands up, and real damage can occur. And there is no reason that the car was stopped because of what the passenger was doing under the circumstances here."

Said Curran: "Yes, Justice O'Connor, I see the point you're trying to raise, and obviously the question of a baby and a young mother out in the rain is obviously not—"

O'Connor again stepped in. "That's just one example and you want an automatic rule."

"Yes, Your Honor," Curran said, "we do want the automatic rule, and I might add the same—"

O'Connor: "And it will work automatically, too."

"Yes," Curran said. But he didn't explain why that might be a good thing.

Scalia had sat quietly as Curran tried to make his case, but the lawyer's failure to make headway with O'Connor became too much.

During oral arguments, Scalia often jumped in to rescue a lawyer struggling to respond to a pointed question from a more liberal justice.
Souter often did the same thing whenever he saw a lawyer stymied by
a question from a conservative justice. Sometimes Scalia and Souter argued through the lawyer, using the advocate to make their own points.
"I think what he's trying to say," Scalia would begin, before he articulated his position. "Isn't it true you really mean this," Souter would
counter, making his own point.

After watching Curran struggle, Scalia leaned forward in his chair
and offered a better explanation. Rules are sometimes necessary so
everyone can see they're being treated the same way, regardless of their
race or sex, Scalia suggested, his voice patient, as if he were talking to a
student. "Because bureaucracies being what they are, in order to protect themselves from claims of discrimination—making some people
get out because of their race or because of whatever else—to be sure
that no such claims will be available, they will make everybody get out,"
Scalia said. "That will be an invariable rule."

Curran: "With respect, Justice Scalia, I appreciate the question."

But O'Connor was not persuaded. She'd thought of another scenario
where a clear rule would operate unfairly against the vulnerable. "Or
suppose the passenger has [a] certain dementia," she said. "It's an old
parent who, left to his own, will just wander away and not even understand what was being said to him, but automatically, you're going to get
this passenger out and require him to stay, and if he doesn't understand,
shoot him."

The courtroom erupted into laughter, but O'Connor was serious
when she continued. "You know, this can be carried to extremes, and
you seem to . . . don't even recognize that there might be a difference,"
she said.

The Court went along with O'Connor in that case, with Rehnquist
writing the majority decision, but it saved Curran's bigger point for
another day. In her long tenure on the Court, O'Connor had become a
limiting force in a number of different ways, worrying about extremes

and pulling back the justices in cases where they would be inclined to write more boldly. When she didn't join with the liberals, she sometimes forced conservatives away from sweeping decisions, especially on social issues conservatives care so much about. In the area of religion, she simply refused to join the four more conservative justices and adopt a clearer test for determining when the government had become too involved in public life. The four justices—Rehnquist, Scalia, Kennedy, and Thomas—had been moving toward a new way of looking at whether religious programs or activities violate the First Amendment's establishment clause, which says the government shall make "no law respecting an establishment of religion."

The division was clear in a case that asked whether the federal government could provide computer equipment for parochial and public schools.[5] A majority said yes, the religious schools could get the equipment. Rehnquist assigned Thomas the opinion. But O'Connor ultimately refused to join it, because Thomas had advanced a new standard to allow the programs if the government had treated the participants neutrally, regardless of whether they were religious or not. O'Connor wanted a more intricate, multistandard test for analyzing whether government had gone too far. She wrote a concurrence. Without her vote, Thomas had no majority, and the Court had no bold new standard for religion cases.

O'Connor changed in her twenty-four years on the Court, becoming more liberal than when she first joined as a reliable conservative, particularly on criminal-law issues and abortion. The shifting dynamics of the institution affected her and pushed her to the middle, with fellow centrist Kennedy. The two were moderates partly because both were pragmatic and approached each case on its own. Kennedy, like O'Connor, eschewed rigid rules. Months after O'Connor had left the Court for good, Kennedy said he found himself missing her. If Ginsburg was the lone woman, Kennedy had become the lone moderate, the justice who sided with conservatives sometimes and liberals others. "Jurisprudentially, I find it much more difficult," Kennedy said in an interview six months after O'Connor left the Court. "There were two of us that would frequently stake out a position, and now I have more writing to do."

O'Connor and Kennedy sometimes parted ways, typically when the cases involved discrimination or women's issues, O'Connor more often siding with the woman or the aggrieved. A sexual-harassment case in 1999 was especially dramatic.[6] The Court was deciding whether a school district could be held liable when one student sexually harassed another student. O'Connor thought the answer was yes, and the Court's four liberals joined her opinion.

Kennedy thought the lawsuit was frivolous, and he harshly criticized O'Connor's opinion in the case. "After today, Johnny will find that routine problems of adolescence are to be resolved by invoking a federal right to demand assignment to a desk two rows away," Kennedy said in dissent. But O'Connor was unusually direct when she summarized her opinion from the bench. To the conservative dissenters who said the ruling "would teach little Johnny a perverse lesson in federalism," O'Connor said the Court instead was assuring that "little Mary may attend class." Kennedy saw the case as one in which little Johnny pulls little Mary's pigtails and then the federal government intrudes in the classroom. But O'Connor saw it differently. To her, it was about discrimination and the harm of sexual harassment.

Beyond the real substantive differences a woman could make, O'Connor thought Bush should nominate another to replace her because having just one woman on the Court—in a country where women are half the population and half the nation's law school students—had the feel of tokenism. She found it hard to believe that the Court would go back to where it was when she joined it, with just one among the nine. She was the only woman for twelve years, until Ginsburg joined her in 1993. Ginsburg's entry onto the Court was far different from O'Connor's. She'd been a judge on the prestigious D.C.-based federal appeals court, as had Scalia and Thomas. She'd taught constitutional law and argued before the Supreme Court, advocating on behalf of women's rights. And with O'Connor on the bench, the spotlight on Ginsburg, the woman, was not as bright.

Ginsburg likes to tell a story about O'Connor's arrival in Washington that she says shows how much times had changed between 1981 and 1993, when President Clinton nominated her. It was O'Connor's first year on the Court, and she and her husband were attending an official black-tie dinner in the State Department's Benjamin Franklin Room. As the couple approached their assigned table, John O'Connor greeted one of the men already seated. "Hello, I'm John O'Connor." Then came this reply: "Oh, Justice O'Connor, I'm so happy to meet you. I've heard so many wonderful things about you."

O'Connor laughs when asked about the story. "That happened many times," she said. "People would come up and say how wonderful it was to meet a justice, and they'd shake John's hand. He'd laugh. He has a good sense of humor."

A decade later, when Ginsburg joined the Court, people didn't make that mistake. Ginsburg says her husband, Marty Ginsburg, has yet to be called Justice Ginsburg.

During that first year on the Court, Ginsburg often sought out O'Connor for advice, saying she was "like a big sister." The counsel began right away. After Ginsburg had been on the Court only a few weeks, she received her first opinion assignment and was completely taken aback by its complexity. As the new justice, she had expected an easy and uncontroversial one for a unanimous Court—as is the tradition when a justice first joins the Court. Instead, she ended up with a difficult case involving an intricate law about benefits for federal employees, a case on which the Court was sharply divided. How should she handle it? Ginsburg asked O'Connor.

"Just do it," O'Connor told Ginsburg, in her trademark blunt way. "And if you can, get your draft in circulation before the next set of assignments is made."

That was O'Connor's approach, as Ginsburg has put it. Waste no time on regrets or resentment. Get the job done. O'Connor ultimately dissented in the case, but she passed Ginsburg a note on the bench when she summarized her opinion. "This is your first opinion for the Court," O'Connor told Ginsburg in the note. "It is a fine one. I look forward to many more."

O'Connor meant it. Ginsburg's arrival came almost as a relief after all those years of being the only woman. And not just because the Court installed a women's bathroom in the robing room, where the justices don their robes before taking the bench. Before, there was only one large bathroom used by the men; O'Connor used the women's room down the hall that the chief justice's secretaries shared. "It made a huge difference when Justice Ginsburg came on. I was so glad to have company," O'Connor said. "Immediately, the media started treating us like fungible justices, not so much focused on a single woman. It made an immediate big difference."

But with Roberts's nomination, it appeared, Ginsburg, who'd spent her career as a lawyer battling for women's rights, would be alone.

Gender aside, Ginsburg, like O'Connor, thought highly of Roberts. Even before Bush nominated him to the D.C.-based federal appeals court, Ginsburg had privately told her colleagues she thought Roberts belonged on the federal bench. Beyond Roberts's obvious intellect and skillful advocacy, which she'd witnessed over the years, Ginsburg also had a personal impression. Her daughter Jane had known him in law school at Harvard in the late 1970s, when Roberts was managing editor of the *Harvard Law Review*. Jane Ginsburg, who was a class behind Roberts, thought he was scrupulously fair and impartial in giving out assignments. She had no idea what his political views were, she had told her mother. Ginsburg took that as an encouraging sign that the Bush appointee would not be ideological.

Despite O'Connor's statement of regret, Bush's decision to nominate a man to replace her stirred little controversy, because most assumed Ginsburg wouldn't be the lone female for long. After all, Bush could nominate a woman or minority the next time, after the ailing Rehnquist retired or died. O'Connor's conclusion that Bush wouldn't nominate a woman as chief justice was beside the point, they thought. Bush could move Roberts or Scalia into Rehnquist's old seat and then tap a woman or minority to take his place. Senator Arlen Specter, the Pennsylvania Republican and chairman of the Judiciary Committee, even urged Bush to ask O'Connor to come back and serve as the nation's first female chief justice when Rehnquist finally left the Court.

With a second nomination on the horizon providing another opportunity for a woman to join the Court, the talk quickly moved on. The morning after Roberts's nomination, when he met Bush for coffee in the White House, the focus was already on other contrasts between O'Connor and Roberts. The differences were stark. A conservative like Roberts could turn the Court in an entirely new direction in areas where O'Connor had cast the deciding vote and determined national policy, including on the biggest blockbuster issue of them all: abortion.

By the time he reached Capitol Hill that afternoon to begin meeting with senators, Roberts's position on *Roe v. Wade* had become the central question in his nomination. The landmark decision that is both a rallying cry and a dividing line, that is passionately viewed as either a key protector of women's rights or a lawless exercise in judicial overreaching, that has reshaped the nation's political parties and has been a core issue in everything from school board elections to presidential contests, that has become the ultimate touchstone in the ongoing conflict over culture and values throughout America, has for more than two decades consumed Supreme Court nominations and confirmation proceedings.

Although abortion involves a fraction of a justice's time once he or she is on the Court, it takes on outsized importance among presidential advisers, senators, and interest groups trying to discern whether a nominee is on their side. It's also become a ready code for the kind of justice a person would be: The nominee's position on abortion becomes almost a marker of his or her liberalism or conservatism, indicating the way he or she views the role of a judge and the proper approach to the law.

The issue of abortion had sparked controversy over O'Connor's nomination in 1981, but not from the women's groups sounding alarms about Roberts. In O'Connor's case, antiabortion groups rightly suspected she would not be willing to overturn *Roe*. As rumors spread through Washington that Reagan planned to nominate her, angry antiabortion and religious groups flooded the White House with telephone calls. They believed she had supported abortion rights as an Arizona state legislator, and they threatened a nasty political protest against Reagan. Senate Republicans like Don Nickles of Oklahoma, Steve Symms of Idaho, and Jesse Helms of North Carolina also weighed in with calls to the White House against her. Nickles told the White House that he and "other profamily Republican senators w[ould] not support" O'Connor if Reagan nominated her.

For religious conservatives, the Supreme Court had become a battleground, and abortion was its defining war. O'Connor's nomination was the first to galvanize the movement, since John Paul Stevens's nomination had come only two years after *Roe,* before there was widespread organized opposition to the decision. Reagan's White House advisers grasped the sea change. "O'Connor aside, and turning more generally to the nomination, it is important to bear in mind the special significance that right-to-lifers attach to Supreme Court nominations," White House adviser Mike Uhlmann told Ed Meese in a July 6, 1981, memo, the day before Reagan announced her nomination. "The federal judiciary in general, and the High Court in particular, have in their view been engaged in a systematic effort to prevent the public from working its will on the subject of abortion."

But the religious conservatives had not yet become a prominent political force, and Reagan ignored the opposition to O'Connor. He liked her personally, and he thought she was the best woman for the job. And he wanted to nominate a woman, putting aside other names, including conservative luminary Robert Bork. Reagan didn't know O'Connor's views on abortion. Like subsequent nominees, she refused to telegraph them, although memos and notes taken by Reagan advisers at the time show she was careful not to leave the impression that she supported abortion rights. She told Reagan she was personally opposed to the procedure, and that she couldn't remember whether, as a state legislator in the days before *Roe v. Wade,* she'd voted to repeal Arizona's law banning abortion. The firmly prolife Reagan was comfortable with that.

Roe and the issue of abortion became more prominent in the later Reagan years, when the administration began urging the Supreme Court to overturn the decision. Groups on both sides of the issue organized to fight. Robert Bork's confirmation hearings, when he effectively killed his nomination by articulating narrow views on the right to privacy, pushed the issue to the forefront. Nominees since Bork have been closely questioned about *Roe,* but have disclosed little.

Senators have focused so closely on nominees' views about privacy because that's what Justice Harry Blackmun, in his majority opinion in *Roe v. Wade,* said provided the constitutional foundation for the right to an abortion.

The constitutional right to privacy, Blackmun said, is "broad enough to encompass a woman's decision whether or not to terminate her pregnancy." He acknowledged that the Constitution "does not explicitly mention any right of privacy" but said the Court has recognized such a right "does exist under the Constitution."

The Supreme Court relied on a constitutional right to privacy in 1965 when it ruled that states could not punish married couples who used contraceptives. In 1972, it again relied on a privacy rationale to strike down state restrictions on distributing or selling contraceptives to single adults. But the Court in *Roe* dramatically extended those rulings. It held that states must have a compelling reason for restricting abortion.

The Court has abandoned Blackmun's trimester analysis in the years since *Roe.* But with O'Connor's critical vote, it has firmly protected the basic right to an abortion, striking down laws that regulate the type of procedure or impose any "undue burden" on a woman's ability to get an abortion. It has allowed only a few state laws restricting abortion, including those that require providers to give women specific information about the procedure, instruct minors to get consent from their parents or a judge, and impose waiting periods.

With the Court so closely divided on the issue, every Supreme Court nomination becomes mired in it as well. Presidents and senators and special interests groups have poured their energies into discerning how a nominee will vote on the issue. They have often guessed wrong. O'Connor put aside her personal feelings about abortion and refused to overturn *Roe* when the Court had the chance in 1992, in *Planned Parenthood of Southeastern Pennsylvania v. Casey*. Kennedy, Reagan's final Supreme Court appointee, who was believed to be a prolife Catholic, joined her, surprising administration lawyers who believed he was a likely vote to overturn *Roe*. On the flip side, abortion rights groups opposed David Souter's nomination in 1990 and printed red-and-white flyers that loudly shouted: STOP SOUTER OR WOMEN WILL DIE. Two years later, in *Casey*, Souter went with O'Connor and Kennedy to uphold *Roe*.

O'Connor supported abortion rights more strongly than her fellow moderate Kennedy did, as her vote in a 2000 case striking down state restrictions on so-called partial-birth abortions made clear.[7] Kennedy would have allowed the restrictions. As a result, O'Connor departed the Court after twenty-four years much as she had joined it: surrounded by talk about the future of *Roe v. Wade* and abortion rights.

In searching for her replacement, lawyers in the White House and Justice Department knew a nominee couldn't be too hot on the explosive issue or too cold. Outspoken opposition to abortion doomed the chances of one of the conservatives' favorite nominees, Judge Edith Jones, of the New Orleans–based federal appeals court. Jones had come close to the nomination in 1990, but George H. W. Bush picked Souter instead, a choice widely viewed by conservatives as one of the most inept decisions by a Republican president in the twentieth century.

In the years since she was passed over, Jones began to write more critically about *Roe*. In a 2004 opinion, she put her cards on the table, calling *Roe* an "exercise in raw judicial power" and one that she "fervently" hopes the Supreme Court will reevaluate.[8] Jones wrote about the "long term emotional damage" abortion inflicts on women and how, even in the early stages of pregnancy, it can cause a fetus excruciating pain. The Supreme Court, she suggested flatly, had no business getting involved in the abortion issue. "[T]he perverse result of the Court's having determined through constitutional adjudication this fundamental social policy, which affects over a million women and unborn babies each year, is that the facts no longer matter."

That kind of ardent opposition would make nominees like Jones almost impossible to confirm without changing the rules of the Senate. Although journalists always featured her prominently among the contenders to replace O'Connor, Jones, in fact, never made it onto George W. Bush's short list. The White House believed moderate Republicans would have opposed her, just as they did Robert Bork.

Jones's experience shows that abortion, for such a controversial and divisive issue, can produce a remarkably lopsided debate during the confirmation process. Republican nominees walk a minefield, knowing vocal opposition to *Roe*, or even criticism of it, could doom their chances. But Democratic nominees are assumed to support the abortion right and have been easily confirmed.

Other prospective nominees to replace O'Connor weren't seen as predictable enough on abortion to satisfy the social conservatives who had become, over the years since O'Connor joined the Court, an important political constituency. Although liberals criticize Attorney General Alberto Gonzales for his position in crafting the administration's policies in the war on terror, conservatives opposed his Supreme Court nomination because they thought he would be sure to uphold *Roe v. Wade*. Before he moved to Washington to become President Bush's White House counsel, Gonzales's opinion in an abortion case in 2000 while serving on the Texas Supreme Court motivated conservative opponents to mount a wide-ranging and long-lasting campaign against him.[9]

The case asked whether a teenage girl could get an abortion without her parents' consent. Texas law allowed teenagers to bypass their parents and go to a judge for permission to get the procedure in certain circumstances. The girl in the case, a high school senior who lived at home, said she was afraid of her parents' reaction, and she insisted she was mature enough to make the decision. A trial judge disagreed, but the Texas Supreme Court—with Gonzales on board—reversed. The case produced strong dissents, including one by Priscilla Owen, President Bush's subsequent nominee to the federal appeals court. Owen insisted the justices were overreaching. Gonzales called that position an "unconscionable act of judicial activism" and clearly not what the Texas legislature intended when it passed the law.

On the issue of abortion, the White House concluded Roberts was just right. He'd left plenty of clues he opposed abortion and, unlike O'Connor, would allow more state regulation of the procedure—perhaps even to the point of allowing states to ban it almost entirely. As a lawyer in the Bush senior administration, he'd signed a legal brief urging the Court to overturn it, but he had not gone on the record with his personal views about *Roe*. It would be a difficult position for moderate senators to oppose.

If the Court overturned *Roe*, the issue of abortion would return to the states. The state legislature in Alabama, reflecting the views of its voters, might choose to ban abortion completely. The state legislature in New York or California might decide to permit it. That was the scenario before the Court stepped in in 1973 and declared a woman had a constitutional right to the procedure and that states could not ban it. Pre-*Roe*, some states allowed it, and others were moving in that direction. Some banned it outright.

When Roberts discussed his views on the role of a judge, he sounded like someone who thought the Court was wrong to take up the issue of abortion in the first place. Roberts had not come to those views recently. Starting in his mid-twenties, Roberts worked as a lawyer in the Reagan administration and frequently criticized judges for taking on issues that he thought should've been left for legislatures, which he believed were best equipped to make policy decisions. Courts, he said, shouldn't be the first place people look to solve social problems. In numerous memos, he often wrote that courts—including the Supreme Court—should be more restrained. Several of his memos implied that he thought that was true on the issue of abortion, too.

Later, when he was a practicing lawyer, Roberts had also said he believed courts shouldn't "have too narrow a view" about protecting constitutional rights. He said courts should not forget about the important right of the people to participate in moral debates over life-or-death choices. Roberts was discussing a 1997 Supreme Court decision that had rejected a constitutional "right to die." He told PBS's Margaret Warner, in an interview on the *NewsHour with Jim Lehrer,* that courts should also respect "the right of the people through their legislatures to articulate their own views on the policies that should apply in those cases of terminating life and not to have the court interfering in those policy decisions."[10]

That sounds almost exactly like a conservative critique of *Roe.* But regardless of Roberts's views on *Roe,* White House lawyers were confident Roberts's overall approach to the law would not have permitted him to sign on to a decision like *Casey,* with its flabby reasoning and grandiose language about the mysteries of life.

The basic right to an abortion seemed secure when Roberts was nominated. Only three justices on the Court would vote to overturn the landmark decision—Rehnquist, Scalia, and Thomas. Even if Roberts agreed, the Court was still one vote short. But Roberts could still have an enormous impact on a woman's right to an abortion. Kennedy had been willing to allow some restrictions, as his bitter dissent in the 2000 partial-birth abortion case made clear. As a result, Roberts, in taking O'Connor's place, could provide the fifth vote for conservatives on cases like the one involving the partial-birth procedure.

Roberts began his career in the Reagan administration, ironically enough, helping O'Connor get ready for her own confirmation hearing. He and other lawyers in the Justice Department went over legal issues with her and anticipated possible questions from the senators. Lawyers also wrote out prepared talking points for O'Connor to use in explaining her judicial philosophy to the senators. In those statements, O'Connor sounded like a principled devotee of judicial restraint. In fact, she sounded an awful lot like a young John Roberts. In one set of talking points the lawyers prepared for O'Connor, she was to stress that she believed strongly in judicial restraint "and will not substitute my beliefs as to a desirable public policy for the judgment of the political branches of government." She would say a "judge should interpret the law, not make it," and she vowed to "recognize the importance of limited government generally and of the institutional restraints upon the judiciary in particular."

Those views mirrored Roberts's own strongly held beliefs. He put them into practice, spending his time in government arguing for policies that would yield a more limited role for the courts. In his early days in the administration, Roberts spent a good deal of time on the debate over legislation by Republicans in Congress that would have stripped the Supreme Court of its power to decide cases involving abortion, busing, and school prayer. Then–assistant attorney general Theodore Olson had taken the position that the bills were unconstitutional. In an April 1982 memo, Olson had written Attorney General William French Smith that the administration would get high marks for opposing the bills and that its stance would "be perceived as a courageous and highly principled position, especially in the press."

On his copy of that memo, Roberts underlined "especially in the press," and he wrote "NO!" in the margin. He then wrote: "Real courage would be to read the Constitution as it should be read and not kowtow to the Tribes, Lewises and Brinks!" Roberts was referring to liberal Harvard law professor Laurence Tribe, *New York Times* columnist Anthony Lewis, and the then–American Bar Association president David Brink. The three had opposed the bills. Roberts thought the legislation was bad policy, but he strongly disagreed with their position—and Olson's legal analysis.

His other handwritten remarks on the margins of that memo proved prescient about the future direction of the Supreme Court. Olson had written that the legislation was unnecessary because the Court had more justices appointed by Republican presidents than it had in the 1960s, when the Court issued sweeping decisions on prayer, busing, and privacy. But Roberts didn't share Olson's optimism. He underlined the name of one of the Republican appointees, Justice Harry Blackmun, who'd crafted *Roe* just three years after President Nixon put him on the Supreme Court. Roberts then drew an arrow from Blackmun's name to the word "abortion."

Some of Roberts's language in other memos is sarcastic, almost snarky, which came as a surprise to people who'd seen him as a congenial, easygoing guy. Before the memos were publicly released, the White House sent a team of lawyers to the Reagan Library in Simi Valley, California, to review them, and they made frequent hurried calls back to Washington whenever they unearthed possibly damaging ones. Miers was particularly displeased by some of his language. She didn't like his pointed, sometimes pointless, criticism.

The administration worried about one memo in particular. While working in the Reagan White House, Roberts leveled harsh criticism at three Republican congresswomen for supporting a proposal to pay women their "comparable worth" to men in similar jobs. The comparable-worth theory was not that women be paid the same as men for doing the same job. It went much further, asking that women be paid the same if they did a comparable job—if the woman was a domestic worker, for example, and the man drove a truck. Roberts wrote that it was "difficult to exaggerate the perniciousness of the comparable worth theory." But his next memo to his boss, White House counsel Fred Fielding, was the real problem: "I honestly find it troubling that three Republican representatives are so quick to embrace such a radi-

cal redistributive concept." He said the three may as well adopt the
Marxist-like slogan "From each according to his ability, to each according to her gender."

One of those Republican representatives was Olympia Snowe of
Maine. She had since become moderate senator Olympia Snowe, and
her vote was considered critical to getting Roberts confirmed. The Republicans could not afford to lose Republican votes and embolden Democrats to rise up in opposition, and Snowe ultimately announced
her support.

But the memos revealed a side of Roberts most people hadn't seen,
especially the journalists who had concluded he was a moderate, since
he patiently returned their calls and explained the law and spoke in such
a reasonable tone. Many journalists had concluded that the super-
smart, supernice Roberts couldn't really be that conservative. It was a
concern some conservatives also shared, since Roberts always kept his
views to himself. But the White House believed John Roberts was no
moderate. "Are you ready for Armageddon?" Miers asked Boyden Gray
several days before Bush nominated Roberts.

If Bush had been looking for the anti-O'Connor, he could hardly
have done better. Roberts was different from O'Connor in almost every
way, and he had little patience for her approach to the law, which he saw
as undisciplined, almost to the point that it bordered on irresponsible.
O'Connor had become the most powerful woman in America, conservatives like Roberts believed, precisely because she lacked a defined
philosophy for interpreting the Constitution or deciding cases. The justices under Rehnquist's leadership were in constant struggle over which
of their competing legal theories was the right one. But O'Connor stood
alone. She took a pragmatic approach, focusing on the facts and merits of each case. She was hard to predict, and lawyers often talked about
how their cases came down to whether O'Connor would be on their
side. In some cases, lawyers crafted their arguments specifically for her,
knowing that if they managed to get her vote, they'd win the case. Con-

servatives complained that she'd become powerful because she didn't have a jurisprudence of her own. Her vote was always up for grabs.

That was not how John Roberts thought a Supreme Court justice should be. Roberts thought the focus should be on the law, not the individual judge or justice. It was like in a baseball game. Fans shouldn't leave the game talking about how great the umpire was or how impressively he'd defined the strike zone on that particular day. They should be talking about the players and the game itself. The Supreme Court was the same. It was about the cases and the law, not how an individual justice could call the outcome. In Roberts's view, a justice needed a consistent philosophy the same way an umpire had to have a consistent strike zone. Without it, judges could become too powerful and take over the game.

Unlike O'Connor, Roberts liked easy-to-apply rules and clear guidelines. He frequently was called a "lawyer's lawyer," and his work as a government attorney and in private practice at a law firm had taught him about the costs of uncertainty. If courts aren't clear, litigants aren't sure how to respond down the road. He thought the justices had a responsibility to decide cases in a way that would give guidance to lower courts and litigants in the future.

But a clear and consistent philosophy wasn't enough. A judge also required the self-control to stick to it, no matter the outcome of a particular case. Roberts, a man so disciplined that he could keep his views to himself for more than a decade—even when sharing steaks with like-minded conservative acquaintances—had both. If confirmed to replace O'Connor, he would move the Court away from the course she had often set. He saw the law differently, and he saw his role as a judge differently.

From the beginning, the groups that typically opposed Republican nominees had worried that Bush would tap Roberts for the Court. They believed that Roberts, of all the nominees on the short list, would be hardest for them to defeat. For one thing, he lacked a visible conservative record. He had friends on both sides of the spectrum. He cultivated relationships with journalists. He was smooth and smart. He also happened to be incredibly well qualified for the job. The Supreme Court's law clerks vote every year on which lawyer has the best oral argument of the term. Roberts won the contest often.

But leading opponents Nan Aron, of the Alliance for Justice, and Ralph Neas, of People for the American Way, knew Roberts was a solid conservative. These highly networked, persuasive advocates just couldn't convince anyone. That first week after Roberts was nominated for the critical O'Connor seat, Neas considered it an enormous victory when he, Aron, and others were able to keep a single Senate Democrat from announcing support.

The memos, in which Roberts emerged as a forceful defender of Reagan's policies on key social issues from abortion to school prayer, gave them something to point to. But they were written so long ago that they barely caused a bump, even as Roberts met with senators and responded to their questions throughout August. As an appellate lawyer and now a federal judge, Roberts handled the Senate visits with ease. He had been immersed in constitutional concepts his entire legal career. As a lawyer, he'd spoken on public panels and frequently helped journalists decipher Supreme Court decisions. He was accustomed to translating complex legal terms into language nonlawyers could understand, and those skills paid off in his Senate visits.

The issue of abortion came to dominate Roberts's private meetings with senators. In almost every session, with senators on both sides, the key question was about his views on abortion. Some of the senators were blunt in expressing their deeply held convictions on the abortion issue and their concerns about whether to vote for Roberts.

"This vote is the only reason I'm here," Senator Tom Coburn of Oklahoma told Roberts during their meeting. "And I couldn't vote for someone who would uphold *Roe*."

Most of the senators knew he couldn't answer how he would decide a legal challenge to *Roe* or any other case that might come before the

Court. So instead they asked for his views on stare decisis, a Latin phrase for "let the decision stand." Principles of stare decisis guide courts when weighing whether to overturn precedents.

Like nominees before him, Roberts was discreet in those private sessions, and people on both sides of the issue took comfort in his responses. He told senators he valued judicial restraint. He stressed the values of "modesty" in a judge. He emphasized that he believed *Roe* was settled law, but added that it was subject to the legal principle of stare decisis—a response that told senators nothing. To suggest *Roe* is settled, subject to principles of stare decisis, means only that *Roe* is settled law so long as the Supreme Court says so.

Supporters of abortion rights, such as Specter, interpreted Roberts's remarks to mean he saw his role as a limited one. A restrained and modest judge, they believed, would surely not wreak massive social disruption by boldly reaching out to overturn landmarks like *Roe*. But abortion opponents, who see *Roe* as a decidedly immodest judicial ruling, also took heart. A restrained and modest judge would surely correct the most lawless decision in modern Court history, without worrying about the consequences. In fact, the less bold approach, as they saw it, would be to toss out *Roe* because it didn't square with the cases before it. The less bold approach would be to look back to those old cases and correct the Court's error with *Roe*.

Roberts's ability to walk those lines set him on a course for confirmation, even as word was trickling out from all quarters that he really was conservative. Judge Harry Edwards, a liberal colleague of Roberts's on the D.C.-based federal appeals court, encouraged conservatives and scared liberals when he privately said Roberts was the "most conservative judge he'd ever seen." And Edwards had served with Scalia and Thomas. As he met with the senators, Roberts also went through grueling sessions at the Justice Department with administration lawyers and others who'd once served in the White House and now were working in law firms, were professors at law schools, or were in corporate America. They pretended to be senators on the Judiciary Committee, and they grilled him for hours about his views on different cases and areas of the law. Each lawyer was responsible for a specific area, such as abortion or civil rights or presidential power. Roberts welcomed those sessions because that's how he knew to prepare for arguments in the Supreme Court. He also studied other confirmation hearings to see how different nominees deflected questions about specific cases. When he'd prepared for his confirmation hearing to be a federal appeals court judge, he'd carefully studied Justice Ginsburg's approach with the senators. He ended up quoting her at his own confirmation hearings whenever senators persisted in pressing for his views on specific cases.

Roberts had spent his career thinking about the big-picture legal issues and analyzing them as a practicing appellate lawyer. But he also knew he could afford no mistakes. He worried that one answer, one ten-second response to one question over the course of fifteen hours of questioning, could doom his chances. Administration lawyers who were working to prepare him wanted him to eschew short, simple answers—the kind of responses he'd given Cheney and the group of advisers back in May—and instead use his allotted time to explain different legal concepts, almost as a law professor would to his students. That was different from his experience arguing cases in the Supreme Court, when the justices fired questions at him with dizzying speed. During an argument, Roberts would barely finish one question when another was hurled his way. "Think of the clock as your friend," Kelley urged him at one point. "The more time you take, the less time they have."

Another difference in the Senate hearing was that he could draw lines wherever he chose. As a lawyer arguing before the Supreme Court, he'd been constrained by the law and precedent, but he didn't have those boundaries before the Judiciary Committee. He could draw his own lines. He could tell senators which of the cases he would discuss and which ones he wouldn't.

Roberts's preparation with White House lawyers included carefully crafting responses, down to the precise words, to expected questions. And they expected multiple ones about *Roe* and the right to privacy. In

his 2003 hearings for the federal appeals court, Roberts said that he believed "*Roe* is the settled law of the land" and that "there is nothing in
my personal views that would prevent me from fully and faithfully applying the precedent, as well as *Casey*." But that answer wouldn't work
in his confirmation hearings for the Supreme Court. As an appellate
court judge, he was required to follow Supreme Court rulings and respect the decisions as binding precedent. As a justice, Roberts would be
in a position to reevaluate *Roe*. In his hearings, as in his private interviews with senators, he had to walk a careful line. If he told senators he
believed it was settled, he would be signaling that he would vote to uphold it once on the Supreme Court. "*Roe* is settled law," he said, "subject to principles of stare decisis." That sounded comforting to everyone.

After weeks of meetings and study and mock sessions, Roberts and
the administration lawyers felt confident he was ready for the intensity
of the first Supreme Court hearing in eleven years. The week before it
was set to begin, he'd endured a daylong, twelve-hour practice session
designed to mirror the intensity of the real thing. It appeared he was
poised for confirmation.

Roberts continued to work that Saturday to prepare for the hearings
now three days away, and he went to bed early that evening. His wife,
Jane, stayed up later and was watching the news on television when a
bulletin announced that Rehnquist had died that evening in his northern Virginia home. She woke Roberts and told him, and the two
watched the coverage on television. Now Bush would have two vacancies to fill, on a Court that hadn't seen one in eleven years. And unlike
his father, he had a commanding majority in the Senate.

10.

"TRUST ME"

William H. Rehnquist died at one of the lowest moments of George W. Bush's presidency. Just five days before, on August 29, Hurricane Katrina devastated New Orleans and destroyed the Mississippi Gulf Coast, killing nearly two thousand people and displacing hundreds of thousands more. Katrina's thirty-five-foot storm surge obliterated the entire region, sweeping away city halls, communities, and cultures that had survived a civil war and countless hurricanes.

The federal government's failure to respond during those first critical days, while televised images from New Orleans showed tens of thousands of people pleading for food and water, proved to be a devastating political blow to George W. Bush. As the floodwaters rose and state and local officials floundered, neither Bush nor his administration seemed to grasp the scope of the disaster or the degree of human anguish. The administration's disaster-management team—led by Michael Chertoff at Homeland Security and Michael Brown at the

Federal Emergency Management Agency—came under outraged attack by Democrats and Republicans alike.

Bush had visited the Gulf Coast on Friday, four days after the storm laid the area bare. In a news conference in Mobile, Alabama, he hit all the wrong notes. He envisioned sitting on Senator Trent Lott's front porch after the Mississippi senator had rebuilt a "fantastic house" from the rubble of his Gulf Coast mansion. And he looked over to his FEMA director and praised the overmatched bureaucrat: "Brownie, you're doing a heck of a job."

The next day, William Rehnquist was dead. But when it came to replacing the legendary chief justice, Bush did not hesitate. Bush called Roberts at home Sunday morning and asked him to meet with him that afternoon in the White House. Roberts didn't know it, but the president had already all but made up his mind.

It wasn't a hasty decision. Since Bush nominated him to take O'Connor's place back in July, Roberts had been his own best advocate for the chief justice position without ever saying a word about it. For six weeks, Roberts had endured a firestorm. Senators grilled him on his views in private meetings. Liberal public-interest groups pored over his record. Journalists interviewed friends and family and old classmates. With his hearings for the Supreme Court's most critical seat now days away, Roberts hadn't morphed into a scary caricature, the way Robert Bork did after Democrats redefined him. Instead, Roberts looked pretty much like the man Bush had nominated: a brilliant, ambitious conservative who'd lived a scandal-free life, made liberal friends, and had no apparent enemies. Had Rehnquist retired before O'Connor at the end of June, when everyone expected him to, Bush's decision to tap Roberts out of a select group of lower-court judges would not have been so clear. But the six weeks he'd been a nominee had enhanced Roberts's stature. After confidently meeting with senators and adeptly articulating the law, he seemed bigger than an appeals court judge with two years' experience on the bench. He had the sheen of a chief executive.

He had demonstrated a keen ability to read people and navigate sometimes contentious conversations without irritating or offending. Those
were the kinds of interpersonal skills that would help him manage the
Court's eight competing personalities, with all their wildly different
views. Although the chief justice has just one vote, he is considered the
"first among equals" and has significant power to help shape the direction of the Court. He assigns opinions when he's in the majority, so
he can help define how broadly or narrowly an opinion is written, depending on which justice he asks to write it. That involves making judgments on which justice can best articulate the position for the majority.
Guessing wrong can sometimes cause a majority to crumble. When a
justice is too bold, he can drive away others. Roberts was savvy enough
to make those judgments and smart enough to walk in commanding
immediate respect from the elder justices.

"How do you feel about being chief justice?" Bush asked Roberts
during their private meeting Sunday afternoon in the White House residence.

Roberts responded in a self-deferential way. "I haven't thought
about it."

"Well, you'd better start," Bush said.

In selecting someone outside the Supreme Court to come in and
lead it, Bush took a well-worn path. Reagan plucked Rehnquist from the
ranks of the associates to be chief justice—and never really considered
anyone else for the job—but presidents typically have looked outside
the Court. Rehnquist was the nation's sixteenth chief, but only the third
associate justice to be elevated in the Court's history. When he disclosed his illness in late October of 2004, many conservatives began a
steady chorus of support for Justice Scalia, urging Bush to follow Reagan's lead and elevate him to take Rehnquist's place. They believed
Scalia deserved the title after twenty years of battling against what he
called "idiotic" liberal approaches to the Constitution.

But the White House realized that elevating a sitting justice like

Scalia or Thomas raised problems. It would mean an additional confirmation hearing, since the Senate would have to confirm both the
chief justice and the new justice who would be taking his place. Administration officials didn't relish the thought of hearings on either
Justice Thomas or Justice Scalia, both of whom they feared would come
under personal attack. They also believed it would be difficult for
the Court, as a group, to welcome a new boss who'd been an equal
for so long.

Bush's advisers also thought the sixty-nine-year-old Scalia was too
old. His moment had passed. He would serve as chief for eight or ten
years, presumably, which meant they ran the risk that a Democrat
would be in the White House and positioned to name his successor.
Bush would not want to take that chance. At fifty, Roberts would lead
the Court for three decades if he lived as long as Rehnquist.

Scalia understood that. He had been ambivalent about the prospect
of becoming chief justice from the beginning, telling close friends he
didn't expect it because of his age. But he found himself feeling surprisingly disappointed when it became evident he wouldn't get the
chance. It would've been nice if the White House had at least asked.
Thomas had gotten a phone call from the White House in the fall to
gauge his interest in the job. Thomas said he had none because he didn't
want to go through another confirmation battle or take on the administrative hassles that come with running a third branch of government.
But no one ever asked Scalia.

Justice Kennedy did not share Scalia's ambivalence or Thomas's ret-
icence. He wanted the title and was widely believed to have been on a
campaign to get it, dating back to a 2002 "Dialogue on Freedom" initiative with Laura Bush and the American Bar Association. Kennedy re-
cruited the first lady to participate with him in the initiative, which
involved a series of conversations with high school students about freedom and democracy. In the years that followed, he kept a high profile
in Washington and spoke often about the Court and the nation's future,
even enlisting former law clerks to call the White House and lobby for

their former boss—as other prospective picks also were doing. But Kennedy was the justice conservatives had come to despise, a view many on Bush's legal staff happened to share. No one in the administration considered it. Chief Justice Kennedy was not an option.

The White House focused its attention outside the Court. Immediately after Bush was sworn in, his staff began putting together a list of potential nominees and conducting extensive background research on them. Officials believed Rehnquist was likely to retire in the summer of 2001, and they were determined to be ready. Each young lawyer in the White House counsel's office, most of whom had clerked on the Supreme Court, was assigned a candidate and made responsible for writing a lengthy report about him or her. In the late spring, then–White House counsel Alberto Gonzales and his deputy Tim Flanigan began secretly interviewing some of those possible replacements.

The advance work was designed to ensure that George W. Bush would be prepared when a justice stepped down. His White House would not make the mistake of his father's administration, which was caught off guard by the retirement of the aging William Brennan in 1990 and in its haste recommended David Souter to replace the liberal icon. Bush's advisers were struck by how deeply his father's nomination of Souter "seared him," as one put it, and made him even more determined to make the right call on the Supreme Court. The early in-depth research and interviews with prospective nominees were important in ensuring Bush would have coolheaded advice, removed from any external political pressure to select a particular nominee in the hours after a retirement.

That wasn't the case in 1990, when White House lawyers had assumed Ken Starr would be the elder Bush's pick, and they didn't take seriously any other replacements until Starr was ruled out. By that time, Souter had emerged as the favored candidate of chief of staff John Sununu, and the White House lawyers were scrambling to reread and process Souter's opinions, conscious of the growing momentum for his nomination. Knowing Souter was a favorite candidate made it easier to believe he was also the right one. It was a terrible miscalculation that the younger Bush was determined not to repeat. His staff would be ready.

Beginning in 2001, the Rehnquist retirement watch became an annual ritual. Every June, as the end of the Court's term approached, the White House anxiously waited for Rehnquist to announce he was stepping down. Gonzales and deputies Flanigan and David Leitch had continued to interview prospective nominees in 2002 and 2003, when the White House thought Rehnquist surely would retire. Administration officials were confident Rehnquist wouldn't want to gamble on Bush losing the 2004 presidential election to Massachusetts senator John Kerry, and they knew justices don't like to retire during the political circus of an election year. Rehnquist shocked—and angered—White House lawyers and many anxious conservatives when he instead opted to gamble on a Bush victory in 2004 and remain on the Court.

By staying on the bench, Rehnquist altered the course of history. There's no question Roberts would not have been nominated for chief justice if Rehnquist had retired, as expected, before the 2004 election. Roberts wasn't in the right place. It's often said that getting nominated to the Supreme Court is like getting struck by lightning, and that even if you've managed to get with a group of people crowded together under a tree during a thunderstorm, you still never know when or where the bolt will hit. Before 2004, Roberts wasn't even with the group under the tree, waiting for the lightning to strike. He wasn't confirmed to the federal appeals court until 2003, and Bush wouldn't have nominated a lawyer in a private law firm to be chief justice of the United States. In those years, J. Harvie Wilkinson or J. Michael Luttig, colleagues and rivals on the Richmond-based federal appeals court, were the most likely prospects to replace Rehnquist. Also a possibility was federal appeals court judge Samuel Alito, who had made the trip to Washington from his chambers in New Jersey to interview with Gonzales and Flanigan.

But the composition of the Senate in those years made the gracious and courtly Wilkinson the most likely contender—even though the more combative Luttig had a strong defender in his old friend Flanigan. Without a solid majority in the Senate, Bush would've been hard pressed to nominate someone as controversial as Luttig. The Senate was divided fifty-fifty when Bush was first elected. Republicans controlled, but only because the vice president casts any tie-breaking votes. They lost power to Democrats in May 2001, after Senator James Jeffords of Vermont defected from the Republican Party to become an independent. But that calculus changed as years passed. Republicans regained a bare majority in the 2002 elections, and solidified it two years later. Now with Republicans comfortably controlling the Senate with fifty-five votes, Bush could afford to nominate someone younger and more conservative than Wilkinson.

Roberts was both. By the time Rehnquist died in 2005, he was also sailing toward confirmation for the all-important O'Connor seat—a prize that Democrats and liberal public-interest groups had spent millions to keep away from a rock-solid conservative like Roberts. Bush knew that Roberts would be a sure bet as chief justice. Ideologically, he was closer to Rehnquist than to O'Connor. Kelley and others believed he would actually be both more effective and more conservative than the old chief. He was more interested in reaching out to the other justices and more attentive to the law and the reasoning than was Rehnquist. It was fortuitous. Because as it was, with the administration's failures on the Katrina disaster, Rehnquist's death came at a time in Bush's presidency when he could ill afford to gamble on anyone else.

Roberts arrived at the White House early Monday morning for another televised announcement with Bush. But this one did not have the drama or the pomp of the first, on July 19, when Bush revealed his decision in a prime-time announcement carried live by all three television networks. The mood was different. Bush was grappling with a disaster unlike any in the nation's history, a cataclysmic storm matched only by the catastrophic failures in leadership at every level of government. People died of neglect after they followed instructions to ride out the storm in New Orleans' Superdome, and anarchy reigned on the city's streets. It also was less than forty-eight hours after Rehnquist's death, and his funeral arrangements hadn't yet been made.

Roberts stood solemnly by the president's side as Bush told the nation that he had "earned the nation's confidence" in the past two months. Senators and the American people had learned about Roberts's career and his character. "They like what they see," Bush said.

Bush left Washington immediately after the announcement to fly back to the Gulf Coast for his second tour of the shattered region. He called O'Connor from Air Force One to tell her he was nominating Roberts to be chief justice, which meant he had to find another nominee to take her place. There wouldn't be time to confirm her successor before the term started in four weeks. She would have to get ready to return to the bench, Bush said.

"Well, I guess I'd better get back to my homework then," said O'Connor.

For Roberts, the sequence of events seemed almost too unreal to believe. Later that afternoon, Rehnquist's children asked him to serve as a pallbearer in their father's funeral. The next day, when his confirmation hearings to replace O'Connor would have been under way in the Capitol, Roberts stood beside Rehnquist's coffin outside the Supreme Court. Six of the justices were standing on the steps of the Court. O'Connor wiped away tears as she watched them carry the simple unvarnished wooden coffin past them and into the great marble building that had defined Rehnquist's life. The pallbearers placed the coffin in the center of the Supreme Court's Great Hall, then joined scores of law clerks already inside for a brief service.

O'Connor wept openly as she stood staring at Rehnquist's coffin. Justices Antonin Scalia and Clarence Thomas also wiped away tears. Only Kennedy and Souter were absent. Kennedy was in China and was unable to get a flight back to the United States in time for the service. Souter was at his home in New Hampshire.

Roberts stood at the edge of the group of former clerks, not really one of them but not yet one of the justices on the other side of the coffin, either. His jaw was tightly set, as if he were clenching his teeth, and his hands were clasped so tightly in front of him that his knuckles looked white. Here he was, in the Great Hall of the Supreme Court, having just carried in the coffin of the iconic man he'd once called "Boss." That title would soon be his, and with it would come the responsibilities for managing the aging group of justices standing nearby and mourning their respected fallen leader. Roberts listened as the Reverend George Evans, Rehnquist's pastor, led the service. "Here, you honored our nation with your service," said Evans, his voice quietly echoing around the soaring marble hall. "Know you are loved."

But outside the stillness of the ceremony, in the Capitol and down Pennsylvania Avenue at the White House, the nominations' machinery was turning at warp speed. Roberts's confirmation hearings to be chief justice would begin the following Monday, just six days away, and Democrats were already promising tougher questions in light of his more prominent role. In the White House, lawyers in Miers's office—having prepared Roberts—had moved on to their next critical assignment, to find a replacement for O'Connor. They had an increased sense of urgency. Card had told Miers and Kelley that Bush insisted on nominating a woman this time. "No white guys," Card said. There was no "unless" that followed his directive.

Bush told reporters that day that the "list is wide open." He wasn't joking. It was so wide open that it had no names on it. White House lawyers had examined all the women and minority candidates in July, when they were first looking for a replacement for O'Connor. They had crossed them all off. They couldn't come up with one who both was confirmable and would be the kind of judicial conservative Bush had said he wanted to nominate. "That should create some good speculation here in Washington," Bush added. He smiled and looked over to his attorney general. "And make sure you notice when I said that I looked right at Al Gonzales, who can really create speculation."

It was a deliberate jab. If a John Roberts nomination had been the liberal groups' greatest fear, Al Gonzales was the conservatives' biggest nightmare. Ever since Bush had indicated he wanted to nominate the first Hispanic to the Supreme Court, conservative groups had campaigned hard against Gonzales. They thought he was either too liberal, like Souter, or would drift to the left once he got on the Court, like Kennedy and O'Connor.

The persistent opposition irked Bush and outraged Gonzales. It was Gonzales, after all, who was responsible for Bush's conservative appeals court nominees, like Roberts and Miguel Estrada, Priscilla Owen and Janice Rogers Brown. Gonzales's defenders in the administration thought the groups had misjudged him. They conceded he could have been shaky had he been nominated straight off the Texas Supreme Court, but they believed his tenure in the administration had solidified his conservative views. He'd helped shape the Bush administration's antiterrorism programs, and he saw how the media could harshly judge the administration's initiatives. That time in government was important. Many former Republican administration officials, looking back at botched Supreme Court nominations, have come to believe that service in the executive branch is one of the surest ways of guaranteeing a justice won't drift to the left once he's on the Court. They point to Rehnquist, Scalia, and Thomas—three solid conservatives who worked in Republican administrations and endured media criticism long before they joined the Court. When they were confirmed, they weren't bothered by what the *New York Times* had to say, because they'd been criticized before. Gonzales's experience as White House counsel and attorney general shored up his conservative beliefs, his supporters argued. "Why do these people come out against me?" an agitated Gonzales asked an associate earlier in the summer. "Part of me wants to get on the Court just to prove them wrong. They think I'd be like Souter? I'd never be like Souter."

But conservatives were convinced, as they liked to say, that "Gonzales" was Spanish for "Souter." Exhibit A was the opinion Gonzales wrote when he was on the Texas Supreme Court that allowed a teenager to get an abortion without telling her parents. Exhibit B was his stance on affirmative action. They blamed Gonzales for the Supreme Court's decision in 2004 that allowed colleges and universities to consider race as one of many factors in college admissions.[1] The case came about when white students challenged the admissions polices at the University of Michigan and its law school because they allowed administrators to consider an applicant's race. Conservatives in the Justice Department wanted the administration to argue that affirmative action was unconstitutional across the board. But in legal papers filed in the Supreme Court, the White House instead took a more watered-down approach, arguing that colleges and universities shouldn't use affirmative action because there are other, race-neutral ways of increasing minority enrollment, such as automatically admitting top students from all state high schools.

Gonzales had argued for that more moderate approach, and the Supreme Court, with O'Connor casting the critical fifth vote with the liberals, eventually refused to ban all affirmative action. Conservatives had believed the case was the best opportunity to end affirmative action in a generation, and they blamed Gonzales for giving the Court wiggle room to evade a ban on racial preferences. But lawyers in the White House counsel's office insist that Gonzales was merely reflecting Bush's views on affirmative action. Those lawyers—typically smart young conservatives who'd clerked for Thomas or Kennedy or Scalia or Rehnquist and opposed affirmative action like their former bosses—often were surprised to see the premium Bush put on diversity. "I don't see any women on here," Bush would say, with displeasure, if a list of executive branch nominees had only male names. Lawyers quickly learned always to include women on any list of possible nominees—even if it meant reordering the lists to pull women off one and add them to another that was deficient.

Now, Bush was engaged in his own brand of affirmative action for the O'Connor seat. After he turned to Roberts to replace Rehnquist, lawyers in the counsel's office, including Miers, had urged him to nominate Alito. He'd been the runner-up to Roberts in July for the

O'Connor vacancy, and they insisted he was the most qualified choice this time. But Bush had told his team to find a woman or minority.

Miers telephoned senators and asked for their suggestions. Several, including influential Republican Mitch McConnell, wanted Estrada. Miers and Kelley believed Estrada clearly would've been Bush's pick to replace O'Connor had the Senate confirmed him as a federal appeals court judge in 2003. But there was the filibuster, and Democrats prevailed, and Estrada was back at his old law firm. He was still a prospect, and Miers continued to press him to throw his hat in the ring. He continued to refuse.

The list was meager. As she made the phone calls and reached out to prospective nominees, Miers didn't know she was edging her way onto it. When it appeared that Bush would move Roberts over to the chief justice's seat, Andy Card took aside Miers's deputy, Bill Kelley, and gave him a highly sensitive, confidential order. Kelley should start vetting Miers for the O'Connor vacancy, Card said. Miers had worked for Card as deputy chief of staff before she became White House counsel, and he knew the Bushes thought highly of her. She might well be the right selection, but Kelley first had to sift through her background and make sure it contained nothing damaging or disqualifying. And he should make absolutely certain, Card warned, that no one—including Miers herself—found out about it.

Card's decision to ask the trusted Kelley to vet his own boss was an egregious managerial mistake. It put both Miers and Kelley in awkward positions and compromised the advice Bush would ultimately get. It also was a dramatic departure from the rigorous system the White House set up in 2001 to vet Supreme Court nominees. White House lawyers had compiled those detailed reports and conducted early interviews of top contenders before a retirement announcement, so Bush could get advice untainted by the turbocharged external pressure that swirls after a justice steps down. But Card had asked Miers's deputy to look secretly at her background—and quickly, without telling anyone.

Now, the pressure was coming from all sides. Outside the White House, there was a loud chorus for a woman to replace O'Connor. Inside the White House, the push was much the same, but with Card's implication that the president's trusted attorney was a viable nominee. That put Kelley in a difficult position. He wouldn't shade his advice if he uncovered anything disqualifying, but he also liked Miers and respected her as a lawyer. Even as he scrupulously examined her record, he would naturally see her experience in the best possible light. That's why vetting typically is done by outsiders without personal knowledge of a candidate. When Gonzales was being considered for attorney general, for example, the administration brought in Reagan's first White House counsel, Fred Fielding, to vet him. David Leitch, Gonzales's deputy, never knew Gonzales was under consideration until Bush offered him the job as attorney general.

But with time pressures mounting, Card realized he just needed someone to make sure Miers had nothing serious in her background. Kelley was capable of doing that. Miers was a longtime friend of the president and the first lady. She was a self-described Texan "through and through" who'd attended Laura Bush's alma mater, Southern Methodist University, for college and law school. From there she'd had a career of firsts, becoming one of the most prominent female lawyers in Texas. She was the first woman hired by her law firm in 1972, the first woman president of the Dallas Bar Association, and, later, the first woman president of the Texas Bar Association. She was managing partner of her four-hundred-lawyer firm, again a first for a woman for a big Dallas firm. She served two years on the Dallas City Council and was general counsel of Bush's gubernatorial campaign committee. As governor, Bush asked Miers to clean up the troubled Texas Lottery Commission by becoming its chair, and she promptly fired two officials, burnishing her reputation as a tough manager.

Miers was with the Bushes on election night 2000, when networks declared—and undeclared—Bush the winner, and Al Gore took back his phone call to concede defeat. After Bush moved into the White House, Miers came to Washington to work for him, but not as White House counsel. That post went to Gonzales, while she became staff secretary, a job that required her to review every piece of paper that crossed the president's desk. Miers kept a low profile but maintained close friendships with more publicly prominent players, like National Security Adviser Condoleezza Rice. When Bush tapped Gonzales to be attorney general, Miers finally got to move into the office of the White House counsel.

As he secretly vetted Miers, Kelley continued to search for other prospective nominees. Shortly after Bush asked Roberts to be chief justice, Kelley and Miers met with the Federalist Society's Leonard Leo in Miers's office in the West Wing. Leo, the executive vice president of the conservative legal group, had taken a leave of absence from his job so he could work full time on judicial nominations, and he met often with White House officials, particularly Kelley, to discuss prospects and strategy. Leo was responsible for representing the views of judicial conservatives, while Jay Sekulow, the well-spoken general counsel of the American Center for Law and Justice, who argued religion cases in the Supreme Court, represented the views of social conservatives.

The two men were completely different in style. Leo was a serious, behind-the-scenes player who had a regular table at the Mayflower Hotel, near the White House, where he ate breakfast nearly every day and always ordered the same thing: bacon and espresso. Before becoming an officer in the Federalist Society, he helped head Catholic outreach for the Republican National Committee. He was also a committed judicial conservative with Ivy League degrees who clerked for the blunt-spoken federal appeals court judge Raymond Randolph. Sekulow, who'd converted to Christianity from Judaism, was the more flamboyant of the two. He spoke frequently to the press and was as comfortable before the television cameras as he was fielding questions from the justices in the Supreme Court. He was a highly regarded legal advocate who was fast on his feet. Those skills translated well to the broadcast media: Sekulow's Christian radio show reached nearly a million people every day.

Leo and Sekulow usually had similar interests and shared the same opinions, but they represented different constituencies—and these differences would become critical as the summer unfolded. On the issue of abortion, for example, many evangelicals and social conservatives who listen to Sekulow oppose the procedure on moral and religious grounds and think it should be banned entirely. But judicial conservatives in Leo's Federalist Society aren't necessarily opposed to abortion. They just don't think women have a constitutional right to the procedure and that state legislatures ought to decide whether it's legal or not. They take issue with the Court's *Roe v. Wade* decision because they believe it to be a lawless judicial exercise without any basis in the Constitution. Social and judicial conservatives both end up in the same place on the issue of abortion, believing *Roe* should be overturned. But they get there in different ways. Social conservatives care largely about the result and want nominees who are strongly antiabortion. Judicial conservatives in the Federalist Society aren't impressed by claims that a nominee is antiabortion. They want to hear his or her views on the Constitution and the role of a judge.

Over the summer, Leo had taken on the most prominent role in discussing prospective nominees with Kelley. He shared his concerns about specific candidates and argued in support of others. But he didn't know whether his arguments had an impact. Miers and Kelley listened, but didn't share their own thoughts or indicate how the president thought. Leo, like Sekulow, often felt as if he were reading tea leaves. Both would leave meetings in the White House mulling over what, if anything, the officials had revealed.

In Leo's meeting with Miers and Kelley in early September, the focus was solely on women and minorities. The field was not big. Clement, whose interview with Bush in July hadn't gone particularly well and who had come across as haughty to White House staff, was off the radar screen. Jones, the runner-up to Souter, was not discussed.

Other federal appeals court judges had problems or pitfalls. Karen Williams, of the Richmond-based appeals court, was the wife of a wealthy trial lawyer and had stirred suspicions among prolife groups when she stepped out of an abortion case because she knew the doctor. The Supreme Court had also reversed a number of her rulings, prompting concerns that she would be seen as a lightweight. Alice Batchelder, of the Cincinnati-based federal appeals court, was well regarded by conservative groups and a favorite of Leo's, but she'd inadvertently decided a few cases in which her husband appeared to have a financial interest because he'd held stocks in the companies involved. Scores of judges, unaware of stocks in a fund or portfolio, had encountered similar problems over the years, but it was considered too risky in the current political climate, when any possible transgression was seen as fair game. Diane Sykes, of the Chicago-based federal appeals court, had a good legal background, but her personal situation was complicated, and the White House believed she would be a better nominee in the future. Deanell Reece Tacha, of the Denver-based appeals court, was seen as too liberal and sympathetic to abortion rights. She had encountered staunch opposition from conservative groups.

Washington lawyer Maureen Mahoney also was mentioned, but Leo strongly resisted. Mahoney, a former Rehnquist clerk who'd worked in the solicitor general's office, was sometimes called the "female John Roberts" because of her sharp intellect and skillful advocacy, but she was not believed to share his conservative outlook. Leo said he was "deeply concerned" about where Mahoney stood on the law. She had represented the University of Michigan in the affirmative action case that had also turned conservatives against Gonzales for good. Mahoney had persuaded the justices that the Constitution permitted some race-based preferences.[2] While it's a mistake to judge a lawyer by the client he or she represents, conservatives thought Mahoney personally believed in affirmative action. Kelley didn't share the administration's views on

Mahoney with Leo, but White House lawyers had already concluded she would not be the kind of judicial conservative Bush was looking for.

At one point during the conversation, Miers stepped out of the room to take a telephone call. Leo took the opportunity to ask Kelley about Miers. "Have you given any consideration to Harriet?" Leo asked.

Kelley equivocated. "The president knows her well," he said. "Obviously there's been some talk."

Leo offered to float her name to the *Wall Street Journal* so it could include her in an article on possible Supreme Court nominees. It was one way they could judge how conservatives would react. The administration hadn't floated names of possible nominees before, but Kelley said he'd think about it. Later in the day, he e-mailed Leo and told him not to contact the *Journal*.

The White House's difficulty in finding a woman or minority was due in no small part to the Senate Democrats' success in eliminating candidates who would have been the top contenders. In 2001 and most of 2002, Democrats controlled the Senate and were able to delay votes on the most prominent nominees, including Roberts and Estrada, as well as state court judges Priscilla Owen, Janice Rogers Brown, and Carolyn Kuhl. When Republicans seized control of the Senate in 2002, those nominees appeared poised for easy confirmation. But Senate Democrats had other ideas.

In a tense closed-door meeting in early 2003, Senate Democrats agreed that they would try to pull off the first-ever successful filibuster of an appellate court nominee and block a vote on the Senate floor. With the Iraq war looming and terror threats an everyday concern, some Democrats strongly opposed the idea as bad timing and bad precedent. Others worried they wouldn't be able to hold together. A filibuster requires sixty votes to overcome. Republicans needed to pick up only five votes, and some Democrats were certain they would lose on the very first nominee in the crossfire: the highly regarded Estrada, who was in line to be the first Hispanic on the D.C.-based federal court of appeals.

Estrada was the classic American success story. He'd grown up in Honduras with his father and stepmother, then moved to the United States as a teenager to live with his mother in New York. Speaking broken English, he enrolled at the State University of New York to learn the language and then transferred to Columbia University, where he earned high honors. He went on to graduate in the top of his class at Harvard Law School and land a Supreme Court clerkship and earn top jobs in government and in the nation's most prestigious law firms. The administration tapped him to be the first appeals court nominee up for a vote after Republicans took control of the Senate in 2002. It fully expected him to be confirmed.

But leadership failures by Republicans in the Senate and in the White House turned the Democrats' early trepidation into triumph. Senate majority leader Bill Frist, only a month into the job when Democrats formulated their strategy, lacked the confidence and legislative skill of his predecessor, Senator Trent Lott, to counter Democrats. But Lott was unavailable to disarm them, having been ousted as majority leader after he made racially insensitive comments during a birthday celebration for South Carolina senator Strom Thurmond, saying that "we wouldn't have had all these problems over the years" if only the country had elected Thurmond president in 1948, when he ran as a segregationist candidate.

Relegated to the sidelines, Lott was highly critical of Frist for failing to move swiftly and forcefully when Democrats began their filibuster against Estrada. A modern-day filibuster is not like the famous ones of old, when senators stood in the Senate and read from telephone books. Today, senators can filibuster simply by joining together and voting against a motion to end the debate. If more than forty of them refuse to end the debate, they've created a filibuster, and the Senate will turn to other business. When Democrats refused to end the Estrada debate, Frist had no plan for cracking their solidarity. He just kept scheduling Senate votes to end the filibuster, and the Democrats kept standing together, growing stronger with each vote. Lott would have played hardball, holding up legislation and putting the Democrats' feet to the fire on other issues until they broke on the filibuster.

The White House, too, failed to grasp the significance of the early filibusters. When outside legal advisers like Boyden Gray and others tried to engage the administration on the issue, they were rebuffed. The outside groups argued that the filibuster was a monumental threat to the president's authority to name judges of his choosing. They wanted Bush to expend some capital on the issue, to pick up the phone and talk to moderate Democrats. But Gonzales, who then was the White House counsel, insisted the battle was a Senate issue.

As a result, Democrats were more successful than they could have imagined. After standing together on Estrada, they set their sights on the next nominee. Suddenly, Democrats weren't asking whether they'd be able to filibuster, but when they would block a nominee. They targeted outspoken conservatives who were potential Supreme Court picks. Not only was Estrada forced to withdraw, but Democrats successfully blocked other potential Supreme Court nominees, including Owen, Brown, and Kuhl. They also made clear they were prepared to do the same on Supreme Court nominations.

Their success in blocking Bush's top women and minority candidates led Republicans to consider changing Senate rules so judicial nominees could not be filibustered. That divisive fight was resolved only after a bipartisan group of fourteen senators came together in compromise. The Senate eventually confirmed Brown and Owen to their appeals court posts weeks before O'Connor retired. But that would be the end of the line for the two. Senate minority leader Harry Reid and other Senate Democrats warned the White House that the nomination of Owen or Brown to the Supreme Court would provoke an all-out fight and likely trigger another filibuster. Republican senators in the group of fourteen concurred. Senator Lindsey Graham of South Carolina told the White House that the Republicans agreed Bush should not consider nominating either woman to replace O'Connor.

As September went by, Leo and Kelley spoke several times about possible nominees to replace O'Connor. A few weeks after Roberts was nominated to be chief, Kelley brought the conversation back to Miers. "What do you think about Harriet?" he asked Leo.

Bush had been weighing the idea for some time. In early July, when O'Connor announced her retirement, Card asked Miers if she was interested, and she declined to be considered. But after Rehnquist died—and all the other women and minority candidates fell by the wayside—the prospect seemed more appealing. The idea picked up momentum on September 21, when Bush invited key Senate leaders to breakfast at the White House to discuss the upcoming nomination. Reid recommended Miers during the breakfast. "If you nominate Harriet Miers, you'll start with fifty-six votes," Reid said, suggesting he would join Republicans right out of the box in supporting her.

Bush broached the idea with Miers later that day. She was reluctant at first, and startled to learn that Kelley had already been sifting through her background. But Card asked her whether she'd consider a prospective nominee with her résumé qualified for the job.

"Yes, I guess I would," Miers said.

That night, Ruth Bader Ginsburg told an audience gathered at the New York City Bar Association that she didn't like the prospect of being the only woman on the Court. She hoped Bush would nominate a woman, but "any woman will not do," she said.

When Kelley brought up Miers two days later, Leo didn't shoot down the idea. His meetings with her to discuss judges and their judicial philosophies had convinced him she was a conservative, and he didn't think she would become another David Souter. She wasn't highly social, like Williams or Clement, suggesting she wouldn't get swept up in the cocktail party circuit that conservatives suspect swayed Kennedy and O'Connor. She was a born-again Christian and had spent her time in the executive branch, making it unlikely she would bend to the will of the opinion elite in New York or Washington. "On judicial philosophy and character, she's okay," Leo said. "She's not an architect, but she knows a good house when she sees it, and she knows the one she would want to live in."

Leo hung up the phone and replayed the conversation in his head. He immediately called Kelley back. "We should talk about this," Leo said.

The next day, Kelley and Leo met for breakfast in Tyson's Corner, an area in Virginia just west of Washington. For about two hours, they discussed the prospect of a Miers nomination. For Leo, it was a wake-up call that Miers was a distinct possibility, although it still seemed a distant one. Kelley hadn't said Bush was going to nominate her or even that she was a leading candidate. "It'll be damn tough," Leo said.

Kelley agreed. "But she's solid," Kelley said. "She'll be a good vote."

Leo asked about her lack of a judicial record. After Souter, conservatives wanted to see a demonstrated judicial record, which Miers didn't have. "We have others with long-standing records," Leo said. "Why not go with the pool of known quantities?"

"The president knows her," Kelley said. "She is a known quantity."

Leo didn't think she would excite conservatives as Owen or Brown would. But Leo didn't know that Senate Republicans had eliminated them both. Owen was too divisive after the filibuster compromise. Brown, who had given provocative speeches indicating that her views were close to those of Justice Thomas, was thermonuclear. Conservatives continued to favor Luttig or Alito, but, unbeknownst to Leo, Bush was adamant about nominating a woman to replace O'Connor. The White House considered the rest of the possible nominees too philosophically unpredictable, too inexperienced, or too inflammatory. But Kelley, acutely aware that Bush did not want any leaks on possible nominees—and certainly not any background information about them— did not tell Leo how woefully bare the short list really was.

Hanging over the entire conversation was the prospect of a Gonzales nomination. Leo thought Bush had gotten the message that conservatives would revolt, but he never heard definitively that the attorney general was off the list. Kelley didn't say so, either. Leo didn't think it was likely, but he also knew that if Bush wanted to nominate a woman or minority and if his advisers couldn't come up with one, the attorney general was always just down the street in the Department of Justice.

Leo went to his office after the meeting and pulled out any file that was remotely connected to Miers. He called several close associates to warn them Miers was in the mix. But Leo didn't think, even after his meeting with Kelley, that Miers would get the nod. Two days later Bush hinted publicly that he wanted to nominate a woman or minority, saying he would "pick a person who can do the job," but adding he was "mindful that diversity is one of the strengths of the country." Leo was hit with a barrage of e-mails from his constituents, asking him to interpret Bush's remarks. He assured a small group of associates that the "internal dynamics right now show that" Bush wouldn't feel compelled to elevate diversity concerns above all else. "It's always been one of many factors for him—and he cannot abandon that now," Leo said. But it wasn't an overriding concern. "As of this weekend, I do not think he was of the view that he has to pick a woman."

That Tuesday, Leo and Wendy Long, the general counsel of the Judicial Confirmation Network, met with Miers and Kelley in her office. Bush's lawyers did not signal what the president was thinking or indicate he was dangerously close to settling on Miers. The secrecy over Roberts's nomination in July showed how seriously Bush valued confidentiality. After Bush told Roberts he wanted to nominate him to replace O'Connor, he ordered Card not to disclose his decision to anyone other than his closest group of advisers. All that afternoon, as Roberts sat in a small office near the president's, preparing his remarks for later that night, the staff lawyers in the White House counsel's office down the hall—who'd labored for months on background reports of prospective nominees—had no idea he was the pick. They found out that night like most everyone else, by watching television.

In that meeting with Leo and Long, Miers led the discussion, solic-

iting their views on what Bush should consider when making his decision. "What do you think is most important?" Miers asked at one point.

"Quality, quality. That's all that matters," said Long, whose Judicial
Confirmation Network was formed to support Bush's judges and supported by the same donors that contributed to the Federalist Society.
Long, who had clerked for Thomas on the Supreme Court, cared so
much about the issue of judicial nominations that she had taken a leave
of absence from the prestigious law firm Kirkland & Ellis to work full
time helping get Bush judges confirmed. "We can handle the rest if
there is quality," Long said.

Miers and Kelley nodded in agreement. The discussion on nominees
was brief. Most of the conversation focused on the strategy for getting
Bush's nominee through the confirmation process and how to ensure
the most widespread support against inevitable attacks by Democrats.
Miers in particular was keen to tap into the grassroots groups and influential commentators outside the mainstream press. "I think the blogs
will be really important," Miers said.

The glaring disconnect was multilayered. Top conservatives in the
administration—but outside the inner circle—were speculating on
other nominees, which made a Miers nomination seem even more remote. That night, Leo and Long had dinner with Alex Azar, the general
counsel of the Department of Health and Human Services, who had
solid conservative credentials, having clerked for Scalia and worked for
Ken Starr on his Whitewater investigation of President Clinton. Azar
told them he thought Bush would nominate Larry Thompson, the former deputy attorney general under John Ashcroft who had since moved
into the corporate world as the top lawyer for Pepsico. Thompson was
a good friend of Clarence Thomas and would be the Court's third
African American justice, but conservatives worried that he lacked a
clear philosophy and would move left like Justice Kennedy. Azar's speculation set off a round of worrying and frantic e-mails from conservatives about whether they should express opposition to Thompson.

No one took the prospect of a Miers nomination seriously. To the group of outside lawyers—most of whom had graduated from the top law schools in the country and clerked for prestigious judges or on the Supreme Court—Miers was seen as such a preposterous pick that they simply refused to believe she was even on the actual short list of contenders. "Yeah, right," said one. "And he's going to nominate Dr. Ruth to be surgeon general." They assumed she was there to show that the White House had considered women. Some even suggested the White House included her to soften the blow to Gonzales when he didn't get the nomination. That way, Bush could say he simply couldn't afford to nominate anyone who would be perceived as a crony.

Leo warned them, but he didn't really think it would happen himself. And no one listened. Even in midweek, when conservatives began to suspect Bush would nominate a woman, they continued to rule out Miers, flatly dismissing her in phone calls and e-mails. She would be the most uncredentialed nominee in history. She would disappoint the base. She would give Democrats a legitimate issue on which to attack Bush: cronyism. Just do an Internet search on "crony or cronyism," one said. You'll get a million hits, especially with FEMA's Michael Brown bumbling the response to Hurricane Katrina and under attack for being a crony pick. Miers just wasn't an option.

They moved on to other nominees. Owen would be the obvious choice unless Republicans had warned the White House off her. They then turned their focus to Karen Williams of South Carolina and began putting together background information on her.

Fueling the skepticism over Miers was the feeling that Leo had cried wolf before. After all, back in July, on the day Bush was to announce O'Connor's replacement, Leo told conservatives in an early-morning conference call that Bush would name Edith Brown Clement, the New Orleans judge. The news landed with a thud. With so many people on the conference call, Leo's discussion and his defense of Clement quickly leaked to reporters, who were desperate for any information about Bush's plans. With the White House in lockdown, Leo's speculation teetered close to confirmation that Clement would be the nominee.

Only in the late afternoon did a White House official finally shoot down the rumor.

Leo's suggestion of Miers this time felt similar. It was speculation, nothing more. Sure, the White House was saying Bush would nominate a woman now. Politically, it had to. But Bush would turn to the most qualified person available when he made his choice, just as he had when he picked Roberts to replace O'Connor.

It would be Luttig or Alito. They couldn't believe he'd do anything else.

11.

DECONSTRUCTING
MIERS

By Thursday, it appeared clear to insiders that Bush would tap Harriet Miers to replace Justice O'Connor. Andy Card had always supported the idea. Karl Rove, counselor Dan Bartlett, and Ed Gillespie, the former head of the Republican National Committee who was advising Bush, had been involved in the discussions and had signed off on the politics. All four—Card, Rove, Bartlett, and Gillespie—told Bush that Miers would be a sound political choice. Most important, she was a woman, and the president had been under enormous pressure to nominate a third female to replace the Court's first. O'Connor and Ginsburg both had said Bush should turn to a woman, as had the first lady.

Miers also would have bipartisan support in the Senate, enabling Bush to avoid a protracted fight at a difficult period in his presidency. Even Senator Chuck Schumer, perhaps the smartest and most aggressive Democrat on the Judiciary Committee, had indicated through a staff member that he would support her. The conservative groups, too, would stand strong. Leonard Leo and Jay Sekulow signed off on Miers, and they didn't signal significant opposition by their constituencies. After all, Miers was an evangelical Christian and staunch conservative herself—and she had the added boost of not being named Al Gonzales. It could be tough, all four advisers told Bush, if Miers was seen as a crony. But she'd make it.

Bush turned to his legal advisers for their views, although his top two lawyers—Miers and Gonzales—were compromised in giving him advice. After her initial reluctance, Miers had warmed to the idea and believed she was qualified for the job. Gonzales wasn't brought into the loop on Miers, even though he'd done all the advance work on Supreme Court nominations. So Bush sought out Kelley, Miers's deputy, who had an elite legal background and sterling conservative credentials, having clerked on the Supreme Court for Scalia and worked for Ken Starr during his Whitewater investigation of President Clinton. Kelley and other lawyers in the White House shared Bush's goal of nominating justices like Thomas or Scalia, and they had argued that Bush should return to his original short list of contenders, even though they were white men. They used sports analogies, contending Bush should pick the best player available, as he did when he nominated Roberts. "You can pick the best player," Card would respond, "but you have to cover all the bases, too."

And Bush wanted to make sure he'd covered all the bases. He was going to nominate a woman, and Miers could do the job. Whenever legal advisers would raise questions, Bush expressed confidence. She was, as he famously said, a "pit bull in size six shoes," and no one on his staff worked harder or longer hours.

But how would she hold up in the hearings?

"She'll do the work," Bush would say. "She's tough as nails."

But she's unknown, they said.

"She's not unknown to me," he responded.

In talking with the lawyers on his staff, Bush only had one question. "Is Harriet qualified?" Bush asked, looking directly at Kelley in one meeting with other advisers.

Kelley did not answer directly. "Mr. President," he said, "Sam Alito is the best nominee."

"But is she qualified?" Bush asked.

"The answer," Kelley concluded, "is yes."

Kelley's vetting had turned up no significant roadblocks. He knew Miers wasn't the strongest writer, but her record as a litigator seemed impressive, as the accolades and awards from her peers in the profession indicated. Kelley respected and admired Miers as a lawyer. He thought she was "plenty smart," in addition to being thorough and insightful, with enough common sense to see different sides to problems. He also knew she was so conservative that she had qualms initially about nominating Roberts. She was suspicious that he'd gone fifteen years without publicly advocating a conservative approach to the law.

Without any of his advisers flatly saying no, Bush moved forward. Conservative advisers Leo and Sekulow had given Miers a green light, so Bush had no reason to suspect conservatives would oppose her. Reid's assurances gave him every reason to think Democrats would support her, and other senators, including Specter, had urged him to nominate a nonjudge—someone with political experience outside what they called the "judicial monastery" of the federal bench. With public support crumbling in the weeks after Hurricane Katrina, Bush needed a consensus nominee like Miers. Beyond the political expediency, Bush was also satisfied that she was capable. After all, his legal advisers had assured him she was qualified for the job. And since Bush knew his friend was smart and tough enough to remain steadfast under pressure, Bush was ready to pull the trigger.

It's impossible to overstate how much the last concern drove Bush's thinking on Miers. He was determined not to repeat his father's mistake with Souter. The elder Bush had relied on assurances by chief of staff John Sununu that Souter would be a solid conservative. But Sununu, a political adviser, had no idea what he was talking about, and his advice led Bush to make one of the most inept political decisions of any modern-day president. In characterizing Souter as conservative,

Sununu hadn't evaluated how he would perform once he got on the Supreme Court—he was just comparing him to other people in his home state of New Hampshire, which was, frankly, not all that conservative a place. By contrast, George W. Bush had known Miers for nearly fifteen years. Although Card got the ball rolling on Miers's nomination, he didn't have to vouch for her conservatism the way Sununu did for Souter. Bush thought Miers was in the mold of Thomas and Scalia, and he could be sure she would stay that way.

With momentum for Miers building, Kelley called Rachel Brand, the assistant attorney general who'd just shepherded through Roberts's nomination. She and other lawyers in the Justice Department had worked tirelessly to get Roberts confirmed, and Kelley thought he owed them advance notice. Bush, he told Brand that Thursday, was seriously contemplating nominating Miers. Brand was incredulous. She had been closely involved in the selection process for years, back to when she'd worked in the White House counsel's office and helped research prospective nominees. A Harvard Law School graduate who had clerked on the Supreme Court, Brand was proud of the list they'd assembled, which emphasized experience and qualifications. For a Supreme Court post, she believed, Miers lacked both.

Brand immediately alerted lawyers in Gonzales's inner circle. Their reaction ranged from skepticism to outright disbelief, but it quickly coalesced into a sense of urgency that Gonzales had to intervene. Brand worried about Miers's credentials and thought she would immediately be seen as a crony. Gonzales's chief of staff, Kyle Sampson, knew immediately how conservatives would react. Sampson had good political instincts, having worked on Capitol Hill for Senator Orrin Hatch before moving to the White House counsel's office to work for Gonzales. After seeing conservatives' ardent opposition to his boss over the years, he sensed Miers would go over no better. "You have to do something," Sampson urged Gonzales. "This is a disaster. Conservatives will revolt."

But Gonzales was reluctant. For several years now, he'd been in the awkward position of vetting prospective Supreme Court nominees and advising Bush on the candidates while he also was a potential pick. Throughout the process, Gonzales, like Miers, never was put on the same list as the other prospective nominees. A couple of years earlier, lawyers in the White House counsel's office had written a memo analyzing Gonzales's old Texas Supreme Court opinions and legal views, just as they'd done for other prospects. But his name was off to the side, and Miers and Kelley never discussed him with Bush. Now that Miers, his old friend and sometime rival, appeared poised to come out on top, Gonzales worried that Bush would think he was criticizing her to enhance his own chances for the job. He did not want to do it. "I don't want him to think this is about me," he said.

But his advisers were adamant. Sampson was the most outspoken. "Your loyalty is with the president," Sampson told Gonzales. "You have a duty to advise him."

The next day, Gonzales went to the White House and presented his concerns to Bush. It was a difficult meeting. Gonzales had known Miers from their days in Texas, where both had been prominent firsts: Miers, the first woman, and Gonzales, the first Hispanic. Their staffers sensed a quiet rivalry at times, exacerbated when Bush named Gonzales White House counsel when he first moved to Washington, a job Miers wanted. But Bush advisers who know them both said Bush always thought he'd eventually tap Miers, his old personal lawyer, as White House counsel, and when he moved Gonzales over to the Justice Department, he did just that.

Gonzales had a keen sense of the other nominees, having vetted and interviewed them for the past four years as White House counsel. Gonzales knew the kind of justice the president wanted, and he knew what it meant to nominate someone in the mold of Thomas and Scalia. Gonzales also had been stung by the conservative backlash against talk of his own nomination, and he believed those conservative groups were no more likely to embrace Miers than they trusted him. He stressed the last point with Bush. But Bush, assured by Kelley and Rove that the conservative groups would fall into place, wasn't troubled by the red flags Gonzales waved. It became clear to Gonzales that Bush had made up his mind. "He's going to nominate Harriet," Gonzales said when he got back to the Justice Department. He was baffled by the decision, but there was nothing more he could do.

Bush went to Camp David with the first lady and several advisers, including Card, the next day. In Washington, Rove started laying the groundwork with the social conservatives who had so adamantly opposed Gonzales. As Republican presidential advisers had known for decades, at least as far back as the O'Connor nomination, social conservatives rallied around the issue of the Supreme Court. As the Court had taken on more of the issues they cared about, like abortion and school prayer, they became committed to influencing the selection process, just as they would a political campaign for the legislature. But social conservatives had never managed to get a seat at the table until George W. Bush was elected president. They had opposed Republican nominees in the past, like O'Connor, because they worried she supported the right to abortion. They also raised concerns about Souter. Both times they were simply ignored.

On Sunday, Rove called James Dobson, considered America's most influential evangelical leader, and said that Miers was a possibility. Dobson's radio program, *Focus on the Family,* is broadcast to six thousand stations worldwide, and he had long been a vocal supporter of Bush judges, blasting Democrats for filibustering the appeals court nominees. The White House wanted his support. Rove explained that Bush had promised to nominate people who would "uphold the Constitution" and "not promote their own political agenda." Miers "fit that bill," Rove told Dobson.[1] He then urged Dobson to call people in Texas who knew Miers, including federal judge Ed Kinkeade and Texas Supreme Court justice Nathan Hecht.

Hecht had known Miers for more than twenty-five years and had helped her join an evangelical Christian church in 1979. He was familiar with her religious views, and in fact had witnessed to her in the 1970s when they were both working at Dallas law firms. Rove had already contacted him and asked that he lend support by talking to the media about Miers's views on social issues, like abortion. In the call with Dobson, Rove also anticipated possible criticism from conservatives and sought to deflect it. He told Dobson that some of the other possible nominees, all highly qualified conservatives, had not wanted their names considered. The process was too bitter and too vitriolic, Rove said, and they just didn't want any part of it.

By that point, Bush had already decided to offer Miers the job. After the weekend at Camp David, Card arranged a Sunday-night dinner for Miers in the White House with Bush and the first lady. Bush offered Miers the nomination, and she said yes.

Hours later, Rove called Leo at home. So abysmally had the White House failed to grasp how conservatives would respond that he gave Leo assurances. "Conservatives," Rove told Leo, "are going to be happy." To Leo, that meant one thing: Sam Alito. He'd come to believe that Alito had edged out Luttig after Bush interviewed both judges in July, and he quickly began making calls to implement plans for the media frenzy that would follow the early-morning announcement. Adam Ciongoli, a former administration official who had clerked for Alito on the Philadelphia-based federal appeals court, flew in from New York to be available to talk to reporters. As word spread that night, several recalled, with glee, that Andy Card had offered similar assurances to Clarence Thomas at a White House dinner in July, the night before Bush nominated Roberts.

The next morning, former Reagan administration official Mike Carvin stepped into the elevator of his office at Jones Day Reavis & Pogue, having hurriedly returned to Washington from New York so he, too, could be in place to support the nominee. Carvin had known Sam Alito when the two worked together in the Justice Department, and for years had said he was the best choice for the high court. With an announcement imminent, Carvin was very happy. But at that moment, one of the law firm's secretaries stopped him cold. "Did you hear?" she told Carvin. "The president just nominated his secretary to the Supreme Court."

"What!" Carvin exploded, processing the news. Then he paused. "Her name's not Miers, is it?"

Throughout town, as the news spread, other conservatives reacted much the same way. The announcement was particularly painful because the promise of change, after years of work and patience, had been so bright. Only four days before, many of them had gathered in the White House for the swearing in of John Roberts and had leaped from their seats with applause after Justice John Paul Stevens delivered the oath. The private reception for Roberts afterward, in the splendor of the East Room, had felt like a celebration, as prominent conservatives from every administration dating back to Nixon's gathered with Republican senators, staffers, and outside advisers, as well as Justices Thomas and Scalia. The mood was almost euphoric, as if all could barely believe that Roberts was positioned to lead the Court for the next three decades and another nominee would soon be joining him. There hadn't been such a sunny celebration for a new Republican appointee in nearly twenty years. Neither Kennedy nor Souter had been a cause for rejoicing, and Thomas was so badly beaten up in his confirmation hearings that his reception seemed more like a sigh of tired relief than a triumphant proclamation.

Roberts would make his first public appearance as chief justice that first Monday in October, when he took his seat in the center of the Court and heard arguments in two cases. But Bush preempted him with the early-morning nomination of Miers. The contrast between Roberts and Miers was stark, and conservatives struggled to understand how the same president had picked them both, back to back. The O'Connor seat was their best chance to change the direction of the Court in decades. Bush had just squandered it, and the realization was a bitter one, made more so because the president himself seemed completely unaware. There he was, in the White House, with Miers at his side, telling conservatives not to worry. "I've known Harriet for more than a decade," Bush said as he announced his selection. "I know her heart. I know her character."

After the announcement, Miers was whisked to the Hill to begin meeting with senators, and conservative commentators began to erupt. Less than three hours after the announcement, *Weekly Standard* editor Bill Kristol blasted Bush on the magazine's Web site for capitulating to Democrats and backing down from a fight on judicial philosophy. He pronounced himself "disappointed, depressed and demoralized." Former Bush speechwriter David Frum also reacted swiftly in his blog on *National Review Online,* calling the nomination "an unforced error." Conservative radio host Laura Ingraham, who had clerked for Thomas, came out with immediate opposition as well.

The White House was forced into full damage-control mode. Vice President Dick Cheney was quickly dispatched to talk radio, where a dubious Rush Limbaugh sharply questioned him. "I'm confident that she has a conservative judicial philosophy that you'd be comfortable with, Rush," Cheney said, adding that Bush "will have done more to change the Court and, in fact, put on it individuals who share his judicial philosophy than any of his predecessors in modern times."

Of course, Bush's father was in that group of modern-day predecessors, and conservatives immediately drew parallels between the two. George H. W. Bush's nomination of Souter was an inescapable comparison. But ironically, that disastrous nomination had, in fact, influenced both sides. It drove his son's decision to select Miers, his known and trusted adviser, in the first place, to avoid putting another Souter on the Supreme Court. It then fueled the subsequent conservative opposition to Miers, who was seen as an unknown Souteresque nominee. Pat Buchanan, after scolding Bush for running from a fight and wasting a "once-in-a-generation opportunity to return the Supreme Court to constitutionalism" and overthrow "the judicial dictatorship imposed on the United States since the Warren Court," took precise aim at the man he ran against in the 1992 Republican primaries. Buchanan and other conservatives noted that like his father, Bush had picked a nominee without a paper trail to avoid a political fight with Senate Democrats.

The paper trail mattered to conservatives. It showed that a nominee had taken a stand on something and could endure the criticism. It showed that a nominee had a philosophy or a theory about the law. As conservatives knew, history proved all too well what happened to Republican nominees without paper trails or clear legal philosophies once they got on the Court. They drifted left. Every time.

Miers's lack of a consistent record also alarmed social conservatives, and White House officials and outside advisers frantically began trying to shore up support. The afternoon that Bush tapped Miers, Dobson and other prominent religious conservatives held a conference call to discuss her nomination. Hecht and Kinkeade joined the call, and someone asked whether the two judges believed Miers, based on their personal knowledge of her, would vote to overturn *Roe*.

"Absolutely," said Judge Kinkeade.

"I agree with that," said Justice Hecht. "I concur."[2]

The White House was so desperate to show that Miers was conservative that insiders and loyalists also began stressing her close ties to Bush. In a conference call with grassroots conservative leaders two days later, Republican National Committee chairman Ken Mehlman said that, unlike with Souter, "we don't have to take someone else's word for it; the president knows her personally." Sekulow, who also was on the call, said that Bush was "keenly aware of what was at stake here" and that Miers understood the Court's "limited role under the Constitution." Leo spoke of her "commitment to conservative judicial philosophy" and her devout Christian views, calling her a "woman of strength, courage, and independence." The Southern Baptist Convention's Richard Land said Texans like Bush and Miers valued loyalty and courage above all. "If she ruled in ways contrary to the way the president wanted her to rule, it would be a deep betrayal," Land concluded. Dobson, also on the conference call, said he was starting to see a change in "the initial shock wave that went through the conservative and Christian community" after the nomination.

But those assurances only served to enrage the judicial conservatives like Kristol, Frum, and Ingraham, not to mention the large group of lawyers like Carvin and Long who had been standing ready to support Bush's nominee. It sharply illustrated the wide chasm between the two groups of conservatives. Judicial conservatives were offended by the suggestion that Miers's religious views or personal loyalty to Bush would cause her to vote the "right" way on the Court. That was the kind of result-oriented approach they'd accused liberals of practicing. They believed true judicial conservatives didn't focus on the result or the outcome of a case. They looked to the Constitution and its words instead of relying on personal views or feelings that there was a "right" way to vote in a case.

Miers couldn't even draw on outraged Democrats to rally conservative support. Conservatives had been skeptical of Souter from the beginning, but liberal women's groups had inadvertently helped galvanize support on the Right for his nomination. The groups immediately announced their opposition to Souter on the grounds that they were certain he would overturn *Roe*. Conservatives interpreted the STOP SOUTER OR WOMEN WILL DIE flyers generated by the Left to mean Souter would, as they saw it, stop the deaths of millions of fetuses by voting to overturn *Roe*—an outcome they very much wanted. But with Miers, the liberal groups held their fire. Disappointed conservatives had only one place to direct their energy: at George W. Bush.

The day after Miers's nomination, Bush held a Rose Garden press conference to assure conservatives that his longtime lawyer and friend could be counted on to champion their causes. Bush's logic was simple: You can trust her because you can trust me. But less than a year after those conservatives turned out in record numbers to reelect him, Bush's right-wing base was no longer in the mood to take him at his word. For nearly five years, conservatives had muted their criticisms of the administration's reckless spending habits, even as Bush took a $155 billion surplus from President Clinton and quickly assembled the largest deficit in U.S. history with unprecedented increases in domestic and foreign spending.

This was the same George Bush who had promised he would do

what few had dared: reform Social Security and Medicare before retiring baby boomers bankrupted those programs. Instead, the only entitlement bill Bush signed into law was a Medicare drug benefit program that caused the greatest expansion in America's welfare state in forty years, with a price tag approaching $7 trillion. Reagan conservatives had started to conclude that George Bush was not in their corner. And in October of 2005, their disillusionment was not limited to spending.

The one thing conservatives had long relied on was the belief that voters would turn to Republicans because of their perceived competence. Whether running against a New England liberal or a midwestern moderate, Republicans would conjure up images of Jimmy Carter's Iranian hostage crisis, Lyndon Johnson's Vietnam War, or John F. Kennedy's Bay of Pigs invasion. Regardless of the opponent, the message was the same: Republicans, not Democrats, could be trusted to defend Americans, protect their tax dollars, and efficiently run their government. But by the time George W. Bush was telling conservatives to trust his judgment in nominating Miers, the entire country had endured nightly scenes of death and destruction from Hurricane Katrina, a tragedy exacerbated by incompetence at the highest levels of government. The same president who was telling conservatives to trust him on Miers had selected Michael Brown to run FEMA. Bush's praise that "you're doing a heck of a job, Brownie" only underscored what liberals and a growing number of conservatives saw as his arrogance and isolation from the political realities of the time.

By October 2005, Bush's base was also growing impatient with a White House that seemed increasingly baffled by the bloody conflict in Iraq. As the country appeared near anarchy, even those conservatives who had originally endorsed Bush's war were losing faith in the Pentagon's ability to execute it. "At the very moment that conservatives have begun to conclude that their bets on Mr. Bush are no longer paying off," wrote the *National Review*'s Ramesh Ponnuru, "Mr. Bush has asked them to double down."[3]

It was a bet few wanted to place. Many had worked for Bush and stayed with him solely because of the Supreme Court. Now he'd betrayed them by nominating a mediocre loyalist. They were fed up with Bush and stung by a history of botched Republican nominations over the years. They were ready to fight him on Miers, in the tradition of Ronald Reagan confronting President Ford over détente and Newt Gingrich squaring off with George H. W. Bush over tax increases.

But others weren't so sure. In that first week, conservatives argued over whether to publicly support Miers out of loyalty to Bush, remain quiet out of respect, or speak out based on principle. Two days after the nomination, George Mason University law professor Nelson Lund sent out a group e-mail to dozens of conservative lawyers and law professors, many of whom, like Lund, had served in previous Republican administrations and had loosely organized to support Bush's judicial nominees. He asked why they should publicly support the nomination, "notwithstanding the complete absence of any external indicia that Harriet Miers should be appointed to the Supreme Court."

"I don't see any basis on which people like me—who don't have first-hand knowledge of whatever her friends, colleagues and client find promising—could responsibly promote her candidacy, or defend the president's decision," Lund wrote. "Am I missing something here?"

Carvin promptly responded with a response designed to separate the group from Leo and his assurances that Miers was an acceptable nominee. "I fully agree with Nelson and, if anything, am more perturbed about this regrettable choice," Carvin wrote. "In this regard, I hope it is being made clear to the White House and the public that no one person is speaking 'for' the people on this email list or, worse still, for the Federalist Society."

Others began to weigh in. Ron Cass, who had replaced Boyden Gray as spokesman for the Committee for Justice, a group formed to support Bush's judicial picks, urged caution. Cass, the former dean of Boston University Law School, had written a piece the day before for *National Review Online,* in which he chastised conservatives for their "off the mark" bashing of Miers. Cass was more direct in his private e-mail to the lawyers. "Unless there is a solid feeling out there that outrage by the conservative base will get Miers to withdraw her name, I just am perplexed at what we are doing to our party and the chances to advance our principles by complaining publicly," Cass wrote. "It's better blushingly to support a friend than boldly to undermine one. We can stand on our principles. But let's be careful to stand there when it's helpful—let's not contribute to further undermining trust in the President."

Cass's tone in the e-mail had the ring of a lecture to it, which only further irritated many in the group. Abigail Thernstrom, the vice chair of the U.S. Commission on Civil Rights, fired off a pointed response. "I don't think any of us are contemplating going public with our doubts about this nomination. We are keeping quiet. And hiding from the media," Thernstrom wrote. "As for undermining trust in the president, I am afraid he has accomplished that all on his own—without any help from us."

Many of those on the e-mail exchange had previously agreed to support Bush's nominee. Dozens had gone through media training at the Mayflower Hotel with an outside public relations company, the same firm that produced the controversial advertisement by the Swift Boat veterans against presidential nominee John Kerry during the 2004 presidential race. Of the more than two dozen originally on the list who had planned to forcefully defend Bush's nominee to the media, only a handful concluded they were willing to speak out in support of Miers. As University of San Diego law professor Gail Heriot put it in another e-mail, "I have to protect my credibility. It may come in handy some day."

Leo held a strategy call the next day with a smaller group of conservatives, including Gray and Sekulow. He said the group needed to make "practical decisions about the basic approach" on the nomination. "There's an internal debate going on about whether this is someone worth supporting," Leo said, before contending that Miers was qualified "both on résumé and judicial philosophy." But he conceded that conservatives "had grounds to be disappointed" that the White House had dodged a fight on a prominent legal conservative. "The White

House and the conservative base are two ships passing in the night," Leo said. "They don't understand why the conservative base wanted a fight."

At the same time, the White House spin machine was doing more harm than good with conservatives weighing their options. It desperately needed White House political operative Steve Schmidt, who'd handled the rollout for Roberts and was a savvy adviser. But he left for three weeks in Iraq the day Miers was nominated, and the White House could not get its footing on the nomination, even with seasoned advisers like Gillespie, the former chair of the Republican National Committee, and Mehlman, its current chair.

Incredibly, Gillespie managed to antagonize the base even more. During another conference call with conservatives, Gillespie went on the attack, saying the opposition to Miers had a "whiff of elitism" and sexism. The former was entirely possible, as Miers didn't have the Ivy League credentials and prestigious clerkships now expected in a Supreme Court nominee. But that didn't explain why conservatives had embraced other nominees without Ivy League degrees, including Priscilla Owen, a Baylor Law School graduate, and Janice Rogers Brown, who graduated from UCLA's law school. As for sexism, if anyone had focused on gender, conservatives believed, it was George Bush. Miers wouldn't be the nominee if she weren't a woman. Gillespie's comments only energized the opposition.

Every day brought more revelations and problems. Though Bush said she wouldn't change once on the Court, Miers had taken remarkably inconsistent positions over the years. She was a Republican, but she had once contributed to Democrats, including Al Gore's 1988 presidential campaign. She pronounced herself a judicial conservative, but had testified in 1989 that she wouldn't join the Federalist Society or any "organizations that were politically charged with one viewpoint or the other." But she'd had no problem joining the liberal Progressive Voters League.

The closer she appeared to Bush, the less impressive her qualifications seemed. Just over a week after her nomination, Miers was confronted with letters she'd written to Bush when he was governor of Texas. She'd proclaimed him the "greatest governor ever" and made liberal use of exclamation points, even describing the Bushes as "cool" parents to Jenna and Barbara. "At least they don't have little hearts underneath them," one conservative, a supporter, sighed with relief when he saw them. But the most damaging commentary was by the *New York Times*'s David Brooks, who wrote an October 13 column that excerpted significant sections of the magazine columns Miers wrote when she was president of the Texas Bar Association. Brooks mocked Miers's writing style and said "nothing excuses sentences like the ones Ms. Miers writes." Brooks then played freshman English professor, dissecting the columns and giving Miers a failing grade, concluding she lacked the "threshold skills" required to sit on the Supreme Court.[4]

Buoyed by the rising tide of anger coming from right-leaning media outlets, and with the White House failing to stem it, Republican senators quietly began raising questions about Miers. She had been meeting with senators since her nomination was first announced, and she had not been well received. In contrast to Roberts, she was ill prepared and uninformed on the law. Unlike Sandra Day O'Connor in 1981, whose dynamic personality carried her through, Miers's voice was soft and quiet, and senators had to strain to hear her. After his meeting with Miers, Alabama's senator Jeff Sessions, a loyal Bush supporter, told her, "Harriet, you're going to have to say something next time." Senator Tom Coburn, another solid Republican on the Judiciary Committee, was more blunt in his assessment.

"How'd I do?" Miers asked him after their meeting.

"Harriet," Coburn said, "you flunked."

Miers's staffers defended her by saying her strengths "take time to appreciate." But time was another thing Miers lacked. While juggling her meetings with senators, she was also working with administration lawyers to get ready for the hearings. George Washington University professor Bradford Clark, who had worked on the Bork nomination in the Reagan Justice Department, came to the White House to help her prepare, but she made little progress. At every mock session, conducted with lawyers inside the administration, she had trouble articulating her views and explaining basic concepts of constitutional law. The Justice Department, which was helping coordinate the effort, had set up sessions with the same private lawyers and law professors who'd helped Roberts prepare, but it kept canceling them. Miers wasn't ready for the outside world. The young associates who worked for Miers and Kelley in the White House counsel's office were demoralized. The preparation sessions had become excruciating, and they would return to their offices wondering how Bush could salvage the nomination. It was like teaching someone French in three weeks and then expecting her to pass a fluency exam. It seemed impossible.

In mid-October, less than two weeks after Miers's nomination, Kelley met with Card to discuss her progress. Advisers had been warning him that Miers was struggling to get ready, but this time Kelley was more blunt in his assessment and mentioned, for the first time, the word "withdraw." Card turned grim at the news, but he remained determined. "We can't quit," Card said.

Like Bush, Card believed Miers could pull it off. But Card failed to appreciate that Miers, though a smart and capable lawyer, had no experience in constitutional law. At her law firm in Texas, she had been more of a manager, without extensive litigation experience. Because she didn't typically handle appeals, she had little understanding of the complex constitutional topics the senators would want to discuss in her upcoming hearings. And the confirmation process had changed since Reagan nominated Justice O'Connor, who was no constitutional law expert herself. The hearings were so contentious and the questions so focused that nominees without a background in constitutional law— either an experienced judge or a Supreme Court advocate like Estrada or Mahoney—would have a very tough time of it. Gone were the days when a president could nominate a practicing lawyer like Lewis Powell or Byron White and watch him sail through.

The growing concern of lawyers inside the White House and Justice

Department reached near panic proportions almost immediately after Kelley talked to Card. Miers had just completed her questionnaire for the Judiciary Committee, and her description of her legal experience was woefully inadequate. The committee had asked Miers to describe the ten most significant litigation matters she had personally handled as a lawyer. Although Miers had the awards and newspaper headlines to show she was a top lawyer, the hard evidence wasn't there. The ten cases she listed were a collection of insignificant, relatively simple disputes that suggested she wasn't the experienced litigator everyone had assumed she was. She had represented some major clients, but only in minor lawsuits. She'd been in court, but typically as the local lawyer who filed papers while the big-city firms in Chicago and New York handled the complex legal work. It came as a jolt to the lawyers in the White House, many of whom had worked in big corporate law firms themselves. They could see immediately from her case list that she was less an attorney than a law firm manager and bar association president. That was not the kind of real-world, in-the-trenches litigation that would enrich the judicial monastery of the Supreme Court.

But if Miers's practice sessions were going poorly, her meetings with senators —even Senate Republicans—were going no better. In a meeting that Monday with Senator Arlen Specter, the Pennsylvania Republican who chaired the Judiciary Committee, Miers said she believed the Constitution contained a right to privacy—or so Specter thought. The point was important to Specter, who supports abortion rights, because a right to privacy is the underpinning for *Roe v. Wade.* He was especially concerned about Miers's views because he'd just learned that in 1989, while a candidate for the Dallas City Council, she had endorsed a constitutional amendment banning abortion. Specter told reporters after his closed-door meeting with Miers that she'd told him she believed there was a right to privacy in the Constitution. When Miers heard Specter's characterization of their conversation, she contacted his office immediately. She denied she'd said any such thing, and asked that Specter clarify his statement. Bill Reynolds, Specter's chief of staff, spent nearly an hour on the phone with Miers that night, trying to figure out what she thought she'd told Specter about the case.

"Do you believe the Constitution contains a right to privacy?" Reynolds, a no-nonsense marine who is also a lawyer, asked Miers. She seemed to indicate yes, but then suggested no. "Well, what do you believe?" asked Reynolds, exasperated. He finally gave up. He told Specter he had no idea where Miers stood on the issue. Specter, accused by Miers of misstating their conversation, was highly annoyed, as his subsequent "clarification" revealed. He said only that he "accepts Ms. Miers's statement that he misunderstood what she said."

The next day, Miers's questionnaire hit Capitol Hill. An already agitated Specter became downright angry when he saw page after page of incomplete responses and missing dates for speeches, newspaper articles, and membership in various organizations. Specter, a scrappy maverick who liked to speak his mind, was the one senator the White House could not afford to alienate. But Miers had done it.

On Wednesday, Specter called an extraordinary joint press conference with Vermont senator Patrick Leahy, the top Democrat on the Judiciary Committee. Both men demanded that she redo significant portions of her questionnaire. "On the balance of her answers, they're incomplete," said Specter, noting she had provided only a "skimpy little group" of cases she had handled. Leahy said reactions to the questionnaire by senators on the Judiciary Committee ranged from "insulting" to "incomplete." They wanted more detailed responses on a third of their original questions, covering almost every aspect of her legal work and continuing through the selection process that led to her nomination.

Specter also doubled back to his private meeting with Miers and implied that he didn't believe he'd actually mischaracterized her views on privacy when he talked to reporters later in the day. Specter, a former prosecutor, said Wednesday that in his years of meeting with nominees, he'd "never walked out of a room and had a disagreement as to what was said." As for Miers, "the sooner we get into a hearing room where there's a stenographer and public record, the better off the process is," Specter said.

Specter then delivered a bombshell: The committee would begin hearings on Miers's nomination on November 7, giving her less than three weeks to respond to questions, continue her meetings with senators, read constitutional law cases, and undergo practice sessions.

Quietly, Republican senators Graham and Sam Brownback began drafting a letter demanding that Miers turn over legal memorandums and briefs she'd written for President Bush. The conservative senators were providing the president and Miers with an escape. They knew the memos were protected by presidential privilege and that the White House could not turn them over. Miers could refuse and then ostensibly step down on principle. At the same time, Senate majority leader Bill Frist also consulted with key Republican senators. They all concurred that Miers was in trouble.

Bush's closest political advisers were working on much the same exit strategy by week's end, believing the best way out for Miers was to point to the Senate's request for the documents. These discussions were tightly held. Miers continued her meetings and preparation sessions unaware, like other top officials in the White House and Justice Department outside the inner circle, of the growing momentum in the West Wing for her withdrawal.

Bush realized the nomination was in trouble, but he wasn't influenced by the critics on Capitol Hill and in conservative circles. He was not listening to them. He wasn't going to back down in the face of criticism, whether it was from opponents or allies, in the press or in the Senate. The conservative revolt did not influence his thinking, because he believed conservatives would ultimately stand with Miers. Like Card, he wanted to fight. Those conservatives who had argued against a revolt against Miers were right. Bush was not going to back away, no matter what they said. They were only hurting themselves and ensuring they wouldn't be invited back to the White House the next time.

But what Bush hadn't counted on was Miers letting him down. He

was so confident of her abilities that he hadn't contemplated her in-
ability to get through the hearings. He had focused on whether she
could perform the job as a justice. His advisers had said yes, she could.
But Bush hadn't focused on whether she could perform as a nominee.
It was becoming painfully clear she couldn't. She wasn't going to learn
constitutional law in three weeks and pass a fluency exam.

Bush had a painful meeting with Card that Tuesday, October 25, in
the Oval Office. Card told Bush the prep sessions were going badly, and
that Miers should consider withdrawing, for her sake and for the president's. She wasn't ready for the hearings, Card said, and she wouldn't
be ready. After Roberts performed so well, expectations were too high.
She had little support from Republicans, and it would be too easy for
Democrats to savage her.

Bush already knew that. He realized how things would unfold. He
agreed it was time to change course.

That night Card went to Miers's office and began laying the groundwork for her to bow out. He didn't tell her to step down. Instead, he
raised concerns. "Things aren't going well," Card said. And the hearings
were less than two weeks away.

The next morning, Kelley visited Miers's office and picked up where
Card had left off. He began the conversation gently, saying her interests
happened to coincide with the president's, and they both pointed in the
same place. Then he paused. "This isn't going to work," Kelley said.
"You have to withdraw."

Miers hadn't interpreted Card's visit as a signal she should quit, so
Kelley's words caught her by surprise. She immediately began to say no,
but Kelley continued. He told her he'd advised Bush that she wouldn't
be able to make it through the hearings, which promised to be brutal.
Democrats who'd held their fire would be unable to resist delivering a
beating. From their perspective, the more unqualified she appeared,
the worse George Bush would look. She wasn't ready for that, and she
shouldn't put herself—or the president—through it.

Miers, far from acquiescing quietly, exhibited the toughness Bush knew so well. She resisted. She wanted to fight, she said. She didn't want to quit. She could do it.

Later in the morning, Frist was in the White House to discuss budget issues, but he made a point of telling Bush that Republican senators had deep concerns about Miers. He suggested that her nomination could fail. But Frist was late to the game; Bush had already made up his mind.

It took one more visit from Card later in the day to convince Miers she needed to get out. She realized it was best for the president, and that he'd been behind Card's visits. That night, she called Bush in the residence of the White House to tell him. She then wrote her letter of withdrawal to Bush. She said she was "greatly honored and humbled" by his confidence in her, but that she was concerned the confirmation process "presents a burden for the White House and our staff that is not in the best interest of the country." She then turned to the face-saving exit strategy Bush's advisers had formulated the week before, pointing to the Senate's request for confidential presidential documents. In the letter, Miers talked about how the Senate's demands could damage the independence of the executive branch. "I have decided," she said, "that seeking my confirmation should yield."

But she couldn't resist defending herself in her last paragraph against all those critics she believed had judged her unfairly. She knew what was at stake with the nomination, and she knew where she stood on the law. "I share your commitment to appointing judges with a conservative judicial philosophy," she said, "and I look forward to continuing to support your efforts to provide the American people judges who will interpret the law, not make it." Before Miers left her office that night, the White House had already found her replacement. The next morning, when news of her withdrawal broke, Miers was fully on board to support him. She would not look back. She was determined to see Bush's next nominee get confirmed. He had been her top choice from the beginning, and she was ready for the next fight.

12.

A FULL COUNT

Samuel Alito was at his desk in the old federal courthouse in downtown Newark when the phone rang. It was late on a Wednesday afternoon, and Alito was working. For the past fifteen years, the studious federal appeals court judge had been writing opinions at that heavy wooden desk, and he had come to accept the fact that he would work there for the rest of his career as a federal judge.

Earlier that summer, Alito had waited for a call from the White House that never came, and he'd moved on. He liked Newark. He liked being a judge. He even liked his old office, with its solid doors and bookcases up to the ceiling. It wasn't fancy, but when an elaborate new courthouse was built across the street in the early 1990s, he'd decided to stay behind in the dilapidated post office and courthouse where he'd begun his career as a law clerk. The windows of his chambers looked out upon the new building's vast plaza, empty but for a grotesquely ugly sculpture of an enormous blindfolded head. Seldom did a day pass without someone posing for a picture with an arm thrust up one of the sculpture's gaping nostrils. Alito was old school, and he didn't like unnecessary change any more than he liked that ridiculous sculpture.

Then came the call in late October. "Are you still interested in a Supreme Court nomination?" asked Bill Kelley, on the other end of the line.

For a split second, Alito was too stunned to speak. He had had many conversations with Kelley in the late spring and early summer about the nomination. He had been to Washington three times since May to talk to administration officials about it. He had even met with Bush in the White House. Sam Alito had gotten so close, but Bush had picked someone else not once, but twice. Alito had tried to absorb the disappointment, which was sharp, and get back to his life.

The month before, Alito had watched some of John Roberts's confirmation hearings. The television was on one night just before Alito and his wife sat down to dinner, and Roberts was still testifying. Alito marveled at Roberts's stamina, enduring a daylong marathon of questioning. He had also followed the controversy surrounding the Miers nomination, but he never thought she would be forced to withdraw. He assumed she would be confirmed.

But Kelley's call seemed to suggest otherwise, that something had gone terribly wrong. Nothing was public, but the president was looking at Alito once again. Was he still up for the job?

"Yes," Alito told Kelley, the surprise registering in his voice. He is a quiet man, but he answered emphatically.

Alito hung up the phone and immediately called his wife, Martha-Ann. Following Kelley's instructions, the Alitos told no one else about the call. As far as anyone else was concerned, the White House was firmly behind Miers's nomination. Only the Alitos and people in Bush's innermost circle knew otherwise.

Even some White House insiders were kept in the dark. The night of Kelley's call to Alito, conservative leader Jay Sekulow called one of Rove's deputies, Tim Goeglein, who served as a liaison between conservatives and the White House. Sekulow was scheduled to go on C-SPAN the next morning to defend Miers, and he didn't want to be blindsided. Goeglein assured him that the president was not backing down. So closely held was the plan that a couple of hours later, just before midnight, White House staffers delivered to the Senate Miers's second attempt to answer her questionnaire from the Judiciary Committee.

Sekulow was one of Miers's few loyal defenders, and he assured C-SPAN viewers early the next morning that she would not withdraw. But an hour later, Miers walked into the Oval Office and handed her withdrawal letter to the president. Bush released a statement shortly thereafter. He'd "reluctantly accepted" her withdrawal, he said. He embraced the same pretext for withdrawing that influential columnist Charles Krauthammer had publicly urged Miers to take and Bush to accept the week before—namely that the Senate's request for documents infringed on executive power.[1] But White House advisers, seeing the writing on the wall, had begun formulating that exit strategy before Krauthammer's column was published.

"It is clear that Senators would not be satisfied until they gained access to internal documents concerning advice provided during her tenure at the White House—disclosures that would undermine a president's ability to receive candid counsel," Bush said. "Harriet Miers's decision demonstrates her deep respect for this essential aspect of the constitutional separation of powers—and confirms my deep respect and admiration for her."

Bush spokesman Scott McClellan held a 9 a.m. press briefing. He told reporters that Miers had called Bush at the residence the night before, leaving the implication that Miers had decided on her own to withdraw. Reporters asked McClellan whether Bush had talked to her before she made the decision. McClellan said that Bush had not. None of the reporters asked whether other presidential advisers had talked to Miers, and McClellan didn't volunteer the information. Instead the focus was on Miers and Bush.

Reporter: Did he talk about this at all—

McClellan: No, this was a decision that she came to.

Reporter: He never—it never came up?

McClellan: No, she was not asked to—this was a decision she came to.

Reporter: Why is he disappointed with the process—

McClellan: And I think it shows the type of person that she is. She is someone who is very selfless and wise, and she recognized that it was more important to protect this important separation of powers and principle than it was to move forward on her personal ambition.

Process notwithstanding, conservatives were euphoric. They didn't buy the excuse about the documents, and they believed they'd driven Bush into a rare capitulation. "It will be a long time before the White House thinks it can use and abuse conservatives again," wrote lightning rod Ann Coulter, who like other Miers critics expected the president now to nominate an intellectual powerhouse with the heft to counter the Court's liberal heavyweights. "Let's move on," said Senator Trent Lott. "In a month, who will remember the name Harriet Miers?"

Democrats had kept quiet for weeks as conservatives savaged Miers. Once she withdrew, they quickly turned their sights on Bush, accusing him of bowing to conservative extremists. "The radical right wing of the Republican Party killed the Harriet Miers nomination," said Harry Reid. Ted Kennedy said Miers deserved a hearing, but that the president had instead sacrificed her to the "extreme factions of [his] own political party." Kennedy solemnly urged Bush to "take whatever time is necessary to find a consensus nominee" to fill the O'Connor seat.

But the White House had already identified its next nominee, and it was moving to put elements in place for an announcement. The administration wanted to put the failed Miers nomination behind it as quickly as possible. Bush had surrendered on his demand for diversity, and consensus was not a concern. The president was going to nominate the man his legal advisers, including Miers, had preferred all along.

That afternoon, after Miers bowed out, Andy Card called Sam Alito at home outside Newark. It was a call Miers typically would have made, as she had earlier in the summer, before Bush offered Roberts the nomination. But that would be asking too much of the White House counsel at this point. Card stepped in to handle the job.

Teenager Laura Alito was on her computer at home, sending instant messages to friends, when the phone rang.

"This is Andy Card calling from the White House," a man said in a pleasant voice. "Can I speak to Sam Alito?"

"He's not here," said Laura, a senior in high school. "He's at work." She gave Card the number in her father's chambers.

It was the kind of mistake Harriet Miers, meticulous and attentive to detail, would not have made. Card had called the wrong number and, in a White House obsessed with secrecy, had shown his hand by identifying himself.

Laura rushed back to the computer and sent her brother Philip an instant message. News of Miers's withdrawal was all over the Internet, and speculation had already focused on a handful of possible nominees, including their father. "The White House just called for Dad," she wrote. Philip, a sophomore at the University of Virginia, shot back: "What? Who?"

Laura couldn't remember the caller's name, so Philip went through a list of possibilities until he landed on Card. "That's it," Laura said. "Andy Card?" responded Philip Alito. "Oh my gosh."

Their father had been thinking for quite some time about being a justice. In 1972, when Sam Alito was just a couple of years older than Philip, his college yearbook caption read, "Sam intends to go to law school and eventually to warm a seat on the Supreme Court." It was written as a joke, but the entry didn't strike anyone who knew the scholarly Alito at Princeton University as preposterous. His senior adviser considered him the "most judicious" student he'd ever had: careful, incisive, and keenly intelligent. The early 1970s, when Alito was a college student, were a turbulent time, but he sidestepped the protests and debates on the Vietnam War. He focused on course work, listened to classical music, and spent part of his senior year in Italy, where his father was born, writing his thesis about the Italian legal system. It was the first time he'd lived outside New Jersey.

After graduating from Princeton, Alito embarked down his path to the Supreme Court, heading to law school at Yale. He clerked for distinguished federal appeals court judge Leonard Garth in Newark, and applied for a Supreme Court clerkship. When Justice Byron White invited him to interview for a clerkship, Alito spent hours and hours reading cases and preparing for an intellectual conversation about the law. But "Whizzer White," a former all-American who had played in the National Football League, wanted to talk about football. Alito didn't get an offer.

With his Ivy League degrees and top grades, Alito could have made a handsome living with a private law firm. He chose instead to work on criminal appeals for the federal prosecutor in New Jersey. His office was one block from the courthouse where he'd clerked for Garth and an hour from his parents' home in Trenton.

In a building replete with colorful characters, Alito was steady and focused. His research work often sent him to the office's law library, where he would throw himself into a chair with gusto and delve into a book. That caught the attention of the law librarian. After she overheard colleagues talking about how Alito was learning Russian for a case involving Russian spies, she passed him a note with her phone number on it. He called two weeks later. They both happened to be reading *Falconer*, the John Cheever novel about a drug-addicted professor who regains his humanity in a grim prison by embarking on a homosexual affair with a fellow inmate.

"Isn't it the greatest?" Martha-Ann Bomgardner gushed. "I hate it," Alito said. The rest of the conversation went much the same way, but Bomgardner told friends she was going to marry Sam Alito, and the couple started dating the next year. Five years after that, when they both were living in Washington, Alito suggested dancing lessons. "Well, we're going to need to dance at our wedding," he explained. They took the lessons and married the following February, in 1985.

Martha-Ann Alito is the kind of warm and vivacious person who meets a new friend every day, while Alito is bookish and quiet. His wife likes to joke that he is "old world courtly" and that he should've been born in 1850, not a century later. He would've been an academician, she thinks, absorbed in his mind and his books and where those things would take him.

In Washington, Alito argued civil and criminal matters before the Supreme Court on behalf of the federal government, then served as the deputy assistant attorney general for the Office of Legal Counsel. He and Martha returned to Newark in 1987, when the first President Bush appointed him the U.S. attorney for New Jersey. Two years later, at a judicial conference in Pittsburgh, Alito heard federal appeals court judge John Gibbons announce he was planning to retire. Being a federal judge was Alito's dream job, and after thinking it over and worrying about sounding presumptuous, he made a few calls to Washington to express his interest. He was fortunate that New Jersey had two Democratic senators, since he had no political activities to speak of—and none of the political ties and connections a Republican home state senator would have looked for. The White House invited him down for a day of interviews. His inquisitors were top Justice Department officials Ken Starr, Mike Luttig, and John Roberts, and Alito can remember only one specific question. "Which Supreme Court justices do you admire most?" Roberts asked during a one-on-one interview with Alito in his Justice Department office.

Alito said Rehnquist. "I'm not just saying that because you clerked for him," he quickly told Roberts, with a smile. He admired Rehnquist's sharp mind. Alito had argued twelve cases on the government's behalf before the Supreme Court, and he always found Rehnquist's mental quickness impressive.

The interview between the two future justices went well. George H. W. Bush nominated the thirty-nine-year-old Alito in January, and when the Senate unanimously confirmed him, he moved down the block to the courthouse where he had clerked before. Alito was full of zeal early on. Casting judgment on his new colleagues, he voted to rehear a case he believed they'd wrongly decided before he'd even written his first opinion. None of the other judges agreed with him, and he wrote a memo saying why he thought the court's decision was wrong. He later came to think his conduct had been disrespectful and inappropriate. As he settled into the new job, he quickly became less aggressive about taking on his colleagues' positions. He wrote fewer separate opinions. He wouldn't support an argument he disagreed with, and he wouldn't suppress one he thought was critically important. But he grew judicious in choosing his battles.

The next year, Alito handled one of his most controversial cases. Pennsylvania had imposed a number of restrictions on abortion, and Planned Parenthood argued they were unconstitutional. Alito thought the Supreme Court's previous abortion decisions signaled that the restrictions were permissible, including a provision that required a woman to notify her husband before getting an abortion. His colleagues disagreed, so Alito ended up in dissent.[2] That was the case, *Planned Parenthood of Southeastern Pennsylvania v. Casey*, which would produce bitter divisions at the Supreme Court, when Justices O'Connor, Kennedy, and Souter would come together and refuse to overturn *Roe v. Wade*.

Alito wrote hundreds of opinions as a federal appeals court judge, and over the years he developed a reputation as a reliable conservative, though not a bombastic one. He was cautious. His opinions were carefully constructed, logical, and unadorned. He didn't write in a captivating style, like Scalia, but he didn't try to. Alito didn't have Scalia's sharp elbows, and he didn't write the kind of sweeping opinions, brimming with rhetorical flourish, that drew attention.

His careful and measured approach to the law corresponded with his personal style on the bench. He was polite, quiet, and respectful. Liberal judge A. Leon Higginbotham, a former colleague, once told a new judge that Alito was "my kind of conservative."

Alito was also far removed from the Washington political scene, in distance and in thought. His law clerks weren't scattered through the Bush administration, and they hadn't gotten automatic spots on the Supreme Court. Alito didn't do the kind of networking and lobbying with justices and former clerks that some appeals court judges— Luttig primarily—did to get their clerks placed on the high court. But Alito impressed enough of the right people during his time in the Reagan administration to keep his name circulating in Washington as a possible pick. When the Bush White House started casting about for replacements for Rehnquist, Alito was on the list.

When Bush's judicial team became serious about Supreme Court replacements, they invited Alito to Washington and interviewed him in April at the vice president's mansion on Massachusetts Avenue. Cheney and the political advisers seemed to ask most of the questions. The vice president wondered about Alito's views on the use of foreign law, which was then a controversial issue that had divided the Court's liberal and conservative justices. Justice Kennedy had consulted foreign laws to bolster the Court's recent decision striking down the death penalty for those who commit murder as juveniles.[3] Scalia had taken strong offense, writing that foreign law was useless in interpreting the U.S. Constitution.

"I don't think that you can interpret the Constitution by taking sort of a poll of the countries of the world and the constitutional courts of the world," Alito told the group. "There are legal issues where it's appropriate to look at foreign law—when you're interpreting a treaty, for instance—but not on that." He sided with Scalia on the question of foreign law.

That led to a question by Rove about Alito's nickname. "What do you think about people referring to you as 'Scalito'?" Rove asked.

Alito had gotten the nickname several years earlier, when he was first mentioned as a possible Supreme Court pick. For journalists, it was a quick and vivid way of saying he'd be just like Scalia if he made it to the Supreme Court. Alito didn't like it.

"I don't think it's appropriate. It's based mostly on ethnicity," he said to Rove. "If they thought I was so conservative, why didn't they compare me to Rehnquist or Thomas? Why did they choose to compare me to Scalia?"

Then he provided an impromptu language lesson. "If they knew Italian, they'd realize 'ito' is not an Italian diminutive, it's a Spanish diminutive," said Alito. "It really shouldn't be 'Scalito,'" he said, pausing. "It should be 'Scalino.'" Rove and the others broke into laughter.

Alito left thinking the meeting had gone well, and he took the train back up to Newark the next morning. A couple weeks later, Miers asked him to come back to Washington, and he met in her office to go over his background information with her—financial statements and questions as to whether there was anything potentially embarrassing in his past. Back home, every time he got a call for more information, he figured it was good news.

He was right. "He's never written a wrong opinion," Kelley told Miers after analyzing all of Alito's decisions. Alito had made fans in the White House, and Miers was a big one. She thought Alito possessed an ideal combination of intellect, conservatism, and quiet confidence. He hadn't campaigned for the job; he hadn't acted like he wanted it too much. In the Bush White House, that was a big plus for Alito—and a negative for Luttig, who was perceived as trying too hard.

Alito heard nothing that last week in June, when everyone waited for Rehnquist to retire. When O'Connor stepped down instead, Alito knew he wasn't the obvious choice to replace her. He remembered a resolution he'd made five years before, when his name was first floated as a possible pick and he'd begun getting calls from Washington. He'd resolved then that he wouldn't allow himself to be mired in disappointment if the lightning didn't strike him. Some federal appeals court judges had been unable to get beyond it. Arlin Adams, a judge on the

Philadelphia-based court, had come close to getting the nomination in the 1970s, and he'd reportedly become sour when he was passed by. Alito told himself he wouldn't succumb to that emotion. If it didn't happen, he was fortunate to be on the appeals court.

But as his prospects for the nomination became more realistic, he found it harder and harder to stick with his resolution.

Alito hadn't heard from the White House for nearly a month when the call came in mid-July for him to come to Washington to interview with President Bush for the O'Connor vacancy. He'd been hearing arguments in Philadelphia that week, so he had to coordinate when he could get to the capital. Bush interviewed him on Saturday, the day he also talked to Edith Brown Clement, the New Orleans judge.

Alito was the last of the five candidates Bush interviewed. Miers sat off to the side, as she did in the other interviews. Since it was a Saturday, Bush met with Alito in the residence, and the president wore casual clothes. Bush thought Alito seemed nervous at first, but Alito wasn't. He was calm, and he felt comfortable answering Bush's questions.

As with the others, Bush sought to put him at ease by talking about personal things. He told Alito he had turned against running—at his age, it was just too hard on his knees. Bush then shifted the conversation to general questions about the role of a judge. His questions were targeted and direct. "I've made all these speeches. I've said I wanted to nominate a strict constructionist," Bush said. "What did I mean by that?"

"You want somebody who will interpret the law," Alito said, "who wouldn't make up the law."

Bush then wanted to talk about the dynamics of working in a large group. He had come to believe that collegiality was critically important on a court that Oliver Wendell Holmes had described as "nine scorpions in a bottle." He wanted to do more than avoid a Souter mistake like his father's. He also wanted a justice who could influence the others, one who would effectively make the case for judicial conservatism to the public, through his opinions and demeanor on the Court. "How can you be a leader on the Court?" Bush asked Alito. "How can you be a good colleague?"

Alito had thought about those questions as a federal appeals court judge. He'd moderated his own behavior on the appeals court after his initial aggressiveness. He saw the value of consensus.

"It should not be personal at any time. You should always try to deal with your colleagues with intellectual respect, with respect for arguments they're making," Alito told Bush. "You totally lose ability to have productive discussions with other members of the court if you convey you don't respect their ideas. Even if you don't think it's a good idea, if you give the impression you don't respect it, you lose the ability to talk with them in the future."

As their forty-five-minute conversation wound down, Bush gave Alito a short tour of the residence. He pointed out the television where he watched baseball games, which Alito thought was an especially nice touch. Alito is a lifelong Philadelphia Phillies fan who coached Little League and once attended a baseball "fantasy camp" to play with the pros—an experience that included dressing in full uniform. But even his love for baseball has a cerebral aspect to it. Although baseball has been known to draw out the sentimental poet in the most unsentimental people, what Alito likes best about it are the statistics.

That afternoon, Alito walked around Washington by himself, turning his conversation with Bush over and over in his head. He was struck that it was easier to talk to the president than he'd imagined it would be. Then he thought of all the things he wished he'd said.

The next call came two days later, on Monday, when Alito was driving his 1999 Ford Taurus to Philadelphia for another argument session. Although his chambers were in Newark, the U.S. Court of Appeals for the Third Circuit is based in Philadelphia and usually hears arguments there. His cell phone rang as he was on the drive down, and he missed the call. He checked the message when he arrived, and saw it was from Miers.

"We're going in a different direction," she told him on his voice mail. She didn't say that Bush had selected Roberts, and she didn't tell Alito he was the runner-up.

His resolution was especially hard to keep that day. It also was difficult during those weeks in September, after Bush tapped Roberts for chief justice, when he knew the White House was again looking for O'Connor's successor and his phone didn't ring. And it was equally hard on the first Monday in October, when Bush announced he was nominating Miers.

Like Arlin Adams, Alito had been passed over. It didn't happen; the lightning didn't strike. He was fortunate, he reminded himself, to be on the appeals court.

Alito never considered the possibility that Miers would withdraw. He thought she'd get through the hearings, then be confirmed to the Supreme Court. Living outside Washington, he was able to escape the relentless chatter about her prospects and what Bush should do. Kelley's call that Wednesday was a flash of lightning, and Alito hadn't even known the storm was brewing.

Andy Card finally tracked down Alito in his chambers late Thursday afternoon after he talked to his teenage daughter Laura. He asked Alito if he would take a call from President Bush, and Alito said yes, he'd be honored to take that call.

When Alito got home that night, he acted as if nothing extraordinary had happened. How was your day? he asked his daughter. Fine, she said. Her father didn't volunteer anything. He's trying to act all normal, Laura thought.

"So, Dad," Laura finally blurted out, "did you get any important calls today?"

The next morning, Alito was in his chambers, waiting on the expected phone call from the president. Martha-Ann was so nervous that she'd gone to the Metropolitan Museum of Art in New York to tour Fra Angelico's fifteenth-century paintings—anything, she thought, to transport herself away from the twenty-first century.

The phone rang in Alito's chambers at the designated time, and Bush was on the line. "I'm thinking about nominating you to the Supreme Court," the president told Alito.

"Well, I'd be very honored by that," Alito said.

"Does that mean you'd accept?" Bush asked.

"Yes," Alito responded.

On Saturday, Alito prepared for the trip to Washington. He told his sister, a top employment lawyer in New Jersey, but not his mother, who was ninety years old. He'd told his mother about his interview with President Bush back in July. "But you are not to talk to anybody. You're not going to tell anybody, right?" Alito said. "Right," responded his mother. But she couldn't resist proudly sharing the information with an intrepid newspaper reporter who called weeks later and asked about her son. To prevent that from happening again, Alito's sister would call their mother Monday morning, just before Alito went on television with President Bush.

Alito went back to his chambers that afternoon and wrote out what he'd say after Bush announced his nomination. He had a lot to say. He would talk of his reverence for the Supreme Court, and of how O'Connor had asked him his very first question at his first oral argument. He would explain that he thought a judge's role was limited. And he would share his wish that his father, who'd immigrated to the United States from Italy as a young child and sacrificed much for his children, had lived to see this day. He would thank his mother, the pioneering educator, and his wife, children, and sister. After he finished writing, Alito practiced saying his remarks aloud. Martha-Ann was back at home, pulling out family photographs the White House had requested for the media. It all seemed surreal.

Alito and his wife and daughter drove down from Newark on Sunday and picked Philip up at Union Station, where he'd arrived by train from Charlottesville. They'd brought along Philip's best suit, since he didn't have one at college. They checked into a hotel in suburban Arlington, Virginia, under a false name the White House had provided, and Alito waited for a car to take him to the White House.

He spent much of the afternoon there with legal and political advisers, going over what to expect the next day. They knew the drill well, and they knew Alito would be scrutinized from day one, as Miers had. Ed Gillespie, who'd signed off on the Miers selection a month before, was there. Steve Schmidt, the communications and strategy guru who'd been so desperately missed during the Miers rollout, was back from Iraq. Both talked about the media and the various senators and what he could expect. Kelley told him about legal issues the senators would want to discuss after the announcement and the kind of questions he could anticipate.

The next morning, the Alitos met Kelley for breakfast in the White House mess. Miers soon came by. "We've got to go," she said. Miers, having stepped aside the first few days after her bitter withdrawal, was firmly back in the middle of the process, where she would remain throughout Alito's confirmation. The family stood up and walked down a hallway with Miers and Kelley. They turned a corner and were astonished to see, right in front of them, the Oval Office and President Bush. The president was waiting to greet them.

Bush made small talk. He told them of the first decision he'd had to make as president: selecting a rug for the Oval Office. "Laura, you're going to have to do this," Bush said, recalling how he'd delegated the task to the first lady.

It was soon time to go to the Cross Hall of the White House, where reporters and photographers had gathered. White House aides positioned Alito's family to the side of the lectern where Bush would stand for his announcement, but the Alitos soon realized a large marble column blocked their view. As cameras clicked, they couldn't see Bush or Alito, just a few yards away. So they listened as Bush began to speak.

Bush stressed Alito's "extraordinary breadth of experience," calling him "one of the most accomplished and respected judges in America."

He talked about Alito's academic achievements at Princeton and Yale and his career as an appellate lawyer, prosecutor, and a judge. He said Alito had "shown a mastery of the law" over the years and had participated in thousands of appeals and hundreds of decisions. In short, Sam Alito was no Harriet Miers.

Miers's nomination had shaken Washington's equilibrium. A Democrat had recommended her. Republicans had opposed her. Interest groups had been noncommittal. But just as Miers's selection had caused political chaos, Alito's put the stars all back in alignment. Within minutes of Bush's announcement, well-funded groups on the left and right, which had raised tens of millions of dollars to try to influence the confirmation process, burst into action. The overwhelming majority had stayed out of the Miers battle, but now they were buying advertising and blanketing Washington with news releases and self-selected lists of experts to shape public opinion.

Conservatives who'd been dubious of Miers were exultant. "The president has nominated someone with a long history of excellence," said Senator Jeff Sessions of Alabama, a member of the Judiciary Committee. "A home run," crowed Trent Lott, the former majority leader. "I commend the president and congratulate Judge Alito on this nomination," said Senator Sam Brownback, a Judiciary Committee member skeptical of Miers. Other Miers critics also weighed in. "Judge Alito is the best," said Wendy Long of the Judicial Confirmation Network. Concerned Women for America, which announced opposition to Miers the day before she withdrew, came out with "wholehearted support" for Alito.

The Democrats and liberal groups who'd held their fire on Miers now lined up for the epic battle they'd expected over O'Connor's replacement. Ted Kennedy said Bush "took the nation a step backward" with the nomination. New York's Chuck Schumer said the choice was "sad" and "likely to divide America." Reid said Bush, in not nominating a woman or minority, was turning the Court into an "old boys' club." They refused to rule out the prospect of a filibuster to block Alito from replacing O'Connor, saying the conservative would certainly change the Court's direction on issues such as abortion, religion, and civil rights.

The leading liberal groups had taken nearly a month to announce opposition to Roberts, and they never took a position on Miers. They denounced Alito within hours.

"Judge Alito would fundamentally change the balance of the Supreme Court, tipping it in a direction that could jeopardize our most cherished rights and freedoms," said Nan Aron, president of Alliance for Justice. Ralph Neas, head of People for the American Way, promised a "massive national campaign" against him. Women's groups that support abortion rights announced marches in protest. "Instead of reaching out to women and/or people of color to make the Supreme Court more diverse and representative, Bush has slammed the door in the face of women and minorities," said Feminist Majority Foundation president Eleanor Smeal. "He has appointed a man who would turn back the clock on women's rights and civil rights." Earthjustice, an environmental law organization, picked up on the date of the nomination, Halloween, and said Alito was a "scary choice." Bush had given a "sweet treat" to the radical Right, the group said, and "played a nasty trick" on the American people.

After the announcement, Alito was thrust immediately into the world of politics and media. He went straight to Capitol Hill, where he met with Frist, McConnell, and Specter, one right after the other. Specter, the chairman of the Judiciary Committee, was an important player, and he talked with Alito for more than an hour.

Specter was a good friend of federal appeals court judge Ed Becker, who served with Alito and thought highly of him, but Specter wanted to know Alito's views on abortion. He launched right into a substantive discussion about stare decisis. Alito said he saw precedent as a sliding scale, and that the longer a decision was in place—and the more times that it had been reaffirmed by different justices—the stronger it was. Like previous nominees, Alito didn't disclose his views, but he was able to talk with ease about the law, and he struck Specter as a careful and restrained judge who wouldn't push the envelope.

The questions Alito faced from other senators were also immediate and substantive. As the advisers had seen with Miers, senators wanted to talk within hours of the announcement. There was no time to prepare. Gone are the days when a nominee would meet with senators and politely listen to their views, as O'Connor had done during her rounds. Today, because the Supreme Court plays such a key role in social issues—and senators tell nominees they ran for office solely because of it—the pressure is more intense. Senators expect a discussion of complex constitutional issues, and a nominee who's spent his career thinking about constitutional law, either as a judge or a top appellate lawyer, starts with an enormous edge.

Lawyers like Miers, who haven't spent their lives planning for a Supreme Court nomination, are expected to do the impossible. At one time, there was a place on the Supreme Court for lawyers like Miers, those with practical experience who handled witness interviews and managed law firms and ran bar associations. Lewis Powell was one before President Nixon nominated him. But those days are gone. The job interview is designed for the appeals court judge or the elite appellate lawyer—someone like a Roberts or an Alito.

Alito ultimately met one on one with eighty-three senators—everyone who had asked to meet with him and anybody who had voted for Roberts. Photographers trailed him to and from each meeting, even walking backward in front of him down the halls of the Capitol to snap his photograph. It was disorienting for Alito, who was accustomed to a cloistered world in Newark, where weeks would pass without his seeing anybody at work but his secretary and law clerks. Even as a federal appeals court judge, he didn't get a lot of attention. When a ruling was newsworthy, the articles focused on the "appeals court in Philadelphia," not the name of the judge who'd written the opinion.

Alito didn't see the process as an opportunity to express his views, and he believed some of the Democrats were merely trying to trip him up. Sometimes Republicans also caused problems, issuing press releases to say they'd felt assured he would take a particular position, when, in fact, he hadn't made any such assurances.

Most of the senators who opposed Alito wanted to talk about the opinions he'd written as an appeals court judge. *Casey,* the abortion case, was the big one. But Alito had written a number of others in areas where O'Connor's vote had made a difference, especially in the areas of states' rights and criminal law. In every case, Alito had taken the conservative path. Democrats argued that he always sided with the government or the powerful against the powerless.

In one case, he voted to strike down a federal law banning the possession of machine guns, believing the Supreme Court had said that issue was up to the states, not the federal government.[4] His colleagues disagreed. Democrats thought that signaled hostility to the role of Congress in protecting civil rights and liberties.

Democrats also questioned him closely on another case, involving the strip search of a ten-year-old girl, where he again parted ways with colleagues.[5] Police had a warrant to search the home of a suspected drug dealer, but when they arrived they found a mother and her daughter there instead of the man. A female officer took them to a bathroom and searched them both, but didn't find any drugs. The mother filed a civil rights lawsuit against the police officers. Alito parted ways with his colleagues and wrote a dissent siding with the police officers. "I share the majority's visceral dislike of the intrusive search, but it is a sad fact that drug dealers sometimes use children to carry out their business and to avoid prosecution," Alito wrote.

As Alito was meeting with senators, lawyers and staff members were working furiously behind the scenes. His former law clerks turned out in droves to support him, some who were liberal Democrats. Some judges, including his rival Luttig, hire only clerks who share their ideological views. But Alito hired both. The clerks arranged a series of meetings with senators and staffers to talk about their experiences working with Alito, whom they saw as open-minded and fair. Some of the liberals and independents actively disliked President Bush and didn't want to work with the right-wing public relations firm hired by the White House. The clerks arranged for the Senate calls on their own.

At the same time, the staffers for liberal interest groups were producing lengthy reports that analyzed Alito's opinions and doing their own outreach on Capitol Hill. The rhetoric of the groups' leaders sometimes sounded heavy, but the staff members had come to see Alito as a radical conservative who would change the direction of the Court. They felt they had a duty to stop him, and they worked closely with the staffs of Senate Democrats, sharing information on Alito's most explosive cases and searching for other information that could help them make the argument against him.

Alito's Senate visits continued through November and into December. He got high marks from Republicans, but Democrats sometimes accused him of being an ideologue. Reid was particularly confrontational, almost as if he were angry with Alito for being the nominee. "You know we're going to have a Supreme Court where everybody's gone to an Ivy League law school?" he asked Alito.

"Well, there's nothing I can do about that," Alito responded with a smile, trying to keep the conversation light. It didn't work.

"Now, someone told me, there would be seven Catholics on the Supreme Court," Reid said.

Actually, it wouldn't be seven, Alito pointed out. He then went through the different justices and their religions. Roberts, Scalia, Kennedy, and Thomas were Catholic. He would be the fifth.

In mid-November, the interest groups believed they'd found their smoking gun, the document that would help derail the nomination. It was a 1985 job application Alito completed when he sought a political appointment in the Justice Department's Office of Legal Counsel. As smoking guns go, it was a big one. In the application, Alito enthusiastically embraced the philosophies of the Reagan administration. He wrote that he "very strongly" believed the Constitution "does not protect a right to an abortion," and he said he was proud of his work as a lawyer in the administration, arguing against *Roe v. Wade*. He also staked out conservative positions opposing racial and ethnic quotas and said he disagreed with Supreme Court decisions that kept a high wall between church and state, as well as those that gave criminal defendants greater procedural protections from police.

Leaving no doubt how he viewed liberal Supreme Court decisions, he said he became interested in constitutional law in college, when he developed a "deep disagreement" with the Warren Court, particularly its decisions on criminal law, church and state, and voting rights. He believed strongly that courts shouldn't try to solve social problems, and that the Supreme Court should have a more limited role in society. He even said he became interested in politics as a youth because he admired Barry Goldwater.

Those comments, taken together, intensified the already contentious battle. There was no doubt about Alito's political or legal views. The White House had gone from an unknown candidate in Miers, who had no judicial philosophy and no background in constitutional law, to one who'd spent a career thinking about the role of the courts and developing an approach to the law—and putting it into practice in his writings and opinions. This time, Neas and Aron had no trouble getting people to listen. Alito was solidly conservative, and they had his own words to prove it.

As Alito continued to visit with the senators, he was also meeting with administration lawyers to get ready for the upcoming hearings. The lawyers gave him briefing books on all the major subjects that might come up, consisting of tabs of leading cases. Each day was a different subject. Alito was familiar with most of the subjects, but not all. He'd never worked on cases involving voting rights and war powers. He had to study those more closely.

The issue of war powers took on increased urgency in mid-December, when the *New York Times* published an explosive account of a secret wiretapping program President Bush authorized in the months after the September 11 terrorist attacks.[6] Bush signed a presidential order in 2002 authorizing the National Security Agency to monitor the international telephone calls and e-mails of hundreds of people in the United States, without first getting warrants, in an effort to find possible links to al-Qaeda. The *Times* said Bush's decision to allow eavesdropping inside the United States without first getting court approval represented "a major shift" in intelligence gathering. It quoted officials questioning whether it "stretched, if not crossed, constitutional limits on legal searches."

The article pushed to the forefront the issue of presidential power, and it gave Senate Democrats a fresh and important legal controversy to use against Alito. Now, they weren't concerned only with abortion. The scope of Bush's power also was on the line. Just the year before, O'Connor had cast a critical vote to reign in Bush's terror policies. She joined Justice Stevens's majority opinion that the American court system could hear legal challenges by foreigners held at the U.S. military facility in Guantánamo Bay, Cuba.[7] A lower court had ruled that U.S. courts had no jurisdiction over the detainees at Guantánamo. Alito's writings as a lawyer in the Reagan administration suggested he had a broader view of presidential power—and a narrower view of the role of the courts. The hearings were an opportunity for Democrats to excoriate Bush's policies and to show how Alito, if confirmed as a justice, would defend them.

White House lawyers also tried to brace Alito for an assault on his integrity and ethics, stemming from his participation in a case involving the Vanguard companies, a stock and mutual fund business. Alito had written on a signed form as an appeals court nominee that he would recuse himself from any case involving Vanguard, since he owned shares in a mutual fund it managed. But somehow, in 2002, Alito ended up on a three-judge panel in a dispute between two individuals over a Vanguard fund. Vanguard was named as a defendant. When one of the parties complained about Alito's involvement, Alito notified the circuit's chief judge. The ethical issue was murky—Alito's involvement probably did not qualify as a conflict under federal rules. But Alito asked that a new panel of judges rehear it anyway. A new group reconsidered the case and decided it the same way. Ethics scholars said the issue was minor—an "oops," as several put it—and not uncommon on the federal courts. But Democrats began hammering Alito for it, as the White House had anticipated. It was ammunition for the upcoming battle, and the Democrats were going to use it any way they could.

By the time the hearings began, the interest groups and the Democrats on the Judiciary Committee believed they were armed with enough information to derail Alito. They had Alito's memos and opinions that showed him to be a solid conservative on every single hot-button social issue—someone who would oppose abortion and affirmative action and vote for sweeping presidential power. He was to the right of O'Connor, and he clearly would move the Court in that direction. They also had the complaint in the Vanguard case, which they could use to question his integrity. And they had his 1985 statement claiming membership in the Concerned Alumni of Princeton, a notorious alumni organization that opposed coeducation and affirmative action in Princeton admissions. Democrats on the Senate Judiciary Committee were united. The liberal interest groups felt confident before the hearings began that none of them would vote to confirm Alito.

For Bush's appeals court nominees, a vote along party lines in the Judiciary Committee had meant one thing when the nomination reached the full Senate: filibuster. If Democrats on the committee unanimously voted against a nominee, they would also be able to block a confirmation vote on the Senate floor. Alito's opponents thought they might be able to pull that off and block his nomination.

The Saturday before Alito's hearings began, Alito got up early and, still in his pajamas, went to his computer. The White House had been pestering him to write his opening statement, and he had put it off until the last weekend. He didn't have a lot of time to spend on it. He sat down and wrote, without stopping, until he finished. Then he e-mailed it to the White House. "What do you think of this?" he wrote.

The White House responded that it looked good.

The day the hearings began, Alito felt a sense of relief. He was more in his element, like a lawyer back in court, and he could speak out publicly. He sat quietly as the senators gave their opening remarks. His wife, children, and sister were in seats behind him.

Senators were aggressive in their opening statements. Leahy talked about Miers, saying Bush had "succumbed to partisan pressure from the extreme right of his party." Kennedy criticized Alito's rulings. "To put it plainly, average Americans have had a hard time getting a fair shake in his courtroom." Russell Feingold of Wisconsin promised "tough questions," saying "no one is entitled to a seat on the Supreme Court simply because he has been nominated by the president." Schumer also looked back to Miers, wondering why the same "cadre of conservative critics" who "called the president on the carpet for naming Harriet Miers have rolled out the red carpet for you."

For the past two months, Democrats had portrayed Alito as a right-wing zealot whose nomination was a sop to Bush's base. He would roll back the clock. He would turn his back on civil liberties. He was, as the group Earthjustice said on Halloween, scary. He was Robert Bork all over again. Now, kicking off his hearings, senators spent the afternoon laying the groundwork for a vicious battle. The stakes were high, and Alito was no stealth nominee. They had the goods on him, and they were going to use them.

But then it was Alito's turn to speak.

He began with thanks and folksy humor. There was an old story, he said, about a lawyer who was making his first argument before the Supreme Court. One of the justices asked the lawyer, "How did you get here?"—meaning how had his case worked its way up through the court system. But the nervous lawyer took the question literally and said, "I came here on the Baltimore and Ohio Railroad." He'd thought of the story a lot in recent weeks, Alito said, when he was asking himself, "How in the world did I get here?"

"I want to try to answer that today and not by saying that I came

here on I-95 or on Amtrak," he told the Judiciary Committee as senators sat quietly. Democrats looked openly hostile. Kennedy's face was
set in disapproval. Most crossed their arms in front of them.

Alito proceeded to talk about his life. He told of his father, who'd
come from Italy as a baby and who grew up in poverty, how he'd graduated at the top of his high school class but had no money for college
until someone got him a fifty-dollar scholarship that paid the tuition
and covered the cost of one used suit. He told of how his father, after
college, in the Depression, found that teaching jobs for Italian Americans were hard to come by, but he'd persevered.

"His story is a story that is typical of a lot of Americans both back
in his day and today," Alito said. "And it is a story, as far as I can see it,
about the opportunities that our country offers, and also about the
need for fairness and about hard work and perseverance and the power
of a small good deed."

He told of his mother, a first-generation American whose father had
worked in a steel mill. She became the first person in her family to get
a college degree, and she worked more than a decade before marrying,
getting a master's degree and working as a teacher—an independent
woman with a deep love of learning that she instilled in her children.

He talked of growing up as a child in an unpretentious, down-to-
earth community, where most of the adults weren't college graduates.
When he headed off to Princeton, twelve miles and a world away, he
"saw some very smart people and very privileged people behaving ir-
responsibly" during the turbulent early 1970s. "And I couldn't help
making a contrast between some of the worst of what I saw on the
campus and the good sense and the decency of the people back in my
own community," he said.

He talked of being a lawyer, of his pride in saying, "My name is
Samuel Alito and I represent the United States in this court." And he explained how being a lawyer is different from being a judge. "A judge
can't have any agenda, a judge can't have any preferred outcome in any

particular case, and a judge certainly doesn't have a client," Alito said. "The judge's only obligation—and it's a solemn obligation—is to the rule of law."

And he talked of his duty. "Fifteen years ago, when I was sworn in as a judge of the court of appeals, I took an oath. I put my hand on the Bible and I swore that I would administer justice without respect to persons, that I would do equal right to the poor and to the rich, and that I would carry out my duties under the Constitution and the laws of the United States," Alito said. "And that is what I have tried to do to the very best of my ability for the past fifteen years. And if I am confirmed, I pledge to you that that is what I would do on the Supreme Court."

The hearing room was still. The Democrats were quiet. Their expressions had changed. Some, like Dianne Feinstein, seemed surprised. This was not the man they thought they'd be subjecting to a brutal cross-examination, the one portrayed as so dangerous to the future of the nation. Halfway through Alito's introductory speech, the fight had completely left the room.

Sam Alito was on his way to confirmation as the 110th justice of the Supreme Court.

The next day, Democrats came back with pointed questions about civil rights, presidential power, ethics. Alito, slouched a bit in his chair, patiently answered every one. To help him prepare, the White House had given him a big binder with Roberts's testimony, organized by subjects, and with the questions from the different senators. Roberts had dazzled senators with his performance, and the White House lawyers were proud of the work they'd done to help him prepare. Alito never got around to looking at it. He answered the questions his own way. Rumpled and soft-spoken, he didn't have the polish of Roberts, but that was not a disadvantage. He was so understated that he never gave Democrats a chance to spark a fight. It was like trying to strike a match off a smooth surface. They couldn't do it.

At one point, Senator Hatch leaned over to Lindsey Graham, who sat to his right. "I think he's better than Roberts," Hatch said.

"He is," Graham whispered back, marveling. "He is better than Roberts."

Graham helped produce the most dramatic moment of the hearings. After Feingold had pressed Alito on his participation in the Vanguard case, and others raised questions about his membership in the Concerned Alumni of Princeton, Graham offered Alito a sympathetic shoulder. "Are you really a closet bigot?" Graham asked.

Alito: "I'm not any kind of a bigot, I'm not."

Graham: "No, sir, you're not. And you know why I believe that? Not because you just said it—but that's a good enough reason, because you seem to be a decent, honorable man. I have got reams of quotes from people who have worked with you . . . Glowing quotes about who you are, the way you've lived your life; law clerks, men and women, black and white, your colleagues who say that Sam Alito, whether I agree with him or not, is a really good man."

It was late in the afternoon on the third day of hearings, and Martha-Ann Alito was tired and growing increasingly upset. Alito's wife is an emotional person who is rarely quiet or motionless more than fifteen minutes at a time. During breaks, she'd walked past women wearing buttons that said NO ALITO and wanted to tell them she says that all the time. She spent some of the hearings trying to catch the eyes of Democratic staffers. She could never get them to look at her.

That afternoon, the questioning was focused more on Alito's integrity, and she'd sent a staffer to get an aspirin because she thought a migraine was coming on. Democrats were pressing Alito on his membership in Concerned Alumni of Princeton. Alito said that apart from his claim on the job application, he couldn't remember being associated with it. Martha remembers volunteering Alito for the group after a friend told her about it in the mid-1980s. She didn't think much of it or know what it was about, and she now felt she was responsible for getting Alito into the mess. As Graham spoke, she felt raging anger at the Senate Democrats. Graham's offer of kindness and support brought her to tears.

"Do you need to compose yourself?" whispered Rachel Brand, the assistant attorney general who'd helped prepare Alito and was sitting beside her.

Martha-Ann got up and went to the back of the room as Alito, oblivious, continued to testify. She then went through a side door and into an office set aside for the administration lawyers, where she sat down, took a deep breath, and put her feet up. The moment was over, the tears were gone, and she felt strong again.

At a break, former senator Dan Coats, who'd shepherded Alito through his Senate visits, told Alito what happened. "Martha got upset," Coats said. "But she's fine."

Coats ushered Alito back to the office where Martha was waiting.

"Are you okay?" Alito said as he walked toward her.

She smiled and shook her head ruefully. "You know me," she told her husband.

They both went back to the hearing room, but the battle was over. Alito would face pointed queries—and ultimately would not win a single Democratic vote on the Judiciary Committee—but he was too qualified, too calm and measured as a witness, with too clean a background and too nice a wife and family. His wife crying at what she perceived to be cheap political shots did not hurt either.

In the end, Samuel Alito was, as Bill Kelley had told the president before the Miers debacle, the best possible nominee. And he would now be taking Justice O'Connor's place on the Supreme Court.

Conservatives had no reason to fear that Sam Alito would be a latter-day David Souter—a nominee so stealthy that he fooled both liberals and conservatives. Alito was also nothing like Anthony Kennedy, an infuriatingly unmoored "eighty percenter" likely to part ways with conservatives in some of the cases they cared about most. Bush had done more than avoid repeating the mistake of his father. After recovering from the Miers debacle, he'd brought the confirmation process back to pre–Robert Bork. After years of White House lawyers trying to slip conservative justices past bitterly divided Judiciary Committees,

Sam Alito proved that even in the face of a filibuster threat, a judge with a clearly delineated, solidly conservative judicial philosophy could get confirmed.

Although he didn't get broad bipartisan support in the Senate, Sam Alito was the conservative equivalent of Ruth Bader Ginsburg. Like Ginsburg, he'd been an advocate for a political change. His deeply held views were well known. He'd established a clear record on the bench. He was a respected judge, admired by his colleagues on both ends of the ideological spectrum. And like Ginsburg, he would be a solid vote for the president who nominated him.

At the time of Alito's and Roberts's appointments, George W. Bush was facing political challenges on all sides: Hurricane Katrina, an Iraq war that was dissolving into civil war, record deficits and federal debts, Republican scandals on Capitol Hill, CIA leak investigations inside his own White House, and approval ratings well below Bill Clinton's at the height of impeachment. But despite all of his missteps, George W. Bush remained steadily focused on doing something his father and other Republican presidents never did: moving the balance of the Supreme Court to the right.

Historians may judge Bush as less than competent on many levels, but none will be able to write that he was unable to follow through on his campaign promises when it came to the Supreme Court. In pushing through John Roberts and Samuel Alito, the Bush White House did indeed give Americans justices closely aligned to Scalia and Thomas.

Roberts and Alito came about through a process that was at times both brilliantly executed and catastrophically blundered. The Bush team's strategy of researching and interviewing in advance of a nomination meant the White House was ready for a nomination when the time came. Unlike his father, Bush delivered a clear command for what he wanted to achieve, and his legal advisers exhaustively researched the prospective picks and responded with solid judicial conservatives. By the time Bush met the finalists, he could hardly go wrong. In deciding between the final contenders, Bush was well prepared for his interviews and had thought about the qualities he wanted to see in a nominee. His questions on judicial philosophy were more penetrating than those Reagan asked, and they were different from his father's. Both Reagan and the elder Bush relied more on their staffs to pare down the list of nominees. They interviewed one or, at most, two prospects before making their decision, compared to the five George W. Bush interviewed to replace Sandra Day O'Connor.

The triumph also came with a certain amount of luck. Bush's insistence on diversity introduced another variable. His decision to set aside his original list of contenders and nominate Miers paved the way for Alito. Instead of Miers, Bush could have tapped a lesser judicial light than Alito—a Karen Williams, for example, or an Edith Brown Clement. Either judge would have been confirmed. But Bush wanted to avoid his father's Souter mistake, and he thought the other women were more likely than Miers to drift left on the high court. He trusted Miers's views. But Miers was such a bad nominee that she couldn't get confirmed. That then freed Bush to turn to Alito, the nominee Miers herself, ironically, had favored for the spot all along. Unlike Reagan in nominating moderate Anthony Kennedy, Bush retained his focus in seeking a staunch judicial conservative to replace his failed nominee. That Bush emerged from the Miers fiasco with Alito, the best possible choice according to his legal team, was a remarkable twist.

It was George Bush's insistence on Court diversity coupled with the Democrats' success in eliminating the most accomplished minorities and women that briefly derailed the process. Liberal court watchers must find it bitterly ironic that their successes in filibustering women, Hispanics, and African Americans in 2003 undermined Bush's plans to replace O'Connor with another woman or a minority and led him instead to replace the trailblazing justice with yet another white, conservative man.

With the unwitting help of his Democratic opponents, George W. Bush ended up placing two of the most conservative justices on the Supreme Court in years. And together with Scalia and Thomas, the Roberts Court is more conservative than any other in a half century. More important for the movement they represent, Roberts and Alito are more than ideological partners. They are collegial and savvy, more so than Rehnquist. They are conservative, but less bold than Scalia or Thomas. They both have an abundance of people skills and political instincts that can help keep moderate Kennedy in check. As Bush and his White House lawyers understood from the beginning, mere conservative votes were not enough. This White House wanted justices who could build alliances and working majorities.

Although their outlook on the law and the proper role of the Court may be similar to that of Scalia and Thomas, their impact on its direction over the next three to four decades will be more substantial. The Court is now poised to recede from some of the divisive cultural debates. George W. Bush and his team of lawyers will be shaping the direction of American law and culture long after many of them are dead.

AFTERWORD

Early on the morning after Memorial Day, Sam Alito walked into his chambers expecting nothing out of the ordinary. He'd been on the Court now more than a year, and after an initial period of bewilderment, he'd adjusted to its rhythms and routines. In the first few months, after assuming Sandra Day O'Connor's seat, he found himself getting lost in the Court's maze of hallways, constantly having to backtrack and retrace his steps. During the public argument sessions, he was reserved, and court watchers wondered when he'd find his voice. And because he'd joined the Court in the middle of a term, as Anthony Kennedy had nearly two decades before, the workload was crushing. He played catch-up.

But by May of 2007, Alito had found his way. His voice—on the bench and in his opinions—was clear and confident, and his vote was solidly and dependably conservative. With new Chief Justice John Roberts at the helm, the Court appeared poised to finally make the dramatic shift to the Right that conservatives had long hoped for and liberals had long feared. Already there had been one clear signal: The month before, Roberts and the new conservative majority had upheld a federal law that banned so-called partial birth abortion. The decision marked the first time since *Roe v. Wade* that the Court had allowed a ban on a specific abortion procedure, and it was Alito's vote that made the difference. Just seven years earlier, the Court had struck down similar state laws. Then, it was O'Connor who had swung the pendulum when she cast her vote with the four liberal justices.

The Court, with its youthful and dynamic new chief and its experienced rookie associate, was turning. Purely by coincidence, the line up of cases in that first full term would provide a quick snapshot of just how much—and how fast. Along with the partial-birth abortion case, the justices also had a docket full of other contentious cases on issues that deeply divide public opinion: race-based school assignment plans, environmental policy, campaign finance laws, and free speech in schools. Every few years brings such a term, when the constellation of cases thrusts the Court into controversy, criticism, and intense media scrutiny. Kennedy's first full year on the bench was that kind of term. So was Clarence Thomas's.

This term—Alito's first full one and Roberts's second—was also shaping up as unusually explosive.

By the end of it in late June, the decisions in those divisive cases would outline, in stark relief, exactly how different a path the new Roberts Court would take than that of the old Court, led by William Rehnquist and directed by O'Connor. Like shifting tectonic plates, the justices in the midst of change would collide and ultimately diverge over those cases with great force. The resulting tension and bitterness spilled into their opinions and public sessions, and lingered after they had left the bench on the term's last day.

The abortion case, by all accounts a barometer of change, was the first rumble of seismic activity. The justices, in a 5–4 decision, voted to uphold the federal Partial Birth Abortion Ban Act, a law that prohibited doctors from performing a rare procedure done in the second trimester of pregnancy. Congress had passed the law with broad, bipartisan support in 2003, three years after the Court's liberal justices—joined by O'Connor—struck down similar state laws as unconstitutional. The federal law banned the same type of abortion procedure the state laws had targeted, and abortion rights groups made the same arguments that it, too, was unconstitutional. They urged the Court not to repudiate a case it had decided just seven years before.

But this time, conservatives prevailed. Anthony Kennedy, who had authored a bitter dissent in the 2000 case, did not waver. He wrote the majority opinion. Ruth Bader Ginsburg, now the Court's only female justice, penned a stinging dissent that accused the court of paternalism and called the decision "alarming." In a rare move on the day the decision was handed down, she read a statement aloud from the bench, her thin voice chastising the majority for endangering the health of women based on archaic and discredited views.

Of all the justices on the Court, Ginsburg felt O'Connor's absence most acutely. The two had become close over the years, and Ginsburg had come to see O'Connor as an older sister of sorts. In the abortion case, Ginsburg also missed O'Connor's vote. Days later, O'Connor called Ginsburg in her chambers to commend her for the dissent, and she expressed her regret at the outcome. Left unsaid between the two women was the obvious point: The Court would never have upheld the law if O'Connor had remained on the Court.

To outsiders, the abortion case was, perhaps, a sign of the inevitable. But the liberal justices knew the case was a marker: the beginning of one conservative victory after another. By the end of April, the justices had cast their votes on all of the term's remaining cases, and conservatives won all the big ones. They wouldn't announce them publicly for another month; they were busy writing majority opinions. The liberal justices, left to divvy up dissents, were feeling helpless and adrift—and increasingly indignant.

A month later, their anger became more evident—and much more public. Sam Alito had no real warning he was about to be taken to task.

Alito arrived at the Court early on that day in late May, planning to read through his summary of a decision he'd be announcing later that morning from the bench. The case involved an Alabama woman who'd sued her employer, Goodyear Tire and Rubber Co., for sex discrimination after discovering she'd been paid less than her male counterparts. A jury took her side. Goodyear appealed the case, arguing she'd waited too long to file her claims under the federal law, and a federal appeals court sided with the company.

The case wasn't seen as controversial, and it was barely noticed at argument in November. Afterward, during the justices' private conference, the liberals made their position clear—they believed Lilly Ledbetter had a valid claim and the jury verdict should stand. But they weren't particularly forceful, and they gave no hint that the case would be a galvanizing moment. Roberts, as is the chief's prerogative when he's in the majority, assigned Alito to write the majority opinion. Ginsburg said she would write the dissent.

When Ginsburg later circulated her dissent among her colleagues, its vehement language and tone caught the conservatives by surprise. Alito reworked his majority decision in response, at one point saying Ginsburg was being "coy," and the case was scheduled to be released the day the Court returned after the Memorial Day weekend.

Unknown to the conservatives, Ginsburg would have more to say. And she was going to say it aloud.

"Justice Ginsburg's reading her dissent from the bench," one of Alito's clerks told him as he entered his chambers. "Her clerk called last night."

Alito was caught completely off guard. It's rare for a justice to read a dissent from the bench. It happens only a few times each term and only in the most controversial and significant cases—like the partial birth abortion case the month before.

But Lilly Ledbetter's case wasn't like that, a splintering argument over abortion—it was a routine discrimination case that was essentially a reprise of a thirty-year-old decision written by liberal John Paul Stevens. Or so the conservatives thought.

Ginsburg's point would become unmistakably clear later that morning, after justices took their seats in the courtroom. Opinions are the first order of business, and, like everything else in the tradition-bound Court, they are announced in order of the justices' seniority. The most junior justice with a majority opinion goes first; the chief, if he has written the majority opinion, always is last. On this day, Alito, as the junior justice, started things off.

In his summary, Alito emphasized that the Court was following the federal law as Congress wrote it, and he cited a long line of cases that were at odds with Ledbetter's arguments. For the spectators and journalists in the courtroom, the case was interesting, but it was not considered especially significant. It would affect only a small number of people, and women like Lilly Ledbetter could turn to different federal laws for recourse.

But then Ginsburg's voice echoed through the courtroom, startling those who had expected to hear Roberts moving on to announce who would be reading next opinion.

"Four members of this Court—Justices Stevens, Souter, Breyer, and I—dissent from today's decision," Ginsburg said, her voice forceful. "In our view, the court does not comprehend, or is indifferent to, the insidious way in which women can be victims of pay discrimination."

The liberals were not about to go quietly.

Ginsburg proceeded to summarize Ledbetter's case in great detail. She had been an area manager at the Goodyear plant and initially had been paid the same as men in similar jobs. But over time, her pay started slipping, and by the end of 1997—eighteen years after she started—she was the only female manager, and the pay disparity between Ledbetter and her male counterparts was glaring. She received 15 to 40 percent less than every other area manager.

Months earlier, when the justices took up the case in conference, Roberts had kicked off the discussion by pointing to the language in the law. It gave people like Ledbetter 180 days to file their claims, and she'd waited too long. Congress had failed over the years to change that provision in the law, even though it had several chances to do so. Moreover, the Court had confronted a similar situation thirty years ago and ruled against the woman.

Ginsburg disagreed in the conference, but she did not seem outraged by the argument, and Roberts decided to assign Alito the job of writing the opinion. Roberts would soon learn a hard lesson about one of the few powers he has as chief: Opinion assignments can be fraught with peril.

It was a complex task, made more so by the fragile nature of the new conservative majority, with Kennedy's vote always up for grabs. Roberts knew he could ill afford to give all of the high-profile cases to Kennedy, which would only enhance his emerging role as the new swing justice. But he also could not assign those cases to Antonin Scalia or Clarence Thomas, since they were often advocating bolder approaches that could alienate Kennedy. He and Alito had a more cautious approach, but he couldn't take every difficult case for himself or, for that matter, turn them all over to the newest justice.

Roberts also was sensitive to putting Alito on the spot with cases that would drive home the reality of O'Connor's departure—cases where it was clear the decision would have been different had she, not Alito, been on the Court. Ledbetter's case raised none of those concerns—in fact, O'Connor's votes in earlier cases suggested she very well would have been with the majority. Roberts never suspected that the relatively obscure case of *Ledbetter v. Goodyear Tire & Rubber Co.* would become a flashpoint that the liberal justices—and the media—would use to show how the newly constituted Court was steering to the Right without O'Connor's more moderate vote.

That all became clear as Ginsburg continued her summary from the bench. Her tone was pointed, almost with an edge to it. She accused the Court of ignoring "real-world employment practices." Ledbetter, she said, could not have known at first that men were receiving more money for the same work—it was only when the amount accumulated over time did it become evident. Ginsburg then referred back to the 1988 term, when the Court—in Anthony Kennedy's first full year—issued a series of decisions that limited the scope of the civil rights laws. Congress responded to those decisions by overruling them with the 1991 Civil Rights Act—legislation widely seen as a sharp rebuke to the new conservative majority.

"Today, the ball again lies in Congress's court." Ginsburg concluded in her statement, pausing to look out at the courtroom—and beyond, almost as if she were addressing her remarks to the lawmakers in the building across the street from the Court. "As in 1991, the legislature has cause to note and correct this Court's parsimonious reading of Title VII."

The next day, the case of Lilly Ledbetter was prominently displayed in newspapers across the country, with most of the articles focusing on Ginsburg's dissent from the bench and many speculating that she had thrown down the gauntlet. *The New York Times* published a second story the next day, with its focus entirely on Ginsburg.

Over the course of the next four weeks, the sense of outrage among the liberal justices became even more focused—almost as if finally dawned upon them what role they would be playing on the Roberts Court in the years to come. With the new line up of justices, Ginsburg and the three other liberals were staring at an equally new reality: they would not be the ones making historic law. They would not be the ones shaping the Court's direction. They would be—more often than not— shouting from the sidelines that the umpires blew the call.

It was not a role they welcomed or one they were willing to accept without a fight.

The realization was made more bitter because they had held out hope—however misguided—that maybe Roberts would not prove to be the solid judicial conservative President Bush thought he was getting.

The pressure on Roberts from his first days on the Court was intense. As the new chief, everything he did was scrutinized or analyzed— even his title was a source of discussion and debate. The justices have long called one another by first names except for the chief justice, whom they address as "Chief." But when Roberts joined the Court in 2005, Breyer suggested that the other justices call him "John" instead of the traditional "Chief." Scalia disagreed, saying "Chief" reflected respect for the office. And "Chief" Roberts would be.

Roberts didn't change the Court's operations much from the Rehnquist era, but his leadership seemed to have a lighter touch. Breyer talked excitedly about how Roberts had relaxed the discussion in their private conferences—Roberts didn't try to silence them with a glare if they went on a little long in discussing a case. At the oral argument, Roberts displayed none of Rehnquist's ruthless efficiency: He allowed lawyers to finish their sentences even when their time expired.

Roberts himself inadvertently raised liberals' hopes after he joined the Court, when the justices were sizing up their new leader and adapting to life without Rehnquist. In one influential article in *The Atlantic Monthly*, Roberts sounded critical of the colleagues he'd just joined, suggesting he thought they had, at times, failed to come together in a way that was best for the Court as an institution. He talked openly about his goals for bringing the Court together, much as the great Chief Justice John Marshall had two hundred years before. He told interviewers that unanimous—or nearly unanimous—decisions were easier for the lower courts and the litigants to understand. He said they also led to greater stability in the law, because they tended to have more staying power than 5–4 decisions, and were therefore better for the Court as an institution.

It was a noble ideal that many, including a few justices, thought suggested he might be willing to moderate his own views. Conservatives, for their part, reacted with alarm or irritation. Scalia groused "lots of luck" when asked about Roberts's comments and privately questioned what the new chief was up to. If consensus meant compromise on the biggest cases of the day, the implications would be profound: Not only was the vote of Anthony Kennedy up for grabs, but perhaps that of John Roberts, as well.

That was not Roberts what meant, which became clear as the term progressed. He was advocating caution, urging the justices to decide the issue before them and no more, if not necessary. But his early comments proved to be a rare misstep for the cautious and savvy Roberts, because they were the catalyst for an internal dynamic that would explode in a spectacular way by the end of the first full term.

For all the talk of consensus, the term would be one of the most divisive in recent years. The Court split 5–4 on the most controversial cases, with Kennedy in the majority in every single one—proof of his powerful new position as the swing vote. Roberts not only sided with conservatives, but he wrote a forceful dissent in the liberals' one big win—a case that rejected the Environmental Protection Agency's refusal to regulate greenhouse gas emissions from new cars and trucks.

By the time Ginsburg was reading aloud her dissent in Lilly Ledbetter's case, the liberal justices knew exactly where Roberts stood on the law and the rightward direction his new Court was headed. Over the course of the next month, the Court struck down school assignment plans based on race, narrowed the scope of a landmark campaign finance reform law, rejected a challenge to President Bush's faith-based initiatives, and sided with a school principal who expelled a student for drug-related speech she found offensive.

Those decisions all were 5–4. Each produced harsh dissents. And every one of the liberal justices would take turns reading aloud at least one of their dissents—sometimes using more pointed and angry language than what they'd actually written in the dissent itself. The press reported their remarks from the bench, adding to the perception that the Court was in almost open warfare.

The anger finally spilled over on the last day of the Court's term.

Roberts announced the decision in one of the most biggest and controversial cases—whether school officials, seeking to achieve racial balance, could consider a student's race when assigning them schools. That issue arose when white parents in Louisville, Kentucky, and Seattle, Washington, challenged the assignment plans after their children were turned away from neighborhood schools because of their race and sent to schools across town. They argued the plans were unconstitutional race discrimination. The school districts—aided by a host of civil rights groups—mounted a fierce defense, saying the plans were necessary to keep the schools integrated and that most children were able to attend the schools of their choice.

Roberts wrote the opinion, and he focused on the words of the Constitution. He emphasized that the document was color-blind and that equal protection of the laws meant treating everyone equally. "The way to stop discrimination on the basis of race," he wrote, "is to stop discriminating on the basis of race." The assignment plans, he declared unequivocally, were unconstitutional.

In the last month, however, Kennedy had wavered. He had been a persistent source of frustration for conservatives in the past on issues of abortion, gay rights, and presidential power, but he was considered a solid vote on race. He had been consistently opposed to race-based preferences over the years—much more so than his fellow moderate O'Connor had been. But Roberts had proposed a clear line: The Constitution prohibits the consideration of a person's race. And Kennedy was not much for definitively ruling something out.

As one justice succinctly put it: "Tony will never say 'never.'" Those five words perfectly capture Kennedy's outlook and explain why he won't overturn *Roe*. And they illustrate why the new Roberts Court—while turning to the Right—will remain unpredictable. Kennedy, more conservative than O'Connor to be sure, nonetheless holds the winning card.

Kennedy agreed that the assignment plans were illegal and supported most of the majority decision. But on the issue of considering a student's race to achieve diversity, he would not say "never." He offered up a separate opinion of his own, suggesting other ways schools could keep classrooms diverse—ideas, incidentally, that Roberts did not reject in his majority. Kennedy's concurring opinion, in fact, was no great departure from what Roberts had written. He just wanted to say something individually, and he announced his views with some drama from the bench.

As he did so, Breyer could barely contain his disdain. He rolled his eyes and put his hand on his head—almost as if he wanted to slap himself.

Breyer then summarized his dissent, taking aim at the new conservative majority, accusing the Court of turning back the clock on decades of racial progress and abandoning the promise of *Brown v. Board of Education,* the landmark case that outlawed separate but equal schools more than half a century before.

By the time the justices finished announcing their opinions that day, there was no doubt about the new Court's direction, and that the liberals were furious about it—and their new chief. Some felt like they'd been had by Roberts and his talk of narrowness and consensus. Breyer was particularly upset, especially since he had written what he thought was a perfect example of a narrow opinion in the student speech case decided that same week. His approach would have dodged the bigger question of whether the student's speech was protected by the First Amendment and focused instead on whether the principal was liable for suspending him.

But Breyer's approach would not have decided the fundamental constitutional issue—and Roberts had never advocated ducking the hard questions to get a unanimous outcome. Roberts wasn't suggesting justices change their views solely for the good of the institution— certainly he wouldn't do that, since he thinks his views on the law are for the good of the institution. When Roberts talked about consensus, he was referring to cases where the justices could put aside whatever bolder views they had on the law to reach a more narrow result—to look first for agreement and common ground. The problem is that the Court considers very few cases where justices can find that narrow ground—and certainly not in the big ones that command most of the media attention.

In the student speech case, Breyer's approach would have resolved the case without providing any guidance to lower courts on the fundamental issue, and Roberts was never advocating that. Breyer got precisely one vote: his own.

Moreover, Breyer's blistering rhetoric in the race case upset justices on the other side. Thomas, who had attended segregated schools as a young boy in the Jim Crow South, found Breyer's comments about the case offensive and paternalistic and he set out to refute them point-by-point in a scathing concurring opinion of his own.

Thomas had come to believe Roberts's efforts at consensus had ended up, ironically enough, driving the liberals further away. Their views on the law had always been too different from Roberts and other conservatives. There was little common ground. Roberts's approach and his talk of unanimity, however well-intentioned, allowed the liberals to think his vote was in play, causing them to overreact at the end of the term when they realized it never was.

The liberals' anger seemed more the result of the recognition they are now in the minority of a firmly conservative Court, and what that may mean for the future, rather than about the sweep and scope of the cases decided that term. Despite their clear outrage, and the even more vitriolic attacks from academics and editorial pages, the Court fell far short of a revolution. It didn't issue sweeping decisions knocking down major legal landmarks—even though Thomas and Scalia would have readily done so. It didn't overrule vast swaths of precedent.

There's no question it was more conservative. It trimmed some obvious cases. In upholding the first-ever ban on a specific abortion procedure, it indicated a clear willingness to allow other regulations and restrictions down the line. In reining in the McCain-Feingold campaign finance law, it laid the groundwork for what are certain to be more attacks on the legislation down the road. In rejecting school assignment plans based on race, it so dramatically limited when schools can consider a student's race for diversity purposes that most school officials are going to scrap those programs.

Those victories, however, came only because Kennedy fell in line. One reason conservatives were so successful in the first full term of the Roberts Court was the constellation of cases. With a different line up of cases on issues where Kennedy is more liberal—when the Court confronts presidential power or major First Amendment challenges or gay rights issues, for example—the outcome could well be different.

A snapshot of a new Court after one term can fade quickly in time.

In Kennedy's first term, the Court appeared firmly and aggressively conservative. Three terms later, it was putting *Roe v. Wade* on more solid ground than ever before and refusing to allow prayer in schools. Kennedy changed.

It's unlikely that Alito, a man of quiet confidence, will have a similar evolution. Roberts, too, knows his mind. But the lasting photograph of the Roberts Court has yet to be taken. For now, the snapshot is clear on one thing: The Supreme Court is and will remain in conflict.

ACKNOWLEDGMENTS

This book is the result of the unwavering trust of my sources and the unwavering support of my editors, employers, family, and friends. Thank you, all.

I take away from this process a profound gratitude for my sources, who were willing to share their experiences and helped bring to life the people whose decisions would shape the face of the Supreme Court and, by extension, the country. Scores of current and former administration officials spent hours of their time with me, some in multiple interviews. I was also fortunate enough to interview more than a dozen federal appeals court judges and nine Supreme Court justices, and those conversations illuminated the memos and notes and documents I'd reviewed during the course of my research. The dedicated group in the Court's office of public information, Kathy Arberg, Ed Turner, Patricia McCabe, and Ella Hunter also answered repeated questions about the Court's history and traditions.

The papers of Harry Blackmun were an invaluable resource, and the staff at the Library of Congress helped me find and focus my efforts.

The knowledgeable Diane Barrie at the Ronald Reagan Presidential Library in Simi Valley, California, directed me toward key documents in the library's impressive and comprehensive collection. Researchers at the George H. W. Bush Library in College Station, Texas, also ensured that I got other papers I needed to tell this story. Thanks also to Steve Wermiel, whose insight helped me better understand Justice Brennan's extraordinary influence on the Court.

I feel incredibly fortunate to have written this book for The Penguin Press, headed by the legendary Ann Godoff, who took a chance on me well before any of us realized how historic a story was about to unfold. Her enthusiasm for the project carried it forward. My editor, the peerless Scott Moyers, provided invaluable comments and was really just a joy to work with. My agent, Melanie Jackson, was a calming voice I trusted instinctively. The book was a daunting prospect, but one friend gets credit (or, as I've told him at various times in this past year, blame) for pushing me to tackle it. Bob Schieffer said it would be the hardest thing I'd ever tried, but that I would be prouder of it than any work I'd ever done. He was right on both counts, as he typically is on all things.

My editors at the *Chicago Tribune* provided continual support and resources. I consider myself lucky to have worked for such dedicated journalists throughout my nineteen-year newspaper career. There is no better editor than Ann Marie Lipinski, and her encouragement over the years—to return to the *Tribune* after law school, to cover the Supreme Court, to work part time after child number 3, to write this book—shaped my career (and my life!). Jim O'Shea was an inspiration. Mike Tackett gave me time, office space, and encouragement. Randy Weissman answered computer queries. Pete Souza provided beautiful photographs. Glen Elsasser, whose knowledge of the Supreme Court is vast, fielded many questions.

My employers at ABC News enthusiastically embraced this work in progress. David Westin's deep knowledge of and interest in the Court and this project helped me make it to the finish line, as did Amy Entelis's support. My new colleagues also gave me space as deadlines loomed large. Thank you, Charlie Gibson, Jon Banner, Robin Sproul, Ian Cameron, Portia Robertson, and Ariane DeVogue.

When I was in law school at the University of Chicago, I used to spend breaks in the Green Lounge talking with Monica Powell, and sometimes we actually discussed the law. Her insights were always startlingly fresh and clear, and when I needed help with the book, I immediately thought of her. Now named Dolin and living across the street from me, Monica is responsible for much of the legal research on Anthony Kennedy's early years on the Court. She did an outstanding first draft of chapter 3. She also provided countless hours reading other chapters and making substantive suggestions.

As I worked through the manuscript, I relied heavily on two other old friends. Steve Daley, a former colleague and flat-out terrific writer, made the book better with his edits and suggestions. His counsel on all matters helped keep me on course, as it has since I first met him in 1994. I also turned to my old college writing partner Joe Scarborough for his keen political insights, twenty years after we took on the campus political machine at the University of Alabama. It's true that some things never change.

Jim Lehrer helped me tackle the "elephant in the room" when I wasn't quite sure where to begin. And Schieffer gave me astute advice when I started writing. "Jan, you know when you're reading a book, and you find yourself skimming over places—just skipping over stuff?" he asked me shortly after I signed on to write the book. "Yes," I nodded, eagerly awaiting Bob's advice on how to avoid those dreaded bypassed passages. "Just leave all that stuff out," he said.

Bob, I hope I did.

I owe all my family and friends a tremendous debt for not yelling at me when I was overtaxed and leaving me to my own devices when I was probably not much fun to be around. My husband, Doug, stoically shouldered the burden and the stress. As he has for almost fifteen years, he picked me up and pushed me on. And he stood in when I wasn't there. He now knows where the lightbulbs are and how much milk to buy at the store. My four children, Carolyn, Louisa, Jack, and Page, were understanding beyond their years and provided unconditional love and support, even when Mom barely had time for a kiss on the top of their little heads. My brother, Ron, isn't holding it against me that I still haven't mailed his birthday present. My in-laws, Joel and Sharon Green-burg, understood. My girlfriends Camilla, Carrie, Catherine, Hattie, Jill, Karen, Micheline, Nancy, Pat, Sharon, Susie, Vickie, and Vivian cut me enormous slack when days, weeks—okay, okay—months passed without returned phone calls.

Finally, an overarching constant has been the support of my parents, Joe and Carolyn Crawford. They took care of my children much of the summer on their farm in Alabama, giving four city kids a chance to ride tractors and four-wheelers and go to cow sales, to run through pastures and streams, just like their mom did. When school started and every-one had to come back, my mother came up to Washington and ran our household better than I ever could, all the while reading chapters and making suggestions, helping with laundry and cooking okra gumbo and lemon ice box pie. My dad told me to "keep your chin up," and his unfailing optimism and belief in me helped me do just that.

Their support always has given me the license to try and the free-dom to fail. They are the best parents in the world, and this book is ded-icated to them.

NOTES

This book is based in large part on more than one hundred interviews with participants in the relevant events who graciously gave their time, some for many hours and in multiple interviews. I was fortunate to interview nine Supreme Court justices and scores of their law clerks, high-ranking White House and Justice Department officials from four different presidential administrations, numerous federal appeals court judges, and other key players in the appointment and confirmation process, including senators and their staffers. Most of the interviews were conducted on background, meaning that I could use the information but not identify its source. I interviewed Justice Sandra Day O'Connor on the record for four hours in two separate interviews in the summer of 2006. I also interviewed Justice Anthony Kennedy on the record in the summer of 2006.

This book also relies heavily on research in contemporaneous documents, including the papers of Justices Thurgood Marshall and Harry Blackmun, which are maintained at the Library of Congress, and documents from past administrations maintained at the Ronald Reagan

Presidential Library in Simi Valley, California, and the George H. W. Bush Library in College Station, Texas.

Some of the direct quotations in the book come from those documents, especially the detailed notes of Justice Blackmun. Other direct quotations are from participants in the conversations or a person who was told directly by a participant. Any thoughts or feelings I attribute to people in this book also come from documents or from interviews with the person or someone who had firsthand knowledge.

I was fortunate to benefit from some excellent writings on the subject by other authors, including Joan Biskupic's *Sandra Day O'Connor: How the First Woman on the Supreme Court Became Its Most Influential Justice;* Ken Foskett's insightful *Judging Thomas: The Life and Times of Clarence Thomas;* Tinsley E. Yarbrough's *David Hackett Souter: Traditional Republican on the Rehnquist Court;* Henry J. Abraham's *Justices, Presidents, and Senators: A History of the U.S. Supreme Court Appointments from Washington to Clinton;* David G. Savage's *Turning Right: The Making of the Rehnquist Supreme Court;* James F. Simon's *The Center Holds: The Power Struggle Inside the Rehnquist Court;* and *Advice and Consent: The Politics of Judicial Appointments,* by Lee Epstein and Jeffrey A. Segal. I also highly recommend Benjamin Wittes's thoughtful new book, *Confirmation Wars: Preserving Independent Courts in Angry Times.*

I have been privileged to work with a fine group of diligent journalists in addition to those named above who have covered the Supreme Court, including Laurie Asseo, Jess Bravin, Richard Carelli, Marcia Coyle, Lyle Denniston, Aaron Epstein, Linda Greenhouse, Steve Henderson, Mike Kirkland, Chuck Lane, Steve Lash, Tony Mauro, David Pike, Jeffrey Rosen, Greg Stohr, Nina Totenberg, Pete Williams, and Jim Vicini. A special word of thanks to the inestimable Stuart Taylor, whose early coverage of the Rehnquist Court and new justice Kennedy proved remarkably dead-on, as have his excellent subsequent reports on the Court, its justices, and other legal issues.

Finally, this book draws on my own knowledge and experience from covering the Supreme Court since 1994 for the *Chicago Tribune,* PBS's *The NewsHour with Jim Lehrer,* and CBS News.

CHAPTER ONE: DAY'S END

1. O'Connor's reaction to Rehnquist's nomination is recounted in Joan Biskupic's comprehensive book *Sandra Day O'Connor: How the First Woman on the Supreme Court Became Its Most Influential Justice* (New York: Ecco, 2005).

2. Andrew D. Martin, Kevin M. Quinn, and Lee Epstein, "The Median Justice on the U.S. Supreme Court," 83 *North Carolina Law Review* 1275 (2005).

3. *Haitian Refugee Center, Inc. v. Baker,* 502 U.S. 1122 (1992).

4. *United States v. Morrison,* 529 U.S. 598 (2000).

5. *Gonzales v. Raich,* 545 U.S. 1 (2005).

6. *McCreary County v. ACLU,* 545 U.S. 844 (2005).

7. *Kelo v. City of New London,* 542 U.S. 965 (2005).

8. *Planned Parenthood of Southeastern Pennsylvania v. Casey,* 505 U.S. 835 (1992).

9. *Grutter v. Bollinger,* 539 U.S. 306 (2003).

10. *McCreary County v. ACLU.*

11. Matthew Mosk, "Gay Unions Fracture Maryland's Black Caucus; Civil Rights Pull as Strong as Church's," *Washington Post,* January 28, 2006.

12. *Dickerson v. United States,* 530 U.S. 428 (2000).

13. *Grutter v. Bollinger.*

14. *Roper v. Simmons,* 543 U.S. 551 (2005); *Atkins v. Virginia,* 536 U.S. 304 (2003).

15. *Lawrence v. Texas,* 539 U.S. 558 (2003).

16. *Rumsfeld v. Padilla,* 542 U.S. 426 (2004); *Hamdi v. Rumsfeld,* 542 U.S. 507 (2004); *Rasul v. Bush,* 542 U.S. 466 (2004).

17. J. Harvie Wilkinson, "The Rehnquist Court at Twilight: The Lures and Perils of Split-the-Difference Jurisprudence," 58 *Stanford Law Review* 1969 (2006).

18. *County of Sacramento v. Lewis,* 523 U.S. 833 (1998).

19. David Cole, "The Liberal Legacy of *Bush v. Gore,"* 94 *Georgetown Law Journal* 1427 (2006).

20. Martin Merzer, "Review of Ballots Finds Bush's Win Would Have Endured Manual Recounts," *Miami Herald,* April 4, 2001; Dan Keating and Dan Balz, "Florida Recounts Would Have Favored Bush; But Study Finds Gore Might Have Won Statewide Tally of All Uncounted Ballots," *Washington Post,* November 12, 2001.

CHAPTER TWO: SETTLING FOR TONY

1. Linda Greenhouse, "The Year the Court Turned to the Right," *New York Times,* July 7, 1989.

2. Al Kamen, "Kennedy Moves Court to the Right; Justice More Conservative Than Expected," *Washington Post,* April 11, 1989.

3. *School District of the City of Grand Rapids v. Ball,* 473 U.S. 373 (1985); *Wallace v. Jaffree,* 472 U.S. 38 (1985); *Thornton v. Caldor,* 472 U.S. 703 (1985).

4. *Wygant v. Jackson Board of Education,* 476 U.S. 267 (1986).

5. James H. Rubin, "Reagan's Judicial Nominees Will Have Rough Time in Democratic Senate," Associated Press, November 10, 1986.

6. *Ollman v. Evans,* 750 F.2d 970 (D.C. Cir., 1984).

7. *Beller v. Middendorf,* 632 F.2d 788 (9th Cir. 1980).

8. *Dronenburg v. Zech,* 741 F.2d 1388 (D.C. Cir. 1984).

9. *U.S. v. Penn,* 647 F.2d 876 (9th Cir. 1980).

10. *Akron v. Akron Center for Reproductive Health,* 462 U.S. 416 (1983).

CHAPTER THREE: FALSE HOPES

1. *Patterson v. McLean Credit Union,* 485 U.S. 617 (1988).

2. *Jones v. Mayer,* 392 U.S. 409 (1968).

3. *Runyon v. McCrary,* 427 U.S. 160 (1976).

4. "Casting a Shadow over Civil Rights," *New York Times,* April 27, 1988.

5. Ted Gest, Gillian Sandford, Erica E. Goode, Jill Rachlin, Marianna I. Knight, "Suddenly, the Conservatives Start Stirring," *U.S. News & World Report,* May 9, 1988.

6. Ibid.

7. Ibid.

8. Ibid.

9. *Patterson v. McLean Credit Union,* 491 U.S. 164 (1989).

10. *Webster v. Reproductive Health Services,* 492 U.S. 490 (1989).

11. *Roe v. Wade,* 410 U.S. 113 (1973).

12. *Rose v. Lundy,* 455 U.S. 509 (1982).

13. *Engle v. Isaac,* 456 U.S. 107, 141 (1982).

14. *Ward's Cove Packing Co. v. Atonio,* 490 U.S. 642, 662 (1989).

15. *Penry v. Lynaugh,* 492 U.S. 302 (1989); *Stanford v. Kentucky,* 492 U.S. 361 (1989).

16. Linda Greenhouse, "The Year the Court Turned to the Right," *New York Times,* July 7, 1989.

17. *Texas v. Johnson,* 491 U.S. 397 (1989).

18. *Allegheny County v. Greater Pittsburgh ACLU,* 492 U.S. 573 (1989).

19. *Atkins v. Virginia,* 536 U.S. 304 (2002); *Roper v. Simmons,* 543 U.S. 551 (2005).

20. Al Kamen, "Kennedy Moves Court to Right; Justice More Conservative Than Expected," *Washington Post,* April 11, 1989.

21. Ethan Bronner, "A New Justice Sways a Court; Consistently, Kennedy Tips Scales to Conservatives," *Boston Globe,* July 21, 1989.

CHAPTER FOUR: THE DEVIL YOU DON'T

1. Warren B. Rudman, *Combat: Twelve Years in the U.S. Senate* (New York: Random House, 1996), 159–60.

2. Ibid., 154.

3. Ibid.

4. Ibid.

5. Ibid., 162.

6. *Opinion of the Justices,* 530 A.2d 21 (N.H. 1987).

7. Rudman, *Combat,* 162.

8. Ibid., 163–64.

9. Linda Greenhouse, "A New Contender Is Seen for Court," *New York Times,* October 29, 1990.

10. Ibid.

11. Karen F. Donovan, "Former High Court Hopeful Joins Circuit," *Massachusetts Lawyers Weekly,* May 28, 1990.

12. *Estate of Dionne,* 518 A.2d 178 (N.H. 1986).

13. R. W. Apple, "Sununu Tells How and Why He Pushed Souter for Court," *New York Times,* July 25, 1990.

14. *World News Tonight with Peter Jennings,* ABC News, July 26, 1990.

15. Ethan Bronner and John Milne, "Souter Calls Himself 'Moderate Conservative,' " *Boston Globe,* October 5, 1990.

16. Bob Hohler and Peter S. Canellos, "Jurist Reveals Little, Even to Good Friends," *Boston Globe,* July 26, 1990.

17. J. Craig Crawford, "Conservatives Do Double Take over Souter's Views," *Orlando Sentinel,* September 16, 1990. Linda Greenhouse, "Filling In the Blanks," *New York Times,* September 15, 1990.

CHAPTER FIVE: "THE YOUNGEST, CRUELEST JUSTICE"

1. Linda Greenhouse, "Thomas Sworn In as 106th Justice," *New York Times,* October 24, 1991; Judy Keen, "Thomas Takes Oath Early and in Private," *USA Today,* October 24, 1991.

2. David Savage, "Thomas Takes Oath in Secret Ceremony," *Los Angeles Times,* October 24, 1991.

3. Tony Mauro, "Bush Jumps Gun on Thomas' Initiation," *Legal Times,* October 28, 1991.

4. *Hudson v. McMillan,* 503 U.S. 1 (1992).

5. *Dawson v. Delaware,* 503 U.S. 159 (1992).

6. *Foucha v. Louisiana,* 504 U.S. 71 (1992).

7. *Hamdi v. Rumsfeld,* 542 U.S. 507 (2004).

8. *Hudson v. McMillan,* 503 U.S. 1 (1992).

9. Editorial, "The Youngest, Cruelest Justice," *New York Times,* February 22, 1992.

10. Mary McGrory, "Thomas Walks in Scalia's Shoes," *Washington Post,* February 27, 1992.

11. *Doggett v. United States,* 505 U.S. 647 (1992); *Cipollone v. Liggett Group,* 505 U.S. 504 (1992).

12. *Doggett v. United States,* 505 U.S. 647 (1992).

13. *Dawson v. Delaware,* 503 U.S. 159 (1992).

14. Linda Greenhouse, "Unusual Use of the First Amendment Overturns a Killer's Death Sentence," *New York Times,* March 10, 1992.

15. *Jacobson v. U.S.,* 503 U.S. 540 (1992).

16. *Lechmere v. NLRB,* 502 U.S. 527 (1992).

17. *White v. Illinois,* 502 U.S. 346 (1992).

18. *Denton v. Hernandez,* 504 U.S. 25 (1992).

19. *U.S. v. R.L.C,* 503 U.S. 291 (1992).

20. *Connecticut National Bank v. Germain,* 503 U.S. 249 (1992).

21. *Wright v. West,* 505 U.S. 277 (1992).

22. *Coleman v. Thompson,* 501 U.S. 722 (1991).

23. Biskupic, *Sandra Day O'Connor,* 257.

CHAPTER SIX: CHANGE OF HEART

1. "The Youngest, Cruelest Justice," *New York Times,* February 22, 1992.

2. *Lee v. Weisman,* 505 U.S. 577 (1992).

3. *Allegheny County v. Greater Pittsburgh ACLU,* 492 U.S. 573 (1989).

4. *Lynch v. Donnelly,* 485 U.S. 668 (1984).

5. Linda Greenhouse, "Another Frantic Finish Looms for High Court," *New York Times,* May 16, 1991.

6. Ned Zeman and Lucy Howard, "Souter: Slow off the Mark," *Newsweek,* May 27, 1991.

7. *World News Tonight with Peter Jennings,* ABC News, May 24, 1991.

8. Ethan Bronner, "Souter Leaves His First Mark as High Court's 'Stealth Nominee,' " *Boston Globe,* May 26, 1991.

9. *Planned Parenthood of Southeastern Pennsylvania v. Casey,* 505 U.S. 833 (1992).

10. *Webster v. Reproductive Health Services,* 492 U.S. 490 (1989).

11. Terry Carter, "Crossing the Rubicon," *California Lawyer,* October 1992.

12. *Gratz v. Bollinger;* 539 U.S. 244; *Grutter v. Bollinger,* 539 U.S. 306 (2003).

13. *Stenberg v. Carhart,* 530 U.S. 914 (2000).

14. *Mitchell v. Helms,* 530 U.S. 793 (2000).

15. *Bush v. Gore,* 531 U.S. 98 (2000).

16. *Roper v. Simmons,* 543 U.S. 551 (2005); *Atkins v. Virginia,* 536 U.S. 304 (2002).

17. *Romer v. Evans,* 517 U.S. 620 (1996); *Lawrence v. Texas,* 539 U.S. 558 (2003).

18. *Roper v. Simmons.*

CHAPTER SEVEN: THE CLINTON WAY

1. Lee Epstein and Jeffrey A. Segal, *Advice and Consent: The Politics of Judicial Appointments* (New York: Oxford University Press, 2005), 138.

2. *Board of Education of Kiryas Joel Village School District v. Grumet,* 512 U.S. 687 (1994).

3. *U.S. v. Lopez,* 514 U.S. 549 (1995).

4. Editorial, "The High Court Loses Restraint," *New York Times,* April 29, 1995.

5. Joan Biskupic, "Top Court Ruling on Guns Slams Brakes on Congress; 30s Commerce Clause Overextended, Justices Find," *Washington Post,* April 28, 1995.

6. *Bush v. Gore,* 531 U.S. 98 (2000).

7. *Stenberg v. Carhart,* 530 U.S. 914 (2000).

8. Robert H. Bork, *The Tempting of America: The Political Seduction of the Law* (New York: Free Press, 1990), 128.

9. Isaiah Berlin, "The Hedgehog and the Fox," *Russian Thinkers* (London: Hogarth Press, 1978; paperback, Penguin).

10. Stephen Breyer, *Active Liberty* (New York: Knopf, 2005).

11. *Stenberg v. Carhart.*

12. *Lawrence v. Texas,* 539 U.S. 558 (2003).

13. *Roper v. Simmons,* 543 U.S. 551 (2005); *Atkins v. Virginia,* 536 U.S. 304 (2003).

14. *McCreary County v. ACLU,* 545 U.S. 844 (2005).

15. *Rumsfeld v. Padilla,* 542 U.S. 426 (2004); *Hamdi v. Rumsfeld,* 542 U.S. 507 (2004); *Rasul v. Bush,* 542 U.S. 466 (2004).

16. *U.S. v. Booker; U.S. v. Fanfan,* 543 U.S. 220 (2005).

CHAPTER EIGHT: THE NATURAL

1. Bork, *The Tempting of America,* 6.

2. *Lawrence v. Reed,* 406 F.3rd 1224 (10th Cir. 2005).

CHAPTER NINE: "EXCEPT HE'S NOT A WOMAN"

1. Rich Landers, "O'Connor: Roberts Good in Every Way, Except He's Not a Woman," *Spokesman Review,* July 20, 2005.

2. Ibid.

3. Ibid.

4. *Maryland v. Wilson,* 519 U.S. 408 (1997).

5. *Mitchell v. Helms,* 530 U.S. 793 (2000).

6. *Davis v. Monroe County Board of Education,* 526 U.S. 793 (2000).

7. *Stenberg v. Carhart,* 530 U.S. 914 (2000).

8. *McCorvey v. Hill,* 385 F.3d 846 (5th Cir. 2004).

9. *In re Doe,* 19 S.W.3d 346 (Tex. 2000).

10. *The NewsHour with Jim Lehrer,* July 2, 1997.

CHAPTER TEN: "TRUST ME"

1. *Grutter v. Bollinger,* 539 U.S. 306 (2003).

2. Ibid.

CHAPTER ELEVEN: DECONSTRUCTING MIERS

1. "Another Look at the Miers Nomination," *Focus on the Family* radio program, October 12, 2005.

2. John Fund, "Opinion Journal," *Wall Street Journal,* October 17, 2005.

3. Ramesh Ponnuru, "Why Conservatives Are Divided," *New York Times,* October 17, 2005.

4. David Brooks, "In Her Own Words," *New York Times,* October 13, 2005.

CHAPTER TWELVE: A FULL COUNT

1. Charles Krauthammer, "Miers: The Only Exit Strategy," *Washington Post,* October 21, 2005.

2. *Planned Parenthood of Southeastern Pennsylvania v. Casey,* 947 F.2d 682 (3rd Cir. 1991).

3. *Roper v. Simmons,* 543 U.S. 551 (2005).

4. *U.S. v. Rybar,* 103 F.3d 276 (3rd Cir. 1996).

5. *Doe v. Groody,* 361 F.3d 232 (3rd Cir. 2004).

6. James Risen and Eric Lichtblau, "Bush Lets U.S. Spy on Callers Without Courts," *New York Times,* December 16, 2005.

7. *Rasul v. Bush,* 542 U.S. 466 (2004).

INDEX